AGENTS OF DISORDER

AGENTS OF
DISORDER

INSIDE CHINA'S CULTURAL REVOLUTION

ANDREW G. WALDER

THE BELKNAP PRESS OF
HARVARD UNIVERSITY PRESS

CAMBRIDGE, MASSACHUSETTS
LONDON, ENGLAND | 2019

First printing

Library of Congress Cataloging-in-Publication Data
Names: Walder, Andrew G. (Andrew George), 1953– author.
Title: Agents of disorder : inside China's Cultural Revolution /
    Andrew G. Walder.
Description: Cambridge, Massachusetts : The Belknap Press of Harvard
    University Press, 2019. | Includes bibliographical references and index.
Identifiers: LCCN 2019010124 | ISBN 9780674238329
    (hardcover : alk. paper)
Subjects: LCSH: China—History—Cultural Revolution, 1966–1976. |
    China—Politics and government—1949–1976. | Political
    persecution—China—History—20th century.
Classification: LCC DS778.7 .W325 2019 | DDC 951.05 / 6—dc23
    LC record available at https://lccn.loc.gov/2019010124

To the memory of Barrington Moore, Jr.

CONTENTS

PREFACE

IT WAS NEVER MY intention to become a historical sociologist. My interest in the upheavals of China's Cultural Revolution was first sparked when I was an undergraduate in the early 1970s. At the time they were very recent events. The startling transformations of the post-Mao era diverted my attention away from this earlier period of upheaval, as they did virtually every other student of contemporary China. In recent years I have returned to this long-neglected subject, and find that I have become a historical sociologist largely through procrastination. It is fortunate that I delayed serious engagement with this topic, because there now are vastly more research materials on these events than were available to researchers some decades ago.

The seeds for this particular study were planted in the late 1970s, when I was a graduate student in the University of Michigan's Department of Sociology. For several years, I occupied a desk at the Center for Research on Social Organization, housed in a somewhat dilapidated former elementary school, which became for a period my primary intellectual home. The Center's director, Charles Tilly, led a large research team gathering data on collective protest from microfilms of old British and French newspapers, coding them into what at the time was called a "machine-readable database." Tilly was then a leading figure in quantitative historical sociology, and also part of a nascent intellectual movement that reshaped the study of collective action and popular protest. Other major figures in this and related efforts—William Gamson, Jeffery Paige, and Mayer Zald—also occupied offices in the Center, along with graduate students engaged in research on political conflict in different times and places. The Center's bag lunches, workshops, speaker series, and conversations over (terrible) coffee made for an exciting intellectual atmosphere, and were as important in my graduate education as the formal coursework.

I originally decided to specialize in the study of China because of a deep interest in the upheavals of the Cultural Revolution. This was a subject close to the heart of intellectual activity at the Center, and I constantly thought about the political conflicts in late 1960s China through theoretical lenses prevalent at the Center. Unfortunately, during those years China was closed to scholars, and documentation about the conflicts of the period was unavailable. I could only dream of pursuing the analysis of China's late-1960s upheaval in the fashion then common at Michigan.

My fascination with this phase of the Chinese revolution never waned. As China opened up in the 1980s, the regime began to examine critically its recent history. During this process, a flood of new information was released, reviving my interest in the conflicts of the period. Early in the post-Mao era, the Chinese government mandated the publication of local annals, many of which contained surprisingly detailed accounts of political events during the Cultural Revolution. Mindful of the potential of these materials for the systematic analysis of rebellion and repression, I began to photocopy sections of annals that contained information about political events. My collection effort accelerated as more local annals were published, making near-complete coverage of the country a realistic goal.

By the time that I joined Stanford's faculty in 1997, my collection included some two-thirds of all cities and counties in China. While the photocopying continued in libraries in Hong Kong, the United States, and occasionally China, I employed a handful of graduate students in trial efforts to code these materials into a database. This work culminated in a concentrated final effort funded by a grant from the National Science Foundation in 2009 that completed a data set covering all but a few dozen counties in the country, and that contains information about close to 34,000 political events in 2,246 cities and counties. This data set, along with the most detailed of the narrative accounts on which it is based, is the primary foundation for this book.

Here I have made a conscious effort to look at this subject primarily through the eyes of social scientists who specialize in the study of rebellion and collective action. My aim is not solely to contribute new historical knowledge and novel interpretations of these still-obscure upheavals, although I am forced to address yawning gaps in the historiography of the period. I also hope to wring from my analysis of these events a set of ideas that will contribute to the way that social scientists analyze phenomena like rebellion and repression. China's Cultural Revolution was highly idiosyncratic, and in many ways historically unique, but it was driven by generic processes that have been observed in different guises in a wide variety of historical settings. My purpose is to lay bare these underlying processes and identify the general processes in the particular.

Barrington Moore, Jr., was one of the undisputed masters of historical sociology, and he was vitally interested in the social sources of political phenomena. His work on the social origins of dictatorship and democracy inspired generations of scholars across a number of disciplines. Quite by chance, during my years at Harvard more than twenty years ago, we formed a close friendship based on shared tastes in academic subjects and sailing excursions out of Salem harbor. Like many scholars of his generation, for him the question of how groups mobilized for political action was distinctly secondary to the more fundamental question of why they formed certain political orientations. This question has receded very much to the background in current work on political movements, especially in sociology. In some ways this book is a throwback to the preoccupations of an earlier generation. Both out of admiration for his intellectual accomplishments and affection for a departed friend, I dedicate this book to Barry's memory.

AGENTS OF DISORDER

1

AN ENIGMATIC UPHEAVAL

IN THE SUMMER OF 1966, the People's Republic of China was approaching the seventeenth anniversary of its founding. Taking power in October 1949 after a two-decade guerrilla insurgency and three-year civil war, the Chinese Communist Party subsequently built one of the most powerfully centralized revolutionary regimes in modern history. Yet within months of this anniversary, the civilian structures of this party-state were on the brink of collapse. Several of the largest cities were paralyzed by street battles between factions of rebel workers that disrupted rail transport and large state enterprises. Soon afterward, a wave of power seizures toppled local governments, spurring the dispatch of the armed forces to stabilize new structures of power. This, in turn, ushered in eighteen months of even more destructive civil disorder and violent factional warfare, which in many regions resembled civil war. A tenuous order was finally imposed near the end of 1968, placing most regions under a harsh regime of military control. When the dust finally cleared in 1969, close to 1.6 million people had died in the upheaval and the suppression campaigns through which political order was rebuilt. What forces generated this remarkable upheaval, and how did such a powerfully centralized state unravel so rapidly?

This dramatic and confusing three-year period was the most violent phase of what would later become known as a decade-long Cultural Revolution. It was set in motion by Mao Zedong's remarkable decision to foment rebellion against his own party-state as a means to halt the bureaucratization that afflicted virtually all regimes modeled after the Soviet Union. This was an audacious act, completely unprecedented in the history of twentieth-century communism.[1] The ultimate result, by 1969, was a new state structure built on a hierarchy of "revolutionary committees" composed of rebel activists, selected veteran officials, and military officers who, in most regions, exercised real control. Without the support of Mao and his enablers in the national leadership, this dramatic series of events would never have gotten underway. But how can we explain the confusing array of conflicts that unfolded over these years, which often appeared to confound Mao himself? Powerful political forces were unleashed. What were they?

More than a half-century on, much about this enigmatic upheaval remains deeply puzzling. There are large gaps in the historiography of the period, leaving basic questions unanswered. Prior to the collapse of civilian governments in early 1967, how widespread was popular mobilization and what forms did it take? How extensive was the wave of power seizures that undermined local governments in early 1967, and who actually carried them out? How did the overthrow of local governments alter political alignments and drive large rebel coalitions to fight one another with increasing violence well into 1968? How extensive was the intervention of military units across China, and what was their role in local politics? How widespread were these violent clashes, and why did they prove so difficult to resolve? How was political order finally rebuilt, and at what cost?

Answers to these questions remain elusive, in part, because past research has focused so heavily on the origins of conflict within schools and workplaces and the political activities of specific social groups.[2] This focus has shed considerable light on a range of previously obscure social cleavages and discontents in China's closed society, but the connections between these grievances and the broader conflicts that later erupted remained largely unexplored. Published regional accounts do address broader patterns of conflict, but they are few in number and skewed toward large cities.[3] The best national-level narratives jump selectively from developments in one region to developments in another, focusing on the ones that shaped the overall political direction of the Cultural Revolution.[4] In this book I shift the angle of vision to the national level, with a focus on mobilizations that undermined state structures, the formation of mass factions during 1967, and the violent regional clashes that culminated in campaigns of suppression in 1968.

Interpreting the Conflicts

What *were* the political forces unleashed during this tumultuous period? For many years we appeared to have a satisfying, if somewhat speculative, explanation. From the outset, researchers viewed these violent factional conflicts as the struggles of interest groups. The new revolutionary order, which aimed to eliminate the severe inequalities of the old society, had nonetheless generated distinctive new patterns of inequality and privilege, based on economic status and political affiliation.[5] The regime's close monitoring of citizens for compliance, its labeling of citizens based on their demonstrated or presumed political loyalties, and its conduct of regular political campaigns that left aggrieved citizens in their wake created reservoirs of discontent and frustration that broke out into violence when the opportunity arose.[6] In the first months of this upheaval, groups that suffered disadvantages frequently protested the limits placed on their opportunities, while those that enjoyed advantages or were tied closely to power structures mobilized to blunt the impact of rebellion and defend the existing order. In later phases of the conflict, large rebel coalitions with opposed stances toward the imposition of military control fought violent battles across large regions of China. Factions that supported military forces appeared to favor the restoration of the status quo and were labeled conservative or moderate. Factions opposed to military control appeared determined to continue the rebellion, and were designated as radical. It seemed reasonable to infer that the former represented relatively advantaged groups, while the latter represented the disadvantaged.[7]

When it first appeared in the 1970s, the evidence for this broad interpretation was suggestive at best, given the limited sources available to researchers during the late Mao era. But its logic appeared to be unassailable, and in the absence of other plausible explanations, it was widely accepted. The interpretation reflected a new trend in the analysis of Soviet-type societies that viewed them, not as totalitarian systems of total power, but rather as differentiated social structures with distinctive patterns of inequality that suppressed, but did not eliminate, interest-based activity.[8] Interest group conflicts were hard to detect in the Soviet Union, but the Prague Spring of 1968 amply demonstrated pluralist political competition and group conflict.[9] The first phases of China's Cultural Revolution seemed to illustrate the core tenets of this appealing new idea.[10]

This interpretation also fit closely with a then-new sociological perspective on political movements. The conflicts seemed to display a pattern familiar to students of protest movements in other settings—mobilization by the aggrieved spurred a countermobilization by those with interests tied to the existing order.[11] The central idea was that the opposed political orientations that defined the factional warfare of 1967 and 1968 expressed divergent interests tied to the social and political positions of actors. The early months of the Cultural Revolution radically changed the structure of political opportunity, permitting the mobilization of dissident challenges while spurring a reaction by those with vested interests in the status quo. The rebel power seizures that overthrew local governments across China in early 1967 were seen as a defeat for the forces of order, while the subsequent factional conflicts were viewed as struggles to shape the new order that would replace it. The conflicts between these two forces became so violent presumably because they were so deeply rooted in structures of power and inequality.

Research over the past decade has eroded confidence in this interpretation. A new generation of scholarship, based on the much richer array of source material made available during the long post-Mao era, has steadily undermined its core propositions. Evidence that once appeared to demonstrate the interest group foundations for factional conflict turned out not to be as convincing as once thought.

In the early months of these conflicts, marginalized groups did indeed take the opportunity to articulate their grievances: these included temporary and contract workers denied the benefits of permanent state employment, urban youth sent involuntarily to the countryside, and demobilized soldiers sent to remote state farms instead of urban jobs.[12] They were among the first to join rebel groups in 1966, and they openly presented their demands. Their protests were prominent for a period, but their cause never defined the main lines of factional division, and their self-interested demands were repudiated in early 1967 and their movements were suppressed.[13]

There was also a fascinating debate about the regime's practice of categorizing individuals based on their family background, which presumably predicted their loyalty to the revolutionary regime. Those in favored "red" categories, especially those whose parents were veterans of the revolutionary struggle, received enhanced opportunities for educational advancement and career opportunities. Stigmatized "black" categories included those whose parents were from exploiting social classes or associated with the defeated Nationalist Party.[14] Students in the favored categories claimed leadership over the early Red Guard movement based on their families' heritage. They debated students from other family backgrounds, especially those with educated middle-class parents, who disputed their claims to be "naturally red." The latter tended to join the early rebellions against local leaders.[15] In one famous case, a widely debated dissident manifesto denounced the entire system of class labels.[16]

Upon closer examination, however, the debate over family background was largely inconclusive, and it was overshadowed by a more consequential debate over violence among high school Red Guards that found students from "revolutionary" households on both sides of an emerging factional cleavage.[17] The famous manifesto that denounced the system of class labels generated widespread support, but it was denounced as reactionary by the elite sponsors of the rebel movement who were close to Mao Zedong, and it was repudiated by the rebel wing of the high school movement that presumably should have embraced its message.[18]

The apparent significance of family class categories was further reduced by the discovery that the issue hardly figured at all in the much larger and more influential Red Guard movement in the universities. Moreover, the leaders and activists on *both* sides of the emerging factional divide were students from politically favored households with records of past political activism and Party loyalty.[19] Students split over political stances taken under rapidly changing and ambiguous circumstances, forcing activists from similar backgrounds subsequently to defend their prior stances.[20] The debilitating split in Beijing between the "Heaven" and "Earth" factions pitted students with identical backgrounds and recent histories of political cooperation against one another. It defied all efforts at reconciliation due to deep animosities toward the most powerful Red Guard leaders on the two largest campuses.[21]

There were, to be sure, those who mobilized to defend local authorities from the early rebel attacks. Party members and favored subordinates appeared initially to remain loyal to their superiors, and Party officials mobilized loyal subordinates as defenders.[22] In the large cities of Nanjing and Shanghai, alliances of workers known as "Scarlet Guards" mobilized near the end of 1966, relying on Party branches and official trade unions. For almost a month they battled with a large alliance of rebel workers that eventually overthrew Shanghai's government.[23] The broader significance of this development, however, was altered by the realization that Scarlet Guard organizations rapidly disintegrated after rebel power seizures were publicly praised by Beijing. Moreover, it has become clear that the factions that engaged in violent warfare after the overthrow of local authorities expressed splits within the rebel movements that had earlier targeted the authorities. The movement-countermovement dynamic so evident in some large cities near the end of 1966, as it turned out, ended with the overthrow of local authorities, and was replaced by an entirely new factional cleavage.[24]

An important reason for the collapse of countermovement activity was that authority figures were divided against one another. In Nanjing, factions originated among workers out of antagonisms between two clearly defined groups in the Party leadership of one of the city's largest industrial enterprises. This, in turn, mirrored divisions between the Party apparatuses in a Beijing ministry and the city of Nanjing.[25] Even more problematic was new evidence that Party functionaries and the staff of government agencies themselves organized rebellions against their own superiors, were also divided into factions, and were active participants in the power seizures that overthrew city and county governments.[26] Divisions among these party-state cadres, and their active participation in rebel activities, undermined any meaningful distinction between forces favorable to, or antagonistic toward, the status quo. The factional battles of 1967 and 1968, as it turned out, were not an extension of rivalries between the defenders and opponents of local authorities in late 1966. Instead, they expressed splits among the rebel groups that had earlier sought to overthrow local governments.

At the core of the idea that factional warfare expressed different orientations toward the status quo was the fact that one faction fought against the imposition of military control, while the other supported military units. In these local struggles, factions that resisted military control appeared inherently more radical; they wanted to rebel "to the end." Factions that supported the armed forces' attempts to impose order appeared by definition to be more conservative. These conflicts were interpreted as familiar movement-countermovement phenomena.

As researchers pieced together local narratives of factional conflict, however, it became evident that these stances did not have the meaning attributed to them. The orientations of rebel factions toward military control, it turns out, did not express preferences regarding the restoration of order, but instead to the restoration of order *on whose terms.* Rebels competed for military support and turned against military units (or supported them) based on whether the military units offered support for their claims in prior disputes with other rebels. In some regions, rebel factions opposed to local military control would call upon and receive support from other military units.[27] In other words, the stance of a rebel group's orientation toward military control did not signal an underlying political orientation regarding the restoration of the status quo. It was a contingent product of the group's history of interaction with local military forces.

A famous example that appeared to contradict this conclusion was a notorious "ultra-left" manifesto associated with a rebel alliance in Hunan that denounced China's entire bureaucratic class in the name of subordinate social classes.[28] The group, known as the "Provincial Proletarian Alliance" (*Shengwulian*), was adamantly opposed to military control, and was part of the last-ditch resistance. Statements that they issued near the end of 1967 called for liberation from oppression by the "red capitalist class." Yet a detailed analysis of the group's history revealed that these ideas did not issue from a coalition of the marginalized, but were instead the product of a split over tactics within the rebel movement, a rhetorical framing of diehard resistance that was not widely shared even within the splinter faction that generated the essay. An in-depth examination of the case concluded, "The birth of Shengwulian was thus impromptu, if not accidental . . . [it] signified the emergence of new political identities and dynamics . . . the immediate causes of the split were relatively minor, the differences over tactics and approaches would later become magnified."[29] Instead, these were "emergent political ideas that granted new meanings to ongoing conflicts"; they were the "contingent consequences of unfolding interactions."[30]

The much more granular view of the formation of political conflict that emerges from recent research suggests that the dominant process was the division of potential interest groups, not their attainment of solidarity, and the formation of new political interests and orientations, not continuity in previously fixed ones.[31] In sociological terms, the political factions that drove conflicts were emergent properties of sequences of political interaction in contexts where political institutions had collapsed, and along with them the taken-for-granted expectations and meanings attached to them.

They were not a function of predefined social and political positions, but rather were a product of interactive processes as conflicts unfolded.

If factions were not a straightforward expression of interests and political orientations that were fixed beforehand, then an explanation needs to specify and document the processes through which these groups and their interests formed. If interest group analysis, and its characteristic focus on mobilization, fails to explain the patterns of conflict during this period, what exactly is the alternative explanation? How does one provide an analysis that does not simply recount detailed narrative histories?

Factions as Emergent Properties

A focus on sequences of political interaction can generate alternative theories about the outcomes of sustained political confrontations.[32] To claim that factions are emergent properties of political interactions requires that we specify clearly the social processes, or mechanisms, out of which factional identities emerge. This implies that we cannot restrict the analysis to the variable characteristics of groups and political settings—the social networks, group political capacities, and features of the political environment. This further implies that narrative accounts comprised of sequences of events are not troublesome details that unnecessarily obscure the clean lines of a causal analysis. Instead, these are the social processes upon which a plausible explanation is based.

A neglected precursor of this line of analysis is Charles Tilly's account of the social origins of the Vendée rebellion against the French revolution.[33] He traced the origins of the rebellion to the local impact of the revolutionary regime's 1791 demand of a "constitutional oath" by Catholic priests. This public oath required clergy to renounce the authority of the Pope and pledge loyalty to the new regime in Paris. This split local priests, some taking the oath, and others refusing, setting off disputes that divided local communities. One of Tilly's most important discoveries was that the rebellion split virtually all social classes, and divided Catholic clergy and their congregants against one another. The rebellion did not express class interests in any meaningful sense. The opposed political factions were an emergent property of sequences of events touched off by the varied reaction of Catholic priests to the demand to take the oath.[34]

At the outset we need to be clear about what exactly needs to be explained. Theories about protest and rebellion typically focus almost exclusively on the problem of collective action—given certain political interests and orientations in a population, how are individuals mobilized to engage in collective action in pursuit of these common ends? These theories are about political mobilization. They assume that groups with shared interests have already formed, or that it is obvious who they are and what interests they have. Our problem, however, is not to explain political mobilization, but political orientation. We need to understand the processes through which opposed factions formed—not how collective action was achieved, but who engaged in what course of political action and why they did so.

To explain the formation of factions we must understand the political choices of individuals and groups. At the individual level, analyses of political mobilization focus narrowly on one choice—whether or not to join with others in collective action, and whether to persist in that activity, once it is underway. There is an extensive and varied literature on recruitment and commitment.[35] To explain the formation of factions, however, the relevant choice is not *whether* to engage in political action, but *what* course of action to take, or *which* group to join, among a set of alternatives. To focus exclusively on the decision to contribute to collective action presumes that political orientations are either obvious or analytically uninteresting.

Theories about protest and rebellion have an equally restricted conception of the problem at the group level. The emphasis of this line of analysis is the *emergence* of mobilized groups, and their capacity to sustain effective mobilization and prevail in political contests with the state or countermovements. Leaders adopt different tactics and rhetorical appeals in the course of these conflicts, but these are analyzed solely in order to understand their impact on the ability of a movement to successfully mobilize in pursuit of group aims.[36] The substantive *aims* of group mobilization—their interests and political orientations—are simply not considered as part of the intellectual puzzle. They typically are treated as a given circumstance inherent in existing structures of power and inequality. As a result, these theories offer little insight into the formation of varied political orientations.

This was not always the case: an earlier generation of scholars was overwhelmingly preoccupied with explaining political orientations. Theories about the origins of fascism and communism, right-wing extremism, political violence, intolerance, and moral crusades were once the major preoccupation of political sociology.[37] Some of the most influential theories of that period lost credibility because they emphasized the impact of social disorganization, hardship and frustration, individual alienation, and the erosion of social ties to family and community.[38] These theories were undermined by empirical research that found a relationship between measures of group solidarity, organizational capacity, and levels of collective protest, but that failed to find a relationship with levels of hardship, deprivation, or social disorganization.[39] Closer examination of political mobilization revealed that it depended crucially on preexisting ties of solidarity between smaller groups of individuals who were organized for other purposes. The observation that mobilization relied on "bloc recruitment" of smaller solidary groups, later reconceptualized as network ties, refuted the proposition that individuals lacking ties to communities are drawn into protest movements.[40]

The refutation of older theories about the origins of political movements led to a subtle and largely overlooked shift of focus. Having demonstrated that political mobilization depends on certain forms of social solidarity, not social disorganization, a new field emerged that designated mobilization as the process of interest. This truncated the analysis of political movements and narrowed the focus. Interest in the formation of political orientations was jettisoned in favor of a quite different stance: "It is taken for granted that a collectivity or quasi-group . . . with common latent interests, already exists and that the members of the collectivity are dissatisfied and have grievances."[41] Theories about political *orientation* were replaced by theories about political *mobilization*. In essence, the then-new wave of theory about collective action moved on to a new question while ignoring the earlier one. This shift has endured in a large and intellectually diverse literature on social movements and collective action.[42]

Interest group explanations of factional warfare in China have the same logical structure. Interests and political orientations are treated as given, or exogenous—determined by a prior pattern of grievances or advantage in the status quo—and they are presumed to be stable motivators of political activity during the entire course of the conflicts. Political orientations are assumed to exist beforehand and provide the basis for collective action, which was facilitated when political opportunities shifted to permit their open expression.

This approach to political conflicts is now being questioned in analyses of ongoing political insurgencies around the world. Theories about civil conflicts routinely posit a unitary actor that is engaged in a contest with agents of a state.[43] Yet insurgencies are often riven with factional cleavages that divide combatants who share common linguistic, ethnic or class characteristics. Insurgents move in and out of alliances with other insurgent groups and with the forces of order and their political orientations and identities shift during the course of conflicts.[44] There is an evident need, in the words of one analyst, "to take seriously the endogenous dynamics of civil wars."[45] How should such an analysis proceed?

Political Orientation as Choice

Political orientations are the product of choices that individuals and groups make among alternative courses of action. In the conflicts described in this book, the primary choices can be stated very clearly. The first is whether to defend or confront individuals in positions of authority, in particular the leaders of local governments. The second is whether a rebel group seeks more than concessions from leaders, and moves to overthrow them in a power seizure. The third, in the wake of such a power seizure, is whether to support or oppose that act, whoever has carried it out. The fourth is whether to support military units dispatched to stabilize order in the wake of power seizures, or whether to oppose them. The fifth, after the formation of distinct political factions, is whether to use armed violence. In simplest terms, these were the alternative courses of action faced by political actors at the time, and they defined political orientations. Individuals who made similar choices coalesced into factions.

In an interest group analysis, the choice among alternative courses of action is a product of the social and political positions of actors prior to the onset of these conflicts. Those who are disadvantaged in the existing system will presumably support attacks on the powerful; they will likely support the overthrow of local officials in power seizures, and after the intervention of the armed forces they will likely resist the demobilization of rebels and the restoration of order by military units. Those who are advantaged, on the other hand, will choose to shield the powerful from rebel attacks; they will tend to oppose their overthrow by rebels in power seizures; and they will tend to support the imposition of order by the armed forces.

If, on the other hand, factions are an emergent property of evolving conflicts, these logical connections are tenuous. Whatever the interests of groups based on their positions in the existing order, choices among alternative courses of action are dependent on evolving political contexts. Under certain circumstances, those who are privileged in the existing order will find it in their interest to form rebel groups and join in attacks on powerful officials, and even to oust them from power—precisely in order to protect their positions. To do so they may willingly align themselves with rebels that express grievances against the existing order. Whatever the origins of a rebel group, their support for a power seizure over the local government will be contingent on their relationship to it. If they were included in a power seizure coalition, they were likely to support it; if they were excluded or preempted by others who acted more quickly, they were likely to object to it. Decisions about whether to support or oppose the efforts of military units to enforce order will be similarly context-dependent. If military commanders support a rebel group's stance in disputes with other rebels over power seizures, those rebels will likely support that military unit; if not, they will likely object to the army's actions. The connections between interests and political choices are defined by context.

Another difference between these two lines of reasoning is whether choice is conceived as interactive. An interest group analysis presumes that individuals and groups will choose courses of action solely based on their own perceived interests, without reference to the actions of others. Factions in this view are essentially aggregations of like-minded individuals that pursue shared interests in concert. If, by contrast, factions are an emergent property of interactions, the political stance of a group will be contingent on the actions of others. Will a rebel group that was excluded from a power seizure become antagonistic to rebels who carried out a power seizure? That depends on whether those who seized power respond to opposition with denunciation and repression, or with compromise. Their response, in turn, may be a function of how the excluded rebels expressed their objections. Will rebel groups subsequently support or oppose military commanders? That depends on decisions taken by these commanders that either support or undermine their claims in disputes with other rebels, and may further depend on whether the armed forces responded with force to criticisms of their actions. The social and political characteristics of members of a group provide little guidance to context-specific choices that are shaped by the actions of others. The process is endogenous to the conflicts themselves—political orientations and their associated identities are emergent properties of the interactions among different parties.[46]

The process is not random, but there is a random element to it, because factions are a joint outcome of contingent interactions in a series of shifting contexts. Statistical theory refers to this as a "stochastic" process. In a deterministic process one can predict an outcome based on the starting point—in this case the attributes of actors. Interest group analysis predicts the political orientation of actors based on their positions in sociopolitical structures at the outset of the period of observation. A stochastic process, by contrast, is one where the eventual outcome is produced by a series of steps, or turning points. At each step, each party faces a choice among alternative courses of action, and these choices are partly dependent on choices made by other parties. This means that it is not possible to determine where an individual or a mobilized group will end up, based solely on their interests or motivations at the outset. This does not mean that we are unable to explain the formation of groups. It simply means that there is no essential or fixed characteristic of actors that permits us to predict their political choices at each step without reference to the interactive contexts within which politics takes place.[47]

Out of a series of choices among alternative courses of action, groups develop political orientations—stances toward authorities, toward military units, and toward other mobilized groups that become allies or opponents. It is out of these choices that factional identities are constructed in the course of ongoing conflicts. These are *insurgent* identities, which define for actors and opponents who they are in relation to other actors.[48] In other words, actors construct collective political identities, often inadvertently, out of the choices they make in evolving circumstances.

To define the problem as one of choice does not imply any stance about the psychology of actors, or *how* they make choices. Usually conceived as questions about the rationality of actors, this issue is often debated as if it has momentous consequences for explanations of social processes. In this context, such debates are a needless distraction. Choice in this setting was highly problematic, whatever we imagine the mental processes of actors to be. Existing political institutions were either collapsing or had already collapsed, and expectations and norms based on prior experience no longer held. A calculating, self-interested actor would find it very difficult to anticipate the likely consequences of a course of action, given the unprecedented and constantly changing nature of the situation. Such an actor would face a high level of *uncertainty* that would make choices highly problematic. Choice is equally problematic for an actor whose choices are presumably shaped by deeply held political commitments, or culturally shaped modes of judgment. This actor would face a situation where the meanings attached to different modes of action, and the evaluation of established institutions, have been thrown into question. This actor would find that the norms, values, and even personal loyalties long taken for granted can no longer be—requiring rapid judgments in novel situations. An actor oriented toward meaningful activity faces a high level of *ambiguity* about how to apply value commitments to an existing situation. The prevalence of both uncertainty and ambiguity makes highly problematic the idea that courses of action, for both individuals and groups, were a product of perceived interests or political orientations at the outset of this period of conflict. Given the contextual and interactive nature of choices, actors driven by presumably different motivations would be as likely to make the same choices as they would different ones.

Even with the best historical evidence it is impossible to distinguish which kind of motives are driving action. Strategic, self-interested actors build moral and political rationales for the correctness of their actions in order to justify them and convince others of their rectitude. Actors driven by political and moral rectitude will be just as determined to prevail in local conflicts as anyone else, and will be fully capable of acting in a highly strategic manner, precisely because they are so convinced of the rectitude of their position. Strategic, self-interested actors can convince themselves of (or deceive themselves about) their moral rectitude. Committed idealists, for their part, can become ruthlessly strategic in pursuing their ends. All actors will make decisions about courses of action in context, partly dependent on the actions of others. Their decisions, however they make them, are the foundation of factions.

An interactive perspective on conflict also implies that the ideals and political commitments that are expressed by groups can themselves be the product of these interactions, rather than an inherent feature of individuals and groups at the outset. To portray interactions as a series of choices does not deny that there are powerful subjective elements and ideals for which groups fight. Studies of these conflicts have already illustrated the ways that new conceptions and political ideals emerged over time. The April 14 rebels at Tsinghua University, for example, in their bitter rivalry with a more powerful rebel faction, eventually developed an explicit rationale for a "moderate" political line that conformed with a recent shift in direction by the Central Cultural Revolution Group. But they did so only after a rival rebel leader objected to that shift, creating a rhetorical opening for this line of attack.[49] The "ultra-left" Hunan rebel group Shengwulian developed an elaborate critique of China's "red capitalists" only near the end of their last-ditch fight against military control.[50]

The observation that ideals and political commitments are the product of political experiences rather than a set of beliefs fully formed prior to participation in politics is familiar in other settings. Studies of antiabortion activists in the United States, for example, have shown that activists initially did not have clear beliefs about conception and unborn fetuses, and developed them only during the course of participation in movement organizations.[51] Similarly, the abolition of feudalism during the French Revolution was not inherent in the lists of grievances initially recorded in assemblies of different estates in 1789. The demands and accompanying ideology shifted over time as popular assemblies in Paris responded to regional protests.[52] The question is not whether ideals and political commitment matter—it is where these political commitments come from and how they develop.[53] These ideals and commitments are part of the process of interaction and identity building that we describe here—they are themselves an outcome of these histories of interaction.

Political Contexts

At the core of any plausible explanation of the endogenous formation of groups, and the subsequent development of violent conflict, must be a clear understanding of the features of contexts that define the choices that actors face. This implies that the dynamic element in these endogenous processes is a sequence of shifts in political contexts over time. Individuals and groups do not constantly face the same choices in a repeating fashion— they face an evolving series of choices presented by contexts that can shift in unanticipated ways.

The idea that contextual shifts are the dynamic element in sustained political conflicts is not a new idea. The familiar concept of "political opportunity structure" is a statement about the context for group mobilization, and it is inherently dynamic. The structure of political opportunity can be defined by trends in national politics that provide elite allies or opponents, legal regimes, levels and techniques of repression, shifting strategies of repression, or the emergence of other mobilized groups that can provide either allies or opponents. The rise and fall of protest movements, their evolution, and their level of success, can be readily traced to the opening up or closing down of political opportunities at the national or local level.[54]

Political opportunity structures are invoked almost exclusively to explain the propensity of individuals to join in collective action, or the success with which a group mobilizes to pursue its ends. But the concept is equally relevant to understanding choices among alternative courses of action, and can readily be applied to understanding these choices. For this purpose, the central puzzle is not limited to the conventional one of explaining the rise and fall of certain forms of political mobilization. It is to help us understand *who* the factional combatants were and *why* they engaged in violent conflict.

In this setting, the first dimension of political context was signals of support or disapproval by actors at the apex of the national hierarchy regarding different courses of action. This was important not only because China had a unitary and centralized political hierarchy that reached down into almost every local community. These signals shifted with regularity, and it was often unclear to local actors which pronouncements reflected Mao Zedong's own preferences. Mao and his associates were the initiators of all rebel activity, and they tried to regulate and steer it over time. Local actors had little prospect of prevailing in courses of action that had the clear disapproval of Beijing. There was, moreover, frequent uncertainty about which actors in Beijing authoritatively conveyed Mao's stance. Younger radical members of the Central Cultural Revolution Group, the ad hoc committee that mobilized rebellions during the Cultural Revolution, often issued directives that encouraged action against civilian and military authorities. Other actors, especially Zhou Enlai, issued directives that countered or moderated these initiatives.[55] Mao Zedong himself shifted his support from one tendency to the other over the course of these conflicts. These signaled shifts in the perceived likelihood at the local and regional level that certain courses of action had a chance to succeed. As we shall see, these signals could have a decisive impact on the courses of action chosen by locally mobilized groups.

The second dimension is the local impact of events at the immediately higher level of the political hierarchy. Events at the province level shaped the choices of actors at the level of prefectures and prefecture-level cities, and events at the prefecture level shaped choices at the level of counties and county-level cities. The relevant shaping influences were most evident within the vertical lines of the political hierarchy. What mattered in a locality were developments at the immediately higher level in the hierarchy. When a provincial government fell in a power seizure, this altered choices faced by actors in cities and prefectures immediately below it; and when the governments of these cities and prefectures were overthrown in turn, this shaped the choices faced in smaller cities and counties below them. After the collapse of provincial governments, it mattered whether the region was placed under military control, or whether it was placed under a new government—a "revolutionary committee"—that had the explicit approval of Beijing. This shaped the choices faced by actors lower in the hierarchy, as military control persisted, or gave way to an approved revolutionary committee, at each step downward in the hierarchy.

A third element of political contexts was the stances of regional and local authorities, both civilian and military, toward mobilized political groups, which could take the form of active support, passive acceptance, the mobilization of defensive countermovements, or aggressive repression by force. These stances, like the activity of mobilized groups, also depended heavily on signals emanating from actors in Beijing, and the actions of both civilian and military authorities during this period shifted repeatedly in response. Given the stances of local authorities—through most of this period and in most regions this meant military units—the decisive element was their capacity to enforce their decisions, and their willingness to act decisively to do so.

A fourth and final element of political contexts was the history of local political interactions among rebel groups and between rebel groups and local authorities, in particular military units. Two aspects were particularly important. The first was the pattern of alignments among rebel groups in support of or in opposition to the power seizures that toppled local authorities, and the way that these alignments were shaped by the actions of local military units when they intervened in local politics. These alignments were the product of contingent encounters, and they created new cleavages that generated political identities. The second was the prior history of conflict between factions, and in particular how long they endured and how violent they became. The choices evolved as violent conflict persisted.

A Focus on the State

The analysis in this book is framed by the architecture of China's party-state, a single hierarchy that encompassed 174 cities of various sizes and more than 2,200 rural counties. I employ an event-based analysis that draws on a database that is extracted from a near-complete collection of more than 2,200 city and county annals, and combine this with an examination of raw material from the longest and most detailed local narratives. By aggregating the political events described in local histories, I trace patterns of conflict across time and space.

This approach to analyzing political conflict has not previously been used in the analysis of China's Cultural Revolution, but it has been widely applied in other settings—to both long-term shifts across historical time, and to relatively brief and intense upheavals.[56] Studies of this sort usually focus single-mindedly on popular insurgencies. My sources, however, also contain a wealth of information about the pattern of collapse of local governments and their subsequent rebuilding, and acts of repression by military and civilian authorities. This facilitates an analysis that portrays conflict as a series of interactions between insurgents and authorities in shifting national and local contexts.

A focus on the state requires us to pay close attention to the structure of this unitary and centralized hierarchy and also the activities of the individuals who staffed it. In 1965, there were 2.4 million office personnel ("cadres") who staffed Party and government organs, and a total of 21.5 million Party members.[57] They were organized into a single hierarchy that reached deeply into the grass roots, well below the level of city and county government. Their reaction to the events of this period, as we shall see, undermined China's party-state far beyond the capacities of the early popular insurgencies, and local cadres continued to play an active role in the factional conflicts that followed.

This implies that we need to focus on the state in a second sense—local state structures are sites of conflict and even rebellion, not just targets of popular insurgencies. Scholarship on this period has been singularly pre-occupied with movements among students, workers, and others who challenged political authorities across China. But there was an equally dramatic political mobilization within the party-state bureaucracy. Beginning in June 1966, the state's structures were quickly thrown into internal upheavals that interacted in complex ways with the unfolding political activism of students and workers. Near the end of 1966, internal rebellions by party-state functionaries against their own superiors destabilized and eventually destroyed state structures far beyond the capacities of the popular rebellions that they faced. As we shall see, the large-scale factional warfare that we associate with this early phase of the Cultural Revolution began only *after* local power structures were overthrown.

The idea that popular mobilizations are intimately connected with state structures is familiar in historical studies of political contention. These publications relate changes in the forms, rates, and styles of collective protest to the expansion of capitalism and the creation of more intrusive and centralized state structures. Charles Tilly's work was notable for its emphasis on the historical evolution of state structures: "The national state's growth entailed increasing control of the resources in a contiguous territory by an organization that was formally autonomous, differentiated from other organizations, centralized, internally coordinated, and in possession of major concentrated means of coercion."[58] This was matched by a parallel evolution in the organization of early-modern economies and societies. The expansion of wage labor and concentration of capital interacted with the increasing scope and centralization of state structures to increase the capacity of urbanized populations to organize and pursue their interests in the form of the modern social movement.[59] Over the course of historical trajectories "we have much to gain from an analysis that singles out the effects of large social changes on ordinary people's interests, opportunities, and organization, then examines how changing interest, opportunity, and organization influence their prevailing modes of collective action."[60] This book is part of that broad tradition of historical sociology, but its focus on the relationship between state structures and political conflict is compressed into a short and intense period of political upheaval. In such a compressed

period of time, the relationship of state structures to popular political mobilization shifts rapidly in ways that requires much closer examination.

This focus on state structures is facilitated by the source materials that
form an important foundation for this book. Throughout, I draw on information contained in local annals *(difang zhi)* that were published in
China by county and city governments after the mid-1980s. The annals
for each local government separately provided its own account of political
events during this period, creating a framework for understanding that
maps directly onto the state hierarchy. These annals revived a practice in
imperial dynasties, when they contained accounts of local history, surveys
of the local economy and society, and biographies of imperial degree holders
and other local notables. Surviving annals from the last two dynasties, the
Ming and Qing, have informed research on popular protest and collective
violence in earlier eras.[61] The new annals contain general chronologies of
major events, and many of them also contain narrative accounts of specific
political campaigns, the local history of the Communist Party and government institutions, and a variety of statistics on the local population,
economy, and social structure.

Accounts from a near-complete collection of 2,246 local annals have
been coded and assembled into a data set of events (see the Appendix: Local
Annals Data Set). Although the quality of local accounts and their level of
detail vary widely, in the aggregate, the annals yielded an extraordinary
amount of information. The data set contains information about close to
34,000 events at the city or county level from June 1966 to December 1971
according to the month they occurred, and more than half of them according to a specific day. It also contains information for more than
twenty indicators of the demographic and political characteristics of the
locality, and the features of the account from which the event data were
coded.

I employ the resulting data to trace the temporal and geographic spread
of certain kinds of insurgent activities and other key political events across
China's cities and counties and their evolution over time, alongside patterns of repression. My aim is to develop a clear, evidence-based description that will illuminate long-standing areas of ignorance and perhaps rec-
tify misimpressions that that may have resulted from the grassroots focus
of past research or the selective nature of regional studies. These broader
patterns will also help to identify puzzles that require further analysis by

addressing other sources. Statistical patterns alone are insufficient. The historical narratives in the longest and most detailed local accounts contain essential information that cannot be expressed in statistical terms. The patterns revealed by the quantitative data frame questions that require a closer look at local narratives, and the processes revealed in the narratives frame questions that will require a closer look at the statistical patterns.

One of the purposes of this book is to fill large gaps in the historiography of this period—to accurately describe and characterize *what* happened. But there is an even more important explanatory agenda—*why* the conflicts of the period unfolded as they did. As broad patterns of political activity come into focus as part of the descriptive agenda, a series of explanatory puzzles come into focus, some of them for the first time. To address these puzzles, it will be necessary to depart from or modify the emphases of influential theories about rebellion, revolution, and other forms of contentious politics. This defines the second task, which is to analyze patterns of conflict from the perspective of social science theory, to treat these patterns as puzzles that require explanation, and to generate ideas that extend theories about political conflict into subjects about which they currently provide little insight.

The first of these puzzles is brought into focus in Chapters 2 and 3, and analyzed explicitly in Chapter 4: why did such a highly centralized and disciplined party-state collapse so rapidly in early 1967? Theories about rebellion and revolution adopt two different approaches to this question. The first views the overthrow of governments as a consequence of the scale of mass mobilization, which overwhelms a state's repressive capacities. In the wake of the unexpectedly sudden collapse of a series of state socialist regimes from 1989 to 1991, threshold models of collective behavior have come to the fore, emphasizing the social processes that generate sudden upsurges of popular protest.[62] The second, an older "state-centered" stream of theory, departs from bottom-up views of revolution as a function of the scale of popular rebellion, and asserts that states are vulnerable only if they have preexisting structural weaknesses that make them vulnerable to mass mobilizations.[63] As we shall discover, local governments collapsed across China in early 1967 well in advance of the spread of popular insurgencies, which at the time were still very limited outside of the largest cities. Moreover, prior to these upheavals the Chinese state did not suffer from the structural weaknesses emphasized by state-centered theories. As we shall see, the answer to this puzzle lies in previously unexamined political processes within the party-state itself—a dimension of politics rarely emphasized in theories about rebellion and revolution. Power seizures diffused downward in the national political hierarchy as party-state officials turned against their superiors as shifting political contexts redefined the choices that they faced. The centralized and disciplined nature of the national political hierarchy was itself a major reason for its rapid collapse.

The second puzzle, addressed in Chapter 5, is why large and antagonistic factional alliances formed in the wake of the collapse of local governments, and in particular why they adopted different orientations toward military units that intervened in local politics. Social science theories about rebellion and other forms of contentious politics—either explicitly or implicitly—typically view conflict groups as expressions of interests defined prior to the activities of interest. I examine detailed local narratives and aggregate data about the formation of factions to reconstruct how factions formed through a series of path-dependent interactions among disparate rebel groups and military units. This is the core of the intellectual problem highlighted earlier in this chapter.

A third puzzle, addressed in Chapters 6 and 7, is why violent factional warfare ensued. To explain how factions formed is not to explain why they subsequently engaged in violent conflict. As we shall see, large-scale factional warfare did not occur everywhere, and the intensity of violence increased the longer that it persisted. What drove this collective violence in certain regions, which proceeded to the point where close to a quarter-million of the combatants were killed? Social science theories about collective violence typically attribute it to the enormity of the stakes for different social classes or ethnic groups, as a reaction to violence initiated by the state's agents, or as a strategy that sustains mobilization and wears down opponents. These explanations all focus—explicitly or implicitly—on how collective action is initiated and sustained. Instead, we will find that the key to explaining the severity of the violence is in understanding how collective action *ends*—in particular, the anticipated costs to participants of failing to prevail over their opponents, or at least fight to a draw. Prolonged histories of unresolved conflicts were the features of local contexts that drove escalating violence. By examining circumstances under which the most severe violence occurred, it will become evident that the problem of exit from collective action explains the most severe and sustained violence. In certain circumstances, combatants were drawn into self-reinforcing escalation traps.

A fourth and final puzzle is addressed in Chapter 8, which examines the process through which state authority was reestablished. Prior work has demonstrated that the restoration of order was far more damaging in terms of lives lost and disrupted than the many months of violent disorder that preceded it. Four to five times as many people died in the campaign to reestablish order, primarily after the end of insurgent activity.[64] In this penultimate chapter I will seek to explain why this was so. Throughout many months of violent regional warfare, China's armed forces always had the capacity to quell armed civilian insurgencies. As 1968 progressed, in one region after another, military units were given freer rein to compel local factions to disarm and disband. Yet death tolls and political victimization rose to unprecedented levels *after* factions were disarmed and disbanded, when they and other citizens returned to their places of residence and work. How to explain the puzzling timing of this upsurge of repression, which went far beyond what was necessary to demobilize rebel combatants?

Scholarship on this period, like many accounts of popular upheavals, has been preoccupied with mobilizations by ordinary citizens to confront agents of the state. In this historical episode, however, the groups that one would ordinarily expect to be bulwarks of the political order—in particular, party-state cadres and military units—contributed to these upheavals in ways that turned them into agents of disorder. The process unfolded in the last half of 1966, when the state's structures were quickly thrown into internal upheavals that interacted in complex ways with the growing political activism of students and workers. It is to the extensive and varied political mobilizations of the last half of 1966 that I now turn.

2

MOBILIZING A NATION

SEVERAL VARIETIES OF political mobilization shaped national politics during the last half of 1966. By the end of the year they had destabilized a number of large cities and had begun to undermine political authority elsewhere in the country. The rapid spread of mass mobilization in the last half of 1966 is not hard to explain. The political movements touched off in China in 1966 were inspired and supported by actors at the apex of a highly centralized and intrusive state structure. Initially students, and eventually workers, were given every encouragement to form independent organizations, and they were provided with the resources necessary for their activities. The security services and armed forces, which normally suppressed such activities with great effectiveness, were ordered not to interfere. State agencies shifted away from systematic repression to active facilitation of certain forms of popular mobilization. Independent political groups were permitted freely to publish their own broadsheets and handbills, and to publish copies of leaders' speeches and transcripts of meetings that would normally be highly classified. They shared this information via networks of like-minded groups across the country.[1]

There was an additional, less obvious structural foundation for the rapid and widespread mobilizations of 1966. The same political structures that permitted the state to penetrate, monitor, and mobilize ordinary citizens toward approved political ends inadvertently created social networks that facilitated independent political mobilization. China's revolutionary regime organized citizens in workplaces and neighborhoods into smaller units that served as sites for monitoring and control. Students were organized by entry cohort into classes of several dozen individuals who stayed together over the years and participated in regular organized activities even outside the classroom.[2] Employees remained in their assigned workplaces for much of their lives, with almost no turnover. These individuals were similarly organized into smaller units based on offices and workshops, and divided into smaller groups for political study and other activities. Members of the Communist Party, roughly 20 percent of the urban adult population, were themselves organized into branches that averaged 12 to 15 individuals, who met regularly for party-directed activities.[3] Even on collective farms, families were organized into production teams that served both as units of residence and units of political and economic organization.[4]

Under ordinary circumstances, these structures facilitated the regime's control, monitoring populations in ways that curtailed the possibility of independent collective action. But these structures also created local solidarities that facilitated independent political activity when political contexts were radically altered in the last half of 1966. Collective action in social movements frequently builds on preexisting solidarities, recruiting adherents in entire blocs rather than as isolated individuals.[5] Individuals who were already organized into classrooms, workshops, small groups, and party branches relied upon these social networks and organized themselves into a variety of small and informally organized independent groups during this period. Larger alliances initially were loose assemblages of these smaller units. Larger factional coalitions across schools and workplaces, in turn, were assemblages of these within-school and within-workplace aggregations.

At the outset, virtually every Red Guard and rebel organization that emerged during this period—whether among students, blue- or white-collar workers, or party-state cadres—exhibited an unmistakable "cellular" structure. Individuals participated in broader political alliances as members of small "fighting groups" *(zhandou dui),* based on the groups they were a part of in their daily life. These groups maintained a separate identity, participating in larger alliances as small solidary groups. This cellular pattern facilitated the rapid expansion of rebel insurgencies, but it also created a recurring problem of fragmentation and division. Not until much later did rebel alliances begin to form cohesive and disciplined organizations. In the early months, the leaders of each of the smaller units could readily become rivals, creating chronic discord and frequent splits. This pattern would eventually have important consequences for the formation of factions after the overthrow of local governments.

There were six separate varieties of political mobilization that unfolded during the last half of 1966. Some were top-down campaigns to investigate political loyalties; some were independent groups that did not threaten political authorities; some targeted political authorities for criticism and removal; and some mobilized to protect authorities from rebel attacks. The first, which was often neglected in accounts of this period, was mobilization within the national bureaucracy for loyalty investigations that netted victims at all ranks in the political system. Spreading rapidly across China beginning in June 1966, this was a conventional loyalty investigation conducted by top party officials at each level of the hierarchy. The second was a nationwide mobilization of university and high school students into a Red Guard movement that had official sanction and support at all levels. Red Guards mobilized to denounce faculty members and school administrators, and attack individuals and physical artifacts that represented reactionary historical legacies. The third was a breakaway "rebel" faction of the Red Guards that turned its critical attention to top officials in local and national governments. The rebel movement grew in scale and militancy after it received the open approval and encouragement of Mao and his followers in October 1966. The fourth, which got underway in mid-November, was a rebel movement among industrial workers and other salaried employees, a development that greatly magnified the scale and impact of popular rebellion in large cities. The fifth was a countermovement in opposition to rebel attacks on authorities. These groups initially formed within party and government offices in September, aiming to secure them against student rebels. In November, this took the form of countermobilization by workers in large state enterprises to confront worker rebels on the streets of large cities. The sixth and final form of mobilization, which spread rapidly in December, was a rebellion by cadres inside the party-state hierarchy against their own superiors. These internal rebellions were critical for the spread of power seizures that toppled regional and local governments across China in early 1967.

Inside the Bureaucracy

At the outset of the Cultural Revolution, China had a highly disciplined and centralized political hierarchy. The opening salvo of a new loyalty campaign was the announcement on May 16, 1966, that an "anti-party conspiracy" had been uncovered in the highest reaches of the party. The head of the Central Committee's Propaganda Department, the Chief of Staff of the People's Liberation Army, the Chief of Staff of the Central Committee, and Beijing's Party Secretary were all condemned as revisionists who sought to undermine Mao Zedong's revolutionary political line. The document launched a campaign intended to root out others with similar political tendencies, and the immediate impact was an unfolding purge campaign that decimated the leadership and staff of the central party bureaucracy and the administration of the nation's capital.[6]

To prosecute these loyalty investigations, large investigative "work teams" *(gongzuo dui)* and smaller "work groups" *(gongzuo zu)* were dispatched to government agencies to examine their personnel, and they were also sent to universities and high schools, research institutes, and large state enterprises for the same purpose.[7] In the schools they mobilized students during June and July in an unfolding campaign to denounce and unmask anti-party elements in educational institutions. In August 1966 the student Red Guard movement was the most visible result. During the same period, a lesser-noticed mobilization for an internal political campaign unfolded within the party-state hierarchy itself. Officials in charge of provincial and local governments throughout China were compelled to respond to the new directive. The Party Center—Mao Zedong—had decreed that "Khrushchev-type bourgeois representatives" that had sneaked into the party in "all provinces, cities, and autonomous regions." For provincial party leaders this was the key passage in the document, indicating it was their responsibility to show zeal in uncovering and punishing such figures in their own jurisdictions.[8] High officials in the nation's capital had already fallen in disgrace, and the vigorous prosecution of loyalty investigations was the only way for regional officials to ensure that they remained above suspicion. In July, Beijing decreed that "the spearhead of this Proletarian Cultural Revolution is pointed at representatives of the bourgeoisie who have snuck into the Party, the government, the army, and various cultural institutions, and especially at the small groups of power-holders who are anti-party, anti-socialist, and anti-Mao Zedong Thought," and furthermore that "all party and government organs at the prefecture level and above must launch this campaign without exception."[9] The process of unmasking and removing anti-party elements would proceed within the organs of the party-state at the same time as it unfolded in schools.

Other high-level victims were soon identified. Two provinces saw their top leaders suddenly removed for alleged anti-party activities. Inner Mongolia's First Party Secretary was summoned to the capital in late May along with other top regional officials and subjected to accusations that he had promoted Mongolian separatism. He was held there until late July and was removed from all of his posts, along with several other members of Inner Mongolia's top leadership.[10] In late June the First Party Secretary of Hebei Province was called to a meeting in Beijing and denounced along with several other leading provincial officials. He was stripped of his posts and the provincial leadership was reshuffled.[11]

The leaders of other provinces displayed their vigilance by hunting for "anti-party elements" in their own jurisdictions. They formed "Cultural Revolution Committees" to conduct loyalty investigations and mobilized thousands of investigators into work teams that were sent into universities, high schools, newspaper offices, and cultural troupes to search for political deviance.[12] Provincial party committees also conducted loyalty investigations within their own ranks, initially focusing heavily on departments responsible for propaganda, culture, and education. They did not limit their attacks to low-ranking officials and intellectuals, although many such figures were also widely targeted. In most provinces at least one ranking member of the top provincial leadership, frequently the official in charge of propaganda, was purged in June or July. The purges typically extended to a number of their subordinates, frequently the editor of the local newspaper, the head of the provincial writer's association, the heads of local universities or the party's training school for its cadres.

Provincial histories are filled with details about these loyalty campaigns. Anhui formed an investigation committee immediately after the first purges in Beijing, and convened a three-week meeting, beginning May 23rd, for all party secretaries of provincial departments, bureaus, prefectures and cities to prepare self-examinations of their political conduct. During these meetings the provincial party secretary in charge of the Propaganda Department was targeted for alleged disloyalty. In early July he was said to have led an anti-party group in his department that included the editorial team of the party's newspaper, *Anhui Daily*.[13] The First Party Secretary of Fujian organized a provincial party congress in mid-June to lay out plans for the Cultural Revolution, and by early July several leading provincial officials were under attack for their work in the Propaganda Department, the Party School, the Culture Department, the Provincial Writer's Association, and *Fujian Daily*.[14] In Gansu, the Party Secretary of Lanzhou University was declared a counterrevolutionary in late June and committed suicide; the head of the Provincial Propaganda Department, a member of the province's Standing Committee, was denounced as a counterrevolutionary along with his deputy, the editor of *Gansu Daily*.[15] In Guangxi a vice-head of the Propaganda Department and the editor-in-chief of *Guangxi Daily* both fell in mid-June.[16] In early July a party secretary who had recently headed Tibet's Organization Department was denounced along with the editor-in-chief of *Tibet Daily*, and was soon removed officially from all posts.[17] Jiangsu's Party Secretary launched the campaign at a mass rally in early July, and soon thereafter more than 400,000 wall posters attacking leading cadres appeared in 57 of the 65 provincial agencies.[18]

These campaigns in provincial governments were replicated in jurisdictions under them. Within the city government of Nanning, the capital of Guangxi Province, more than 1,000 leading cadres and intellectuals, primarily in propaganda, news, and cultural organizations, were targeted by the end of June as "anti-party elements" and subjected to abusive mass meetings known as "struggle sessions" within the organs of the city's party and government.[19] These campaigns extended as far as the party bureaucracy reached, even into remote regions. Officials in Linzhi County, a prefecture capital in eastern Tibet, were already mobilized for an internal criticism campaign in late May. They were informed that anyone in the party and government organs could be criticized, "no matter how high their position."[20] These are just a sampling of the many cases detailed in published histories, and they suggest that the bureaucratic organs of provincial governments and their capital cities were disrupted by divisive and threatening loyalty investigations that netted prominent officials and their close associates.

Often lost in accounts of this period that focus on student activism is the fact that the national bureaucracy itself was already thrown into upheaval.

These events put all government functionaries on notice that their loyalty was subject to challenge, and that their positions were potentially at risk. The potential consequences ranged from a ruined career to a harsh term of imprisonment or expulsion to a labor camp. This forced party and government functionaries at all levels to be closely attentive to political signals emanating from Beijing, and to adjust their behavior to ensure that they would not be swept up in the purge campaign. As the months wore on, however, it also forced them into difficult choices, and as signals from Beijing shifted, they adjusted their behavior in ways that would undermine the political order.

Student Red Guards

As the national bureaucracy mobilized during June and July for internal loyalty campaigns, investigators were also sent into universities and high schools to mobilize a campaign against political deviance. They proved to be highly disruptive. Those sent to schools typically orchestrated accusations against at least some leading school officials, and many of them conducted purges that were radical and extensive. They also mobilized student activists and younger faculty to denounce senior faculty and school officials. However, unlike the intra-bureaucratic campaigns, these work teams met with spirited opposition and struggled to maintain control. Militant students and young instructors vied with work teams over the designation of targets and their treatment. In some settings the struggle was over the direction of the campaign, especially the designation of political targets among the school's leading officials. In some settings students who formed independent organizations were warned that they were forbidden. In other settings the conflicts were over the treatment of targeted individuals, particularly the extent to which student militants would have free access to them for humiliating and violent "struggle sessions" that could result in severe injury and even death. The conflicts in schools became so sharp that many work teams actually fled from their campus, only to be replaced later by more militant work teams that counterattacked against student activists who continued openly to defy authority. In many cases the work teams retaliated against the most defiant students and faculty, labeling them as anti-party elements for their disruptive behavior.[21]

This initial mobilization, and the conflict that it inadvertently spawned, served as the launch pad for the Red Guard movement when it burst onto the scene shortly after work teams were withdrawn at the end of July and denounced by Mao for "suppressing the student movement". The students who defied work teams earned Mao's praise, and they were held up as models for student militants across the country. Mao took several steps to signal that independent student mobilization was permitted, and in fact strongly encouraged. After this point no local leaders could contemplate obstructing the formation of independent Red Guard units among students. This was now official policy, backed by China's supreme leader. Local officials typically provided encouragement and support for the burgeoning student campaign.

An assembly of student militants was held in the Great Hall of the People, at which Liu Shaoqi, Zhou Enlai, and Deng Xiaoping, three of the top seven ranking officials in the party hierarchy, apologized for the work teams' alleged suppression of student activism. Mao himself appeared on the stage and greeted the students.[22] At a subsequent party conference that began on August 1, Mao had wall posters authored by some of the first student Red Guards reproduced and distributed to participants along with his editorial praise, and he issued one of his own that encouraged students to "bombard the headquarters."[23] On August 18, Mao appeared at the first of a series of eight mass rallies held for Red Guards on Tiananmen Square. Appearing on the rostrum with a range of student leaders from the nation's capital, he donned a Red Guard armband, engaged in friendly conversations with student leaders, and had several of them give impromptu speeches.[24]

The state media praised the militant students and made clear Mao's strong approval of their organizations. In the weeks to come Mao's radical associates established ties with student leaders in the nation's capital. Students were permitted free travel on the railway system, and reception centers were set up in the nation's capital and other large cities to provide lodging and food for traveling students. To make absolutely certain that the student movement would be given free rein, two separate directives were issued in late August that forbid public security agencies and the armed forces from "interfering" with or "suppressing" Red Guard activities.[25] The same message was hammered home after reports of popular resistance to

Red Guard activities. On September 11, Mao issued an instruction, distributed nationwide as a central party document, that forbid the incitement of workers, farmers, or soldiers to try to block the activities of student militants.[26]

With this level of official support, the Red Guard movement grew rapidly. Beijing was the epicenter, with Red Guard organizations spreading across high schools in early June, and with imitators soon to appear in the provincial capitals. Figure 2.1 charts the spread of this initial surge of student political activism, as recorded in local annals. The trend lines trace the cumulative percentage, by month, of the first mention of local Red Guard activity at different levels of China's political hierarchy, from provincial capitals to other large "prefecture level" cities, to smaller "county-level" cities, and rural counties. Red Guard activities typically were expressed in critical wall posters, the subjection of teachers and school officials to public denunciation meetings known as "struggle sessions," or the destruction of temples, churches, artwork, and books deemed to be remnants of the reactionary cultures of feudalism and imperialism. Red Guards were rare across China in June and July, but this changed dramatically after the nationwide publicity given to the first Red Guard rally on Tiananmen Square on August 18. Students rushed to form Red Guard organizations, make political accusations against faculty and administrators in their schools, vandalize temples and artwork, and take advantage of free travel around the country—especially the coveted opportunity to travel to Beijing and attend the Tiananmen Square rallies. Almost all of China's cities reported Red Guard activity by the end of August, as did the majority of counties. By October more than 85 percent of counties reported local Red Guard activities.[27]

These figures represent a remarkable level of popular political mobilization. At no point in the previous history of the regime were ordinary citizens permitted, much more encouraged, to form independent political organizations. Citizens were urged to air their criticisms of official behavior during the Hundred Flowers period a decade earlier, in 1957, but independent political organizations were never authorized, and retaliation against those who attempted independent political activity was swift and severe, leading instead to a draconian "anti-Rightist" campaign after only a few weeks.[28] Now less than a decade later, students all across China, beginning in the large cities and soon spreading into rural counties, formed Red Guard

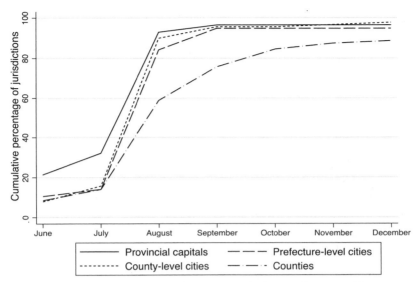

Figure 2.1. The Spread of Red Guard Activity, 1966, by Jurisdiction Level
(N = 2,246)

groups and engaged in activities associated with that movement. These numbers do not convey the relative size of student mobilizations—they simply record the first reports of *any* local Red Guard activity. One might suspect, given the large differences in the size of local student populations, that the Red Guards were a more disruptive force in the larger cities. Clearly, however, students were mobilized nationwide for activities that had the approval of the highest political authorities, and they were free to organize themselves to do so.

The Rebel Movement

Red Guard activists initially focused on their own schools and nearby neighborhoods, and early Red Guard actions were directed primarily at school faculty and administrators, remnants of former "exploiting" classes in nearby residences, and the destruction of historical artifacts and buildings that represented China's old "feudal" culture. But a minority of Red Guards, led by university students who had clashed with the officials who staffed work teams, began to target these officials and their superiors in the government agencies that had sent them. This new trend began in Beijing, when students who had clashed with work teams marched to national ministries and demanded that the officials who had staffed work teams return to their universities to be criticized, apologize for their errors, and turn over dossiers that they compiled on students that had challenged their authority. The students engaged in demonstrations and sit-ins outside government compounds, and in some cases, they invaded the offices and occupied them.

This set off a split in the Red Guard movement about the correctness of these actions. Mao and members of the Central Cultural Revolution Group intervened decisively in early October on the side of the students who took the struggle to the higher officials in the government, and publicly threw the weight of their support behind these student activists. Those who turned their rebellion against the political authorities adopted a new identity; a more radical branch of the Red Guard movement known as the "rebel faction" *(zaofan pai)*.[29]

This rebel insurgency marked a decisive shift in the direction of the student campaign. Student militants targeted government officials who had organized work teams, and by extension their bureaucratic superiors, who were accused of attempting to obstruct Mao's Cultural Revolution. Figure 2.2 traces the spread of the rebel orientation among Red Guards. It displays the cumulative percentage of jurisdictions, by month and jurisdiction level, whose annals first mention activity by "rebels" *(zaofan pai)* in opposition to local authorities. Red Guard groups had become almost universal across China's cities by September, but at that point barely more than half of the provincial capitals, and well under half of all the other cities, had yet to report any activities by "rebel" students. Rebel activity in counties was still very rare, with barely 20 percent of them reporting it by September.

The incipient rebel insurgency received a major boost during the Central Party Work Conference in Beijing from October 9 to 28, which was attended by regional and provincial party leaders from across China. The key document for the session was delivered as a speech by the Maoist radical Chen Boda, who harshly criticized all efforts to blunt rebel attacks on political officials, including local officials who feared the disorder that they increasingly faced. Chen referred to this as a "struggle between two lines," and he asserted that any actions to obstruct or redirect the student rebellion or deflect attacks on authorities were in total violation of Mao Zedong

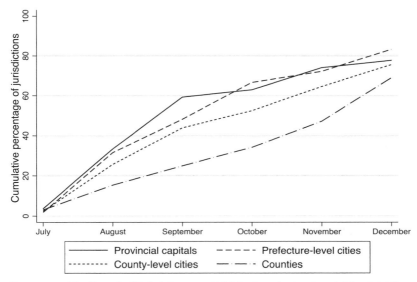

Figure 2.2. The Spread of Rebel Activity, 1966, by Jurisdiction Level (N = 2,246)

Thought. Near the end of the meeting, Liu Shaoqi and Deng Xiaoping, who had been designated as responsible for this "bourgeois reactionary line" *(zichan jieji fandong luxian),* gave self-criticisms; immediately afterward they were demoted in the party hierarchy, and they soon disappeared from public view.[30]

From this point on, Mao and his allies signaled their strong support for the rebel movement. In mid-November, two central directives met the primary demands of rebel factions: that all rebel activists who had been punished after earlier clashes with work teams or other authorities would have the charges against them withdrawn, and that the related "black materials" would be destroyed and removed from their permanent files.[31]

As Figure 2.2 makes clear, only after October did rebel activity begin to approach the levels of Red Guard activity seen in Figure 2.1. The rebel movement spread earliest in the provincial capitals and large cities, more slowly in the small cities, and slower still in the counties. By the end of December, it appears to have been established in most jurisdictions, though the percentage reporting rebel activity was still well below the percentages reporting Red Guard actions. In counties, only two-thirds of the annals mention any rebel activity at all during 1966.

Rebel Workers

As long as rebel insurgencies were limited to universities and high schools, their impact was relatively modest. Should industrial workers and other salaried employees form rebel groups, however, this would greatly magnify the levels of political disruption. There were only 674,000 university students in China in the spring of 1966, but there were 52 million urban workers and staff.[32] If urban workers joined in the rebel attacks on local government officials, their sheer numbers could fundamentally alter the scale and impact of the popular rebellion. Unlike the student rebellion, the large-scale mobilization of rebel workers could potentially lead to shutdowns of factories and paralyze the national transportation networks. The entry of workers into the rebel movement threatened to greatly escalate both the scale and impact of the rebel insurgencies.

These implications were well understood by officials in charge of managing China's economy, and they argued against the spread of independent political activities into productive sectors of the economy. The limits proved very hard to enforce, because a minority of workers challenged their factory leaders almost from the outset. In Shanghai, where work teams were sent into large state factories to conduct the campaign in June and July 1966, worker opposition emerged in ways that paralleled that in the universities. Individuals who would later establish a citywide alliance of worker rebels challenged the work teams sent to their factories during June and July. These workers sympathized with student rebels who confronted the city authorities, and they watched from the sidelines as students organized protests in the streets. These militant workers became thorns in the side of the work teams and the factory's management, as they put up critical wall posters challenging them, fought for positions on Cultural Revolution Committees, and disagreed about who the targets of the campaign should be. In August and September these incipient rebel leaders began to form small "fighting groups" that mimicked the student rebels, and they openly contested with work teams over control of the campaign.[33]

In Nanjing a somewhat different pattern of conflict emerged, and one that generated a prominent campaign against the Nanjing party authorities much earlier than in Shanghai. The workers' rebellion in Nanjing was sparked by cleavages created in large state factories by work teams sent in two years before, during the Socialist Education Movement—in particular at the Yangzi River Machine Works.[34] The earlier campaign had divided the factory's management and workforce, with one side bearing the brunt of a draconian loyalty investigation. Large percentages of the staff and management were subjected to humiliating struggle sessions and charged with political crimes, along with significant numbers of workers and technicians who were associated with them. The campaign was halted in mid-course in 1965 for being too harsh, and an uneasy compromise was fashioned that permitted a factory director who had been attacked in the campaign to retain his post, while the factory's party secretary, one of his tormentors, continued in office. When the Cultural Revolution began in June, the factory's party secretary renewed the campaign against those he had tormented two years earlier, and activists who supported him called for the firing of the factory director for trying to "restore capitalism." Several hundred of the factory director's supporters marched to the Nanjing Municipal Party Committee to submit a petition demanding his reinstatement in mid-August, and in response more than 2,000 workers who supported his purge marched to the Nanjing party offices to oppose his reinstatement. The Nanjing authorities refused to ratify the purge, leading to another large demonstration on August 22 by more than 2,000 supporters of the factory Party Committee who denounced the decision of the Nanjing city authorities.

This group of rebel activists, who called for the purge of their factory director but who supported their factory's party secretary, and who now were in rebellion against the Nanjing party authorities, formed a rebel organization—Red Flag—near the end of August 26. Three days later their opponents in the factory formed their own rebel organization—Red Workers—who opposed their factory's party secretary but supported the Nanjing Party Committee. Red Flag sent a delegation to confront the Nanjing authorities at the end of August, and after failing to change the Nanjing party's decision, they sent more than 1,000 members by train to lodge a complaint with national authorities in Beijing. The Red Flag rebels, opposed to the Nanjing authorities, played a leading role two months later in organizing the first citywide worker rebel alliance in opposition to the city and provincial authorities. The Red Workers, who found the Nanjing authorities sympathetic to their stance, played a major role in the large alliance of workers who supported the city authorities and fought in the streets against the rebel workers near the end of 1966.

Responding to incipient rebel activity in factories, Beijing issued a directive in late September that reiterated official disapproval of independent political activity by workers. It restated the prohibition against independent political groups in workplaces, public institutions and party and government agencies. Groups that had already formed were told to disband. Contacts with groups in other workplaces and travel away from their places of residence were both forbidden.[35]

This prohibition had little effect in cities where workers were already organizing into rebel groups. This was especially evident in Shanghai, where events would soon have a major impact nationwide. Rebel activities among Shanghai workers, which eventually led to one of the first citywide coalitions of rebel groups, accelerated in early October. A factory security officer named Wang Hongwen put up a wall poster that accused his factory's work team of carrying out the "bourgeois reactionary line." On October 10 he formed the factory's first rebel organization, issued a proclamation to all workers in the factory, and led a small delegation of rebel workers to Beijing to lodge a complaint against the factory's work team. After Wang returned to Shanghai in late October, he pulled together disparate rebel groups into an alliance and pushed for the work team to withdraw from the factory. His group took over the factory loudspeaker system and invaded the offices occupied by members of the work team.[36]

In the wake of the October Party Work Conference and the intensified new campaign against the "bourgeois reactionary line," opposition to workers' involvement softened in Beijing. Near the end of October, Mao stated that workers should get more actively involved in the campaign, raising the question of what form this involvement should take. The issue was brought to a head in Shanghai by the formation of a citywide alliance of worker rebel organizations, the Shanghai Workers Revolutionary Rebel General Headquarters, in early November. In their founding proclamation, they charged that the Shanghai party authorities had followed the bourgeois reactionary line. The group made three demands of the city authorities: that they recognize their coalition as a legal organization; that the Mayor attend their planned mass rally and hear their criticisms; and that the authorities provide resources and support.[37]

This placed the Shanghai authorities in a bind. They had turned a blind eye over previous weeks to the formation of rebel groups within individual factories, even though Beijing had reiterated the prohibition against such activities only weeks before. Now, however, they were faced with demands for the recognition of a citywide alliance of such groups—something that went far beyond Beijing's policies. The Mayor phoned officials in Beijing about the demands, and they informed him that alliances of workers across factories were still prohibited. The Mayor then refused to meet any of the workers' demands. On November 9, Wang Hongwen led several thousand of his alliance's members to the city's party headquarters to press for recognition of their group. Receiving no response, they decided to board Beijing-bound trains en masse to petition national authorities for approval of their demands.[38]

This action precipitated a standoff that required intervention by the Beijing authorities and that led to a shift in official policy. The large delegation of rebel workers departed on November 10, overwhelming trains bound for Beijing. Thousands walked along the tracks and eventually blocked the rail lines near a station in the Shanghai suburbs. Beijing authorities, alarmed by the disruption of a major railway line, had Chen Boda, the head of the Central Cultural Revolution Group, send a telegram to Shanghai declaring that the blocking of rail traffic was forbidden, that the workers' alliance was illegal, and that they should not travel to Beijing. The workers refused to relent, declaring the telegram a forgery. The next day another member of the Central Cultural Revolution Group, Zhang Chunqiao (who had until recently been the head of the Shanghai Party Committee's Propaganda Department), was sent to Shanghai to convince the workers to drop their planned trip to Beijing. In the course of the negotiations, Zhang instead agreed to their demands in return for their agreement to go back to work. The agreement recognized the legality of the Workers' General Headquarters, granted official support for its activities, and blamed the crisis on the Shanghai Party Committee.[39]

Zhang's actions surprised other leaders in Beijing and prompted a debate about the consequences of his action, but Mao quickly expressed support. The question then became whether the Shanghai agreement applied to the rest of the country. Officials in charge of the industrial economy argued vehemently that making this a general policy would rapidly disrupt the economy. Mao was not persuaded and decided to rescind the prohibition on worker participation in rebel groups. The resulting 10-point directive, issued December 9, finally gave official sanction to worker rebels, but it tried to limit potential disruptions to the economy. The document did not explicitly sanction citywide coalitions of worker rebels, but for the first time it made clear that workers could form independent groups.[40]

By the time this document was issued, it had already fallen behind developments elsewhere. In Nanjing, worker rebels opposed to city authorities imitated the actions of the rebel workers in nearby Shanghai. They demanded recognition of their alliance on November 14, only days after Zhang Chunqiao agreed to the Shanghai rebels' demands. After the Nanjing city and Jiangsu province authorities failed to respond to their demands, they sent a delegation to Beijing to seek support. On November 16, Zhou Enlai agreed to their demands (Mao already having approved the Shanghai agreement).[41] Alliances of worker rebels spread to other major cities in December. This opened the door to larger and more threatening rebel insurgencies, especially in cities with large industrial sectors.

Loyalist Countermobilization

Local political authorities, targeted by incipient rebel movements, were forbidden from using the security services or armed forces to resist student and worker rebels. Any moves to protect themselves from rebel threats would have to take the form of countermobilization that mimicked rebel insurgencies. This took the form of nominally independent political organizations among workers and staff that frequently adopted an older and more orthodox term for "Red Guard," commonly translated as "Scarlet Guard" *(chiwei dui)*. This term was used to refer to Red Guards that fought for the victory of the Bolsheviks during the civil war in Russia. The term for "Red Guard" invented by students early in the Cultural Revolution— *"hongwei bing"*—was entirely new and not based on standard usage. The adoption of the older term signaled a more orthodox stance of groups whose aim was to "defend Red power."

There were two common forms of Scarlet Guard mobilization. The first was widespread but relatively short-lived: Scarlet Guard brigades of loyal staff within party-state organs. Their avowed purpose was to defend party and government offices from incursions by student and worker rebels, and to protect their leaders from confrontations with them. The second developed somewhat later and was limited to the major cities. This variety mobilized large numbers of industrial workers, utilizing the organizational capacity of the Communist Party and their subordinate trade unions in large state firms. This became much more disruptive, because it involved large numbers of workers who left their workplaces to engage in street protests and confrontations with rebel forces. They eventually fed local disorders, after these Scarlet Guards turned against the local authorities.

The first type of Scarlet Guards responded to rebels that staged protests at party and government office compounds, and that declared their intention to "drag out" the top leaders. A typical example was the reaction of Guangxi provincial officials to the first sit-in protest by rebel students at the party headquarters on September 9. Cadres and staff who worked there formed Scarlet Guards "in order to protect the security of the regional party committee's compound, guard against Red Guard invasions of the offices, and preserve normal office operations."[42]

Scarlet Guard organizations proliferated across Guangxi Province in September 1966, and they were organized at all levels of the government hierarchy. They claimed to be rebel groups within party and government offices, and they occasionally confronted student rebels who tried to invade party and government offices.[43] In Qinzhou Prefecture the party committee announced on August 29, in compliance with Beijing's directives, that it would withdraw all work teams sent to conduct loyalty investigations, but it also called for the establishment of Scarlet Guards in administrative units to protect offices and the documents they contained. The head of the prefecture's Public Security Bureau was put in charge of the effort.[44] In Wuming County, Scarlet Guards were established in early September, immediately after local Red Guards put up a wall poster declaring their intention to "burn alive" the county's party secretary. The heads of the county's Organization and Propaganda departments were put in charge of Scarlet Guard units, whose task was summarized as the "four protects": "protect Chairman Mao, protect the Party Center, protect the Cultural Revolution, and protect Party and government organs."[45] Lingui County had a militant student insurgency influenced by Beijing student rebels. On August 24, after rumors that a rebel group was preparing to invade the party headquarters of nearby Guilin city, one of the county's leaders convened an urgent late-night meeting. Scarlet Guards were to confront the student rebels, treat them politely, but tell them firmly that there was no need for them to meet with the county's leaders.[46]

This type of Scarlet Guard activity was short-lived. This was exactly the kind of activity that was denounced at the October Party Work Conference as a typical example of the "bourgeois reactionary line." After October it was impossible for local officials to encourage such groups without openly defying Beijing, and office workers who persisted in Scarlet Guard activity now risked accusations that they were "reactionary."

The second type of Scarlet Guard activity became more prominent after October and grew rapidly in reaction to the permission granted rebel workers to form cross-factory alliances. These Scarlet Guards were mobilized within workplaces, relying on party and trade union organizations, party members, and other politically loyal workers.[47] They mobilized workers for confrontations with rebel groups both within large enterprises and eventually on the city streets. Scarlet Guards in Nanjing had a major impact on events there in the last months of 1966. Already during the first week of September there was a violent clash in one of the city's districts between rebel workers and Scarlet Guards—the first mention of this variety of countermobilization in Nanjing.[48]

Nanjing's Scarlet Guard movement escalated during November in reaction to the rough treatment student rebels meted out to top officials when they were seized for interrogation and "struggle sessions." After rebels from Nanjing University captured and interrogated one of the provincial leaders during the first week of November, workers from a large state factory put up wall posters denouncing its brutality. A group of them invaded the university campus to free the official, touching off violent confrontations with students. This touched off a series of clashes between student rebels and Scarlet Guards in factories, on campuses, and in the city streets. A city-wide Scarlet Guard coalition was formed on November 19 to coordinate resistance to the rebels. This escalated the conflicts, and violent confrontations continued into mid-December.

Although they were formed to defend the party establishment, the Nanjing Scarlet Guards soon turned against the local authorities. As the rebel movement continued to grow, it forced provincial officials in mid-December to sign a document that recognized the rebel movement and agreed to their demands—one of which was that they confessed to inciting Scarlet Guards to protect them as part of the "bourgeois reactionary line." This was a repudiation of the Scarlet Guards, who responded by sending several thousand members to the provincial party headquarters, invading the office compound, and demanding that provincial officials repudiate their agreement with the rebels. A crowd of more than 10,000 Scarlet Guards assembled at the party headquarters, and they seized a provincial party secretary and forced him onto a Beijing-bound train, where they planned to plead their case with central authorities. Clashes between rebels and Scarlet Guards intensified in street battles that deeply disrupted public order and transportation networks to the end of the year.

In Shanghai, Scarlet Guard mobilization took on a much more dramatic form.[49] The groups originated in factories when loyal workers and managers responded to rebel attacks against factory officials. After the Workers' General Headquarters won their demands for recognition in mid-November, the Scarlet Guards spread rapidly. They distributed handbills denouncing the rebels for disrupting rail traffic and stranding thousands of student Red Guards who were on the trains. Angered by the outcome of this confrontation, which ended with the Shanghai officials caving in to all demands, the party and union organizations of state factories began to mobilize workers to "protect the Shanghai party committee."

Relying on the existing infrastructure of the party and official trade unions, Shanghai's Scarlet Guards grew with astonishing speed. Immediately after the Workers' General Headquarters won their battle for recognition, Scarlet Guards popped up all across the city, and were strongest in factories that had large rebel movements. The Scarlet Guards held a meeting to plan for a citywide alliance on November 23, and two weeks later it already claimed 200,000 members. At their December 6 founding rally there were an estimated 300,000 in attendance. By the end of December, they claimed 800,000 in a total workforce of 2.7 million. This remarkably rapid expansion, which contrasted with the long and slow struggle by rebel workers to build their organization, attested to the effectiveness of party and trade union structures in mobilizing a countermovement.

Although initially intended to protect local authorities, Shanghai's Scarlet Guards, like their counterparts in Nanjing, eventually turned against them. Despite clear signs that Mao and his radical associates favored the rebels, the Scarlet Guards objected that the Shanghai Party Committee was coerced into signing agreements. They turned out huge numbers for large street confrontations with rebel workers in December, disrupting factories and transportation networks to a degree that rebel activities alone could not have achieved. They demanded that the Shanghai authorities recognize them also and repudiate agreements earlier signed with the rebels. They pressed these demands with a massive demonstration at the party headquarters in mid-December. The Shanghai authorities could not comply, because the rebel alliance had the clear backing of Beijing. Open support for the Scarlet Guards would further implicate them in a "bourgeois reactionary line." The Scarlet Guards then turned against the Shanghai authorities, staging large demonstrations at the party headquarters that touched off the confrontations with rebels that led to the collapse and overthrow of the Shanghai Party Committee in early January.[50]

Cadre Rebels

A final type of mobilization developed much later than all of the others, and until recently has been almost entirely neglected in research on this period—rebel movements among party and government functionaries.[51] As we shall see, this type of mobilization played a decisive role in the nationwide collapse of party-state structures and in the subsequent factional conflicts that raged across China for more than a year afterward. At first glance, rebel bureaucrats would appear to be something of a contradiction in terms—especially if one conceives of rebellions as popular movements against states. As an interest group, party-state officials had vested interests in defending their organizations from rebel attacks, and in preserving the structures to which their relatively privileged positions were ostensibly tied. The Scarlet Guards that formed within government offices in September expressed this fact. Yet in the wake of the mounting nationwide campaign to target top officials for carrying out the "bourgeois reactionary line," individual bureaucrats turned against their superiors in growing numbers, forming rebel groups that repudiated their superiors.

Cadres in party-state organs began to criticize the "bourgeois reactionary line" carried out by their superiors shortly after the October Party Conference in Beijing. In Zhejiang Province, a mass meeting was held on October 21 to denounce the actions of the provincial Cultural Revolution Committee. At a mass meeting attended by more than 8,000 office personnel who worked in more than 60 provincial departments, 45 "revolutionary cadres" from 22 provincial party and government organs read out their denunciations of the province's "bourgeois reactionary line." The criticisms focused on the official in charge of the province's Cultural Revolution Committee, and the mass meeting was attended by many of the province's top officials.[52] Following the mass meeting, organizations of rebels who worked in party and government offices (referred to as *jiguan zaofan pai*) spread across the province, and held some 850 mass meetings with a total of more than 30,000 in attendance.[53] This kind of officially sponsored activity, a clear reaction to the recently concluded October party conference, was designed to cast blame on specific individuals within the regional leadership. But as rebel bureaucrats began to mobilize on their own in the following weeks, it would eventually prove impossible for top officials to control the process of accusation and to limit blame to a small handful of scapegoats.

The idea that bureaucrats might rebel against their own superiors was not entirely absent from the thinking of the Cultural Revolution's sponsors in Beijing. They had, from the beginning, encouraged bureaucrats to expose their superiors for revisionist or anti-Mao attitudes and behavior. In the first days of 1967, Mao Zedong himself emphasized the crucial role of cadres in aiding the rebel movement: "The Great Proletarian Cultural Revolution in party and government organs is very important. If . . . the cadres in party and government organs do not actively throw themselves into the Cultural Revolution, it will not succeed. There are many important problems that can only be revealed by the cadres."[54] Mao appears to have had in mind the ability of cadres to expose inside information about the behavior of top officials that was inaccessible to students or workers. From this perspective, cadres could be indispensable allies of outside rebel groups in their efforts to expose the alleged political crimes of top officials. In many cities that had large popular insurgencies, this is exactly the role that rebel cadres would play. But the rebel movements within party-state agencies went significantly beyond this conception, and it is unclear whether Mao was aware at the time he made this statement that the cadre rebellion had already advanced far across China over the previous month.

Rebel cadres played a major role in the collapse and eventual overthrow of the Shanghai Party Committee. A December rebellion by a high-profile "writing group" in the Shanghai Party Committee Propaganda Department—described as "literati rebels" in one account of the period—has long been considered a key development in the crumbling of the Shanghai leaders' authority.[55] But well before this group's public denunciation of Shanghai's top officials, there was an active rebel movement in "party and government organs." An authoritative history of Shanghai's Cultural Revolution describes this internal rebel movement as a crucial breakthrough. Without an internal rebellion within the Shanghai party and government headquarters the contest between the rebels and Scarlet Guards would likely have ended in stalemate.[56] The internal rebellion grew after the establishment of the Workers' General Headquarters, and especially after the issuance in early December of the document that signaled an approval of rebel movements within factories and other workplaces. As the internal rebellion gained force, it shook the resolve of top officials, sapping their ability to withstand the demands of rebel students and workers, and it undermined their authority over their own subordinates.

When in mid-December one of Shanghai's ranking party secretaries declared his support for the rebel cause and the writers' group openly challenged their superiors, cadres at lower ranks in the party apparatus reconsidered their positions, and rebel groups expanded rapidly within various departments. But this was just the last and most public manifestation of a rebellion of lower-ranking bureaucrats that had slowly grown over the previous weeks. On December 16 these rebel bureaucrats held a large meeting to coordinate the formation of an alliance—the main leaders were cadres in the editorial committee of a local party magazine, the Propaganda Department, and the administrative office of the Shanghai Party Committee itself.

The cadre rebellion began even earlier in Nanjing. On November 14, rebel bureaucrats from the city's youth league offices entered the party headquarters to recruit rebels in the Finance Bureau, post office, and the administrative office of the city government. They formed rebel groups across a range of party and government departments and held a mass meeting to denounce the Nanjing Party Committee. They declared their intention to take control over the party's archives and to supervise the activities of the municipal party secretariat. On November 18, close to 500 cadres who had been conducting a purge campaign in suburban villages returned to the city to denounce that campaign as an expression of the bourgeois reactionary line. On November 24, several hundred of them assembled at the provincial party headquarters to denounce top officials, and they seized a Vice-Mayor and forced him to accompany them to Beijing. A coalition of rebel bureaucrats in provincial organs was established on December 5, and rebels inside the city organs followed suit on December 9. On December 20, the latter coalition held a mass meeting at a stadium to denounce the city authorities. The rebel cadres intensified their activities until the provincial and city authorities were overthrown in late January.[57]

Inside Guangxi's provincial party organs in Nanning, the earliest rebel groups formed in late November in the Organization and Propaganda Departments. By mid-December a reputedly "large majority" of the cadres who worked in the provincial party headquarters had joined rebel groups. Even the staff office of the Provincial Party Committee, which served the party secretariat, was riddled with rebels—there were no fewer than eight small fighting groups, many of which had only a handful of members. On December 11 more than 20 fighting groups in the provincial party and government offices formed a coalition of rebel cadres in the provincial organs, with its headquarters in the Propaganda Department. They proceeded with a campaign to denounce the top provincial leaders for carrying out the bourgeois reactionary line.[58]

Internal insurgencies by cadres spread across the party-state hierarchy in Guangxi. After the Beijing authorities issued the document approving the formation of rebel groups in factories and other workplaces, Nanning's municipal party secretary issued instructions to organs under the city's party and government that extended this authorization to their cadres and support staff. Rebel organizations and small "fighting groups" soon mobilized within the city's bureaucracy to criticize the Nanning Party Committee for its complicity with the bourgeois reactionary line. In mid-December the cadre rebels convened a large meeting of all cadres in the city's administration to hear the party secretary's self-criticism, and the following week they joined with student and worker rebels in a mass struggle session against the city's top officials.[59]

The cadre rebellions spread into Guangxi's prefectures and even rural counties. Cadre rebellions appeared as early as mid-October in the offices of Qinzhou Prefecture, and they continued to plague local authorities as they gained strength in December.[60] By late November county-level cadres were also flocking to newly formed rebel "fighting groups" that aimed criticism at their own superiors. By the end of November, in the 29 government offices and departments in Lingui County, there were more than 50 small fighting groups with a membership of 520 out of the county's 883 cadres and support staff.[61] Fusui County had more than 80 rebel organizations, 22 of them in various county party and government offices, including the party's Organization Department, the party committee's staff office, and the Propaganda Department.[62] In Tiandong County, cadres and staff organized a number of fighting groups and one cross-department alliance that had more than 100 members. Led by cadres from the public security bureau, discipline inspection commission, and the court system, it coordinated the cadres' rebellion against their superiors.[63] In Pubei County the Scarlet Guards turned on their masters, reinventing themselves as a rebel group devoted to repudiating the bourgeois reactionary line—an attempt to absolve themselves for their earlier support of it.[64]

The last half of 1966 saw an unprecedented level of political mobilization both within the state bureaucracy and in society at large. Most visible was the spread of the Red Guard and rebel movements, the first becoming almost ubiquitous across China by September, and the second spreading more slowly and becoming widespread only after October. After permission was granted to industrial workers and other employees to form their own organizations and take part in rebel activities in early December, rebel groups formed quickly in workplaces and cross-city alliances of worker rebels began to appear. This greatly increased the scale and potential disruptiveness of the rebel campaign.

Rebel activity sparked active countermobilization by those who sought to blunt their impact. Within workplaces and government offices, "Scarlet Guard" organizations formed to protect their organizations from rebel disruptions and to shield their leaders from rebel attacks. In some major cities, like Shanghai and Nanjing, Scarlet Guards in the industrial sector spread rapidly, utilizing the authority of party organizations and official trade unions to rapidly mobilize large numbers, perhaps reluctantly, to confront rebels. Street battles between these opposed groups disrupted public order and reduced local authorities to powerlessness. Finally, by December it appeared that officials and staff within party and government offices were rapidly defecting to the rebel cause. Rebel groups dedicated to the denunciation of their own superiors in party-state organs began to form on a large scale.

One way of gauging the overall scale of this activity during this period is to trace the number of reported victims of these various forms of political mobilization. An important, if not sole purpose of much of this political mobilization was to identify and punish individuals who had allegedly revisionist if not "anti-party" political leanings. A "victim" is someone who is accused of revisionist or reactionary political leanings, subjected to

coercive interrogation, or who is subjected to public humiliation, forced iso-
lation for investigation and confession, coercive interrogation, beatings,
imprisonment, or expulsion from jobs or urban residence. Local annals
frequently describe these activities, sometimes providing numbers.

Figure 2.3 traces the cumulative number of reported victims described
in local annals from May 1966 through January 1967. It separates victims
according to the actors responsible. "Insurgents" refers to the victims of Red
Guards or rebels, in this period almost always students and workers, and to
a lesser extent cadre rebels. "Authorities" refers to the actions of civilian governments or party organizations, almost always in the form of officially
organized loyalty investigations, for much of this period carried out by investigative work teams.[65]

The figure traces the overall impact of political mobilization in the last
half of 1966, but it also suggests that the social impact of Red Guard and
rebel activity far outstripped that of party-state authorities. By September,
the cumulative reported number of those victimized by Red Guards and
rebels was close to 250,000, and the number would approach 350,000 by
January 1967. The number of those victimized in campaigns conducted by

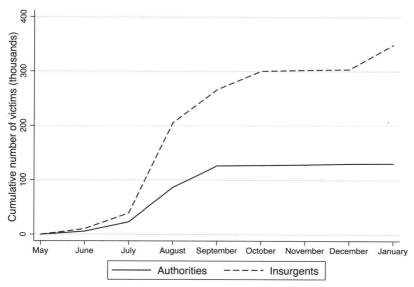

Figure 2.3. Cumulative Number of Reported Victims of Insurgents and Authorities,
May 1966–January 1967

political authorities leveled off after it reached 126,000 in September and increased only slightly afterward. The apparent halt in victimization by political authorities surely reflects Beijing's condemnation of the "bourgeois reactionary line" in October, which undercut activities controlled by regional and local officials.

One might suspect that officially published sources would tend to exaggerate the impact of insurgent activity, while concealing the damage caused by officials, and this may be true to some extent. But existing scholarship on this period, which draws on an array of interviews, memoirs, and documentary sources, makes clear that officially organized loyalty investigations were more focused than Red Guard and rebel activity. Indeed, by all accounts, in the early months of this period the authorities struggled to contain violent Red Guard and rebel activity, and to narrow its scope. These same authorities would later be condemned for their efforts to contain student and worker insurgencies and limit the number of victims. These trend lines are consistent with what we know from other sources.[66] Another consideration is that these same official sources, as we shall see, reported vastly more victims at the hands of authorities than insurgents near the end of the period of mass mobilization.

Another notable feature of Figure 2.3 is that the rapid rise in the number of victims tapers off after September. The initial wave of Red Guards broadly targeted lower-status authority figures and large numbers of individuals with historical ties to politically stigmatized households. The rise of the rebel movement, which first appeared in September, meant that attacks by insurgent groups became increasingly focused on a much more restricted group of ranking officials in all localities (and perhaps also that insurgents had exhausted the potential supply of lower-ranking targets). Not until December 1966 did the number of those victimized by insurgents resume an upward climb, due to escalating attacks on local authorities. The shift toward rebel attacks on authorities, increasingly focused on the way that they had carried out their loyalty campaigns, also accounts for the apparent halt in victimization by the authorities, who increasingly were put on the defensive in the final months of 1966. How far had these trends, so pronounced in major cities like Shanghai and Nanjing, spread across China by the end of 1966? And to what extent had local insurgencies developed to the point where they seriously undermined political authorities?

3

THE PACE OF REBEL INSURGENCIES

THE POLITICAL MOBILIZATION THAT swept across China in the last half of 1966 suggests a nation in turmoil. But the descriptive accounts in Chapter 2 draw on developments in selected locations, with the most dramatic from provincial capitals. Accounts in local histories suggest that through the end of 1966 most local governments were not similarly disrupted. Here I will examine this issue in more depth: how far had rebel insurgencies developed prior to 1967, and how serious were the challenges they presented to authorities? As we shall see, the dramatic upheavals experienced in major cities like Shanghai and Nanjing were very unusual, and until the end of 1966—the eve of the early 1967 wave of power seizures that overthrew local governments—rebel insurgencies remained small, poorly organized, and highly fragmented, and they were very late in developing.

Statistical Patterns

Statistical patterns that summarize accounts in local annals help us trace the scale and impact of local insurgencies. Whatever their overall impact, we should expect that they were likely to be more developed and more threatening to local officials in urban than in rural areas. There are large differences between cities and counties in the size and concentration of the populations that generated early rebel insurgencies. The cities had much larger and more concentrated populations, and much larger numbers of the students and workers who propelled the early rebel insurgencies.

The more than 170 cities in our database contained an average of just over 500,000 people and 140,000 salaried workers. Twenty of the largest cities had populations in excess of 1 million, and ten of them had more than half a million salaried workers. On average, two thirds of their residents were concentrated in urban districts, while the rest lived on collective farms in the nearby suburbs.[1] The counties are a striking contrast. Fewer than 9 percent of their residents lived in urban settlements, primarily in the county seat. The rest were scattered widely across collective farms, most of which were far from the county's party and government headquarters. The average county had a total population of more than 311,000 residents, but fewer than 23,000 urban residents and 6,500 salaried employees. The student populations were much smaller—in most cases they were limited to a few hundred junior and senior high school students. The populations capable of supporting significant rebel insurgencies in most county seats were very small—in most cases much smaller than the workforce of a single industrial complex in a large city.

There are several types of events that might indicate the degree to which the local party and government authorities were seriously challenged by rebel activity. The first is an invasion of the local government headquarters by rebel groups as part of a protest, whether or not the invasion was followed by a prolonged occupation. The second is the seizure of at least one party or government leader by rebels for denunciation at a mass meeting or any other purpose, whether or not the individual was subsequently held captive. The third is the first mention of an alliance of student or worker rebels for the purpose of confronting local authorities. Together, these three types of events provide a broad sense of the extent to which local governments were challenged, the degree to which the personal security of leaders was threatened, and the scale and level of coordination of local rebel activity.

Previously I traced time trends for the percentage of *all* local jurisdictions that reported the presence of any kind of Red Guard or rebel activity. These activities were so widely reported by the end of 1966 that there was little concern about the underreporting of events in local annals. Here, however, we are interested in specific types of rebel activity, reports of which are much more dependent on the level of detail provided in local annals.

These three types of events are reported far less frequently than broad references to rebel activity, and in order to be included in our data set, a specific event had to be described and dated at least to the month that it occurred. By these criteria, only one third of local annals (753) contain descriptions of a rebel office invasion; two thirds (1,471) describe the seizure of a local leader, and half (1,066) report the formation of a coalition of rebel groups. Even smaller numbers of local annals describe these events as occurring prior to the end of 1966.

Given the likelihood of high levels of underreporting, how can we make use of this information to trace the impact of rebel activity on local governments? What is most useful about these reports is *when* these actions occurred, *if* they were reported. If we assume that the timing of the *reported* events is representative also of the timing of the *unreported* events, we can treat time trends as an estimate of the upper limit of the impact of rebel activity on local governments. In other words, the aggregate trends that I report here are fairly confident estimates of the maximum likely impact of rebel activity during the last half of 1966.

Office Invasions

The first indicator is an action that targeted party and government offices. In late 1966, these attacks initially took the form of a demonstration at the gates of the government compound, or an invasion and temporary occupation of the government headquarters. The objective of the rebels often was access to files earlier collected by government agencies on rebel students. Later on, rebels demanded that leading officials be surrendered for mass denunciation meetings. In our data set there were a total of 753 reported demonstrations at or invasions of the compounds that housed the party and government headquarters of some level of government.[2] Only 125 of these occurred during 1966.

Figure 3.1 illustrates the cumulative percentage, by month, of reported office invasions during 1966. There are vast differences across jurisdictions: while close to 67 percent of provincial capitals reported an office invasion by the end of 1966, only 40 percent of prefecture-level cities had done so, and only 25 percent of county-level cities. Rebel office invasions were extremely rare in counties—slightly more than 10 percent of those that reported such an activity did so before the end of 1966. By this summary measure, rebel insurgencies were just beginning to have a significant

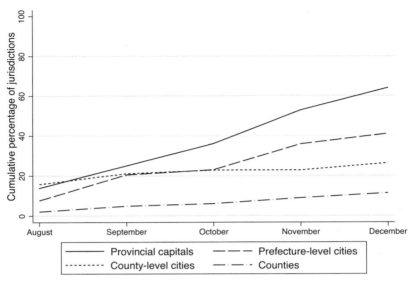

Figure 3.1. First Reported Rebel Invasions of Party-Government Offices, by Month, 1966 (N = 125)

impact in the provincial capitals and larger cities, but through the end of 1966, their impact in the small cities and rural counties was negligible.

Seizures of Officials

The second indicator is the reported seizure of at least one official by a rebel group for a public "struggle session" or any other purpose. In a struggle session—a standard repertoire of protest during the Cultural Revolution—the targeted individual was forcibly placed on a stage and subjected to shouted accusations and ritual humiliation of varying degrees of brutality. Faculty and administrators of schools were widely subjected to such treatment from the outset of the Red Guard movement. As rebel insurgencies grew, leading officials in local party and government organs were seized and subjected to the same kind of treatment. As we have seen, rebel groups also took officials hostage in order to extract confessions, or they forcibly escorted them to Beijing as part of a rebel delegation to plead its case in the capital. When such treatment was suffered by the top officials in a city or county, this was a clear indication that a rebel campaign had begun to shake the local power structure.

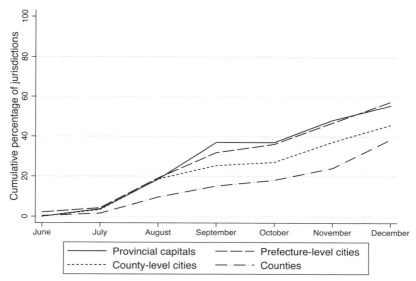

Figure 3.2. First Reported Rebel Seizures of Leading Officials, by Month, 1966
(N = 584)

Figure 3.2 traces the timing of the first reported seizure of a ranking member of a local government (province, city, or county). Reports of this kind were roughly twice as common as reports of office invasions—there were 1,471 reports that could be dated by month, 584 of which occurred during 1966. Roughly half of the cities reported the seizure of at least one official, while counties lagged somewhat behind. These figures only indicate differences in the timing of *first* report of this kind of event—there were surely multiple and repeated events of this kind after the first report, and these are not reflected in these numbers. But rebel movements clearly had yet to seize *any* ranking officials in roughly half of China's cities by the end of 1966, and some two thirds of counties.

Rebel Coalitions

The third indicator of the impact of rebel insurgencies is the reported formation of a local rebel coalition. A coalition is established when rebel groups from different schools or workplaces join together to coordinate their actions under a new name (which frequently contained the term "rebel headquarters," *zaofan silingbu*). The establishment of a rebel coalition

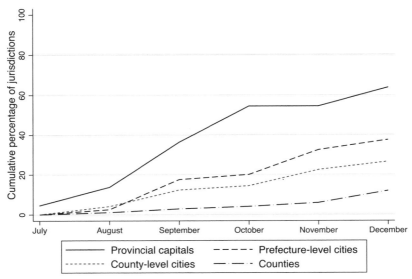

Figure 3.3. First Reported Appearance of Rebel Coalitions, by Month, 1966
(N = 155)

represents a level of organization and coordination that could result in larger and more threatening collective action against local party and government authorities. It therefore provides us with a marker of the scale and level of organization of rebel insurgencies and the potential threat they represent as challengers to local authorities.

Figure 3.3 traces pronounced differences across jurisdictions in the timing of the first reported rebel alliance, and it suggests clearly that by the end of 1966, the rebel insurgencies were still relatively unorganized and fragmented outside of China's provincial capitals. The first appearance of a local rebel alliance was recorded in a total of 1,066 local annals, but only 155 of these reports were during 1966. Almost 67 percent of provincial capitals reported rebel alliances by the end of the year, but the percentage falls steadily as we move to lower levels in the political hierarchy, dropping to some 12 percent for the counties.

These quantitative patterns in local annals are, to be sure, only rough indicators of fairly complex patterns of local events. The three trends that I have described provide a summary sketch of the development of local rebel insurgencies over time. They do not convey anything about what happened after the first event, or the frequency and depth of the event's impact. They do tell us one thing that is very important—that these signature events had not occurred at all in a great many places by the end of 1966, and that only the largest cities, especially provincial capitals, were beginning to be seriously affected.

Variation in Local Narratives

What do these differences look like in concrete terms? To convey a more nuanced understanding of the varied scale and impact of rebellion across jurisdictions, I will sketch capsule summaries of events up to the end of 1966 across four different levels of China's state hierarchy: provincial capitals, other prefecture-level cities, county-level cities, and county seats. To ensure that variation in these portrayals is not the product simply of different levels of detail in local annals, the narratives are drawn only from the longest and most detailed of the available accounts. As we shall see, there are many localities where it appears that little had occurred by the end of 1966, and that local authorities were still either firmly in charge or were only beginning to be challenged by local rebels. In such case descriptions, this is not because the published narratives are short and uninformative. It is because the vast majority of relevant political events described in local annals took place only *after* the end of 1966.

As we shall see, some of China's largest cities were deeply disrupted by the end of 1966 and had already become ungovernable, with local authorities literally powerless to exercise authority or even to protect themselves. Other cities, and some counties, had only gone partway down this path. Many other jurisdictions, primarily small cities and counties, however, had seen only the beginnings of rebel activity, and some none at all, with the authorities still very much in control. The differences across jurisdictions were in part due to their different demographic makeups—large cities often had dozens of universities and hundreds of high schools out of which student rebellions could emerge, and they had hundreds of factories and salaried workforces that ranged from hundreds of thousands to well over a million. At the opposite extreme, the rural towns that often served as the seats of county governments typically had only a handful of middle schools and salaried urban workforces that numbered in the hundreds or a few thousand. The consequences of these differences for the development of local

insurgencies will become evident as I sketch a range of local cases, beginning with China's provincial capitals and ending with remote agrarian
counties.

Provincial Capitals

In 1966, China's provincial capitals averaged 1.3 million urban residents
and 493,000 salaried workers. The four described here—Shanghai, Nanjing, Guangzhou, and Nanning—range from China's largest to the relatively small. Except for Shanghai, a city that was administratively equivalent to a province, provincial capitals were the home of two different levels
of government (province and city), and the headquarters of both were targeted by rebel insurgencies.[3]

Shanghai.   China's largest city had an urban population of 6.4 million
and a salaried urban workforce of 2.7 million in 1966.[4] There were 52,000
students enrolled in its 24 institutions of higher learning, and 726,300 students enrolled in its 519 middle schools.[5] The first Red Guard organization
was established on August 11 at Fudan University, and it eventually formed
the core of a citywide alliance of university rebels known as the Red Revolutionaries, an alliance that would play a central role in later developments.
Others followed in quick succession later in August. A rebel orientation in
the Red Guard movement developed early, under the influence of student
rebels from Beijing. The city was a magnet for traveling Red Guards: 13,500
of them arrived via train on just one day in mid-September, and more than
4 million had visited by mid-December. On the last day of August, Red
Guards from Beijing presented a list of demands to the Shanghai Party
Committee. After receiving no response, they demonstrated at the party
headquarters and demanded that the city's leaders come out to hear their
criticisms. They tried to force their way into the building but were rebuffed
after a violent confrontation with staff and workers. This "August 31 Incident" turned into a cause célèbre for the student rebel movement—a symbol
of the reactionary nature of the Shanghai Party Committee. Handbills critical of the student radicals appeared in the name of Shanghai's workers,
and the party and trade union organizations of factories mobilized veteran
workers to go to the Shanghai Party headquarters to protect the building.[6]

The first local alliance of student rebels that defied the Shanghai authorities' right to supervise their political activities was formed on September 29.

The first citywide alliance of university rebels appeared on October 12, and it eventually turned into the largest student organization in the city, the Red Revolutionaries. It became the dominant student alliance in Shanghai, publishing its own newspaper that by the end of the year had a print run of 800,000 copies. Two more alliances of university rebels were formed on November 3 and November 22. By end of year there were more than 5,400 separate student rebel groups in Shanghai.[7]

During the last half of October, due to the influence of students returning from trips to Beijing, the student movement turned decisively against the Shanghai authorities. Their primary demand was that the Shanghai Party Committee must turn over "black lists" of students classified as troublemakers by work teams sent into schools in June and July. The authorities balked at turning over their confidential files, arguing that their release would spur retaliation against student informers and create deeper conflicts among students. During November, rebel students invaded offices in universities in search of these files, and soon turned their attention to the Shanghai Party Committee, which had organized the work teams and where many of the files were transferred after work teams were withdrawn.[8]

After the confrontation over the recognition of the Workers' General Headquarters in mid-November, rebel students shifted from demands to inspect the files to the overthrow of the Shanghai Party Committee. The student rebellion continued to grow, while the Workers' General Headquarters rapidly expanded and aggressively confronted Shanghai's Mayor and its Party Secretary with a series of demands. In late November the student rebel alliance, the Red Revolutionaries, demanded that their newspaper be distributed along with the party's local newspaper, *Liberation Daily*. After this demand was refused, the students invaded the newspaper's offices and halted its publication. The occupation continued into the next week, during which the Workers' General Headquarters declared its support for the occupation, and the nascent Scarlet Guards, who pulled together their citywide alliance on December 4, sent hundreds of workers to surround the building and force their way in, touching off a violent confrontation. The occupation of the paper's premises was not resolved until December 6, by which point the lines of conflict between Shanghai's student and worker rebels and the Scarlet Guards had hardened.[9]

As the confrontations between these groups escalated, the Shanghai authorities were helpless in the face of their conflicting demands and increasingly violent street confrontations. The authorities had already entered into agreements that recognized the demands of the rebel workers, and they could not agree to Scarlet Guard demands that they repudiate them, fearing a backlash by the Workers' General Headquarters, who had clear backing from Beijing. They warned the Scarlet Guards that their organization should be disbanded, but this did little more than turn that group against them. The Scarlet Guards mobilized 20,000 of their members on December 12 to demand the repudiation of the agreement with the rebel workers. They also demanded recognition of their alliance, the provision of assistance and cooperation on an equal basis with the Workers' General Headquarters, and an official apology.[10]

Shanghai's leaders could not comply—this was precisely the period when rebels within the city's bureaucracy were turning against them. After it became clear that they were being cast aside in favor of the rebel workers, the Scarlet Guards mobilized an estimated 30,000 workers for a mass rally in People's Square on December 23. During the rally, they forced Shanghai's Mayor to sign a formal agreement acceding to their demands. Before the document could be published, Shanghai's Party Secretary called an emergency meeting of the Party Committee and repudiated the pact.[11]

The Scarlet Guards then decided to send a large delegation to Beijing to lodge a complaint, and on December 27 an estimated 30,000 of them assembled at the Shanghai Party Headquarters to demand a reinstatement of their agreement with the Mayor. They remained there for several days, leading to a violent confrontation with rebel workers who surrounded them. These events touched off sporadic fighting between Scarlet Guard and rebel groups across the city, in the streets and in schools and factories. Close to 10,000 Scarlet Guards then set off to board trains for Beijing, with many of them marching along the tracks. When they reached a station in the nearby suburbs, a large contingent of worker rebels, arriving in a convoy of trucks loaded with their activists, intercepted them and another violent clash followed, again blocking railway traffic in and out of Shanghai. As the year ended, hundreds of thousands of Scarlet Guards and rebel workers had left their jobs to engage in protests and street battles with their opponents, and the city's transportation networks and many large enterprises had ground to a halt. The impact on the city was similar to a general strike. Shanghai's Party Committee and government had completely lost control and were helpless in the face of two large and violently opposed popular movements.[12]

Nanjing.   Jiangsu's provincial capital, 190 miles by rail from Shanghai, was disrupted in similar, if not quite so dramatic a fashion. Nanjing had an urban population of close to 1.7 million in 1966, and 573,000 salaried workers and staff. It had 108,000 students enrolled in 147 middle schools, and 30,000 students in 19 universities.[13] With a large student population and industrial workforce, the city was a hotbed of rebel activity.[14] The Jiangsu Province and Nanjing city authorities were both beleaguered by rebel confrontations as early as September, and by December they had almost completely lost control of the city.

Office invasions at the provincial and municipal government headquarters began in early September. On September 9 more than 3,000 student rebels invaded and occupied several offices at the Provincial Party headquarters and began a hunger strike. The first large coalition of Red Guards formed in early October, and a second broad alliance formed the first week of November. Top provincial officials soon found themselves at the mercy of rebel groups. On October 10 rebels from Nanjing University attacked the provincial party offices, demanding that a member of the party secretariat be turned over to them for criticism. They took him into custody on October 31 and publicly humiliated him at a mass meeting on November 2, where he was beaten and forced to kneel before a bust of Chairman Mao to "ask forgiveness."

On October 29, student rebels invaded and occupied the offices of the Jiangsu Party Committee, sealing up the archives while searching for the files compiled by university work teams on rebel students. In mid-November, a large student rebel alliance held a mass denunciation meeting against Jiang-su's First Party Secretary along with other members of the provincial party secretariat, during which he was physically abused and lost consciousness. After another leader gave a public speech to apologize for the province's "bourgeois reactionary line," rebel students judged his self-criticism "insincere," took him into custody, and escorted him forcibly to Beijing to plead their case with the central authorities. In early December these rebel students, who had forcibly taken yet another leading Jiangsu official to Beijing, obtained a decree from the Beijing authorities ordering the Jiangsu leaders to agree to all rebel demands. The most important of these was that all political charges made against rebel students in June and July be officially withdrawn, and that all files kept on the rebels be removed from the archives.

The Nanjing city authorities were similarly beleaguered. In early September, after repeated confrontations with rebel students and workers at the Nanjing Party headquarters, some operations were shifted to a compound of the Bureau of Public Security for protection. After this move student rebels invaded the party headquarters repeatedly, and on October 12 worker rebels occupied the building. Student rebels seized a Vice-Mayor and held him captive on their university campus near the end of November. In mid-December, rebel students invaded the city's party headquarters and assumed control of its telephone switchboard, controlling its ability to communicate with district and neighborhood officials.

Beginning in late November, and continuing through the middle of December, the Nanjing authorities tried to defuse local antagonisms by sending ranking officials to factories to read self-criticisms for carrying out the "bourgeois reactionary line." They apologized for their prior actions and retracted all charges against workers lodged earlier in the fall. A member of the party secretariat went repeatedly to the Yangzi River Machine Works to read a self-criticism on behalf of the city authorities. After the third time, rebel workers hauled him off to Beijing.

With both the provincial and city governments paralyzed by office invasions and kidnappings of top officials, matters worsened when Scarlet Guards, composed of industrial workers, began to fight back against the rebels. They had begun to resist rebel attacks on provincial and municipal leaders as early as October, but in late December, angered that the authorities had repeatedly caved in to all rebel demands, they turned against the Jiangsu authorities and *also* accused *them* of carrying out a "bourgeois reactionary line." On December 21, they held a mass meeting to denounce and "crush" the Jiangsu authorities, demanding that they repudiate all prior agreements with the rebels, especially their confession that they had conspired with Scarlet Guards. Unable to induce the authorities to repudiate these agreements, thousands of them assembled at a major railway terminus on the Yangzi River on December 25 and set off to lodge their complaints in Beijing. More than 10,000 reached a railway station in northern Jiangsu before the trains were halted, where most were convinced to return to Nanjing. After their return, street battles erupted between rebels and Scarlet Guards, disrupting transportation networks and paralyzing the city. As 1966 ended, Nanjing was in disarray, with political authority having vanished entirely.

Guangzhou. Guangdong's provincial capital had a large and active rebel movement, but it developed more slowly than in Shanghai and Nanjing.[15] By the end of the year it had not seriously undermined local authority to the same extent. Guangzhou had an urban population of 2.2 million in 1966, and a salaried workforce of close to 900,000.[16] It had more than 110,000 students enrolled in its 107 middle schools, and 21,000 students enrolled in its 14 universities and colleges.[17] The city's large Red Guard movement showed a rebel orientation in early September, when the first citywide alliances of student rebels appeared. By mid-October there were three separate Red Guard alliances. In late November and early December, groups of worker rebels formed in individual factories, but they did not form citywide alliances until the very end of 1966. Popular resistance against rebel students' violent campaign against remnants of the old society—pedicab drivers, street vendors, and people with relatives in nearby Hong Kong—was expressed as resistance to outside troublemakers from the north, and factory Scarlet Guard organizations formed in response.

The first recorded seizure of a ranking city official by student rebels was on September 5, and the first cross-city alliances of student rebels appeared at the end of October. Despite the growing scale and organization of the student movement, the provincial and city governments still operated. The provincial party committee convened a large cadre conference in early November without incident, at which they discussed the implications of the recent October Party Conference.

By late November, however, the security of the provincial and city authorities deteriorated. On November 23, a large force of student rebels invaded the office compound of the provincial party committee, and they did so twice later that week in search of files kept on individuals punished by the work teams. These materials were used as evidence in mass rallies held on December 11 and 14 to denounce the provincial party committee's bourgeois reactionary line. On December 13 rebels invaded and shut down the two local party newspapers. This stimulated counterprotests organized by trade unions in large factories. More than one thousand workers demonstrated at the newspapers' offices to protest the closing of the papers, shouting slogans declaring their intention to "protect the Party Center and Chairman Mao."

The newspapers' closings unleashed simmering resentment against outsiders, especially among party members and members of trade unions, because the action was led by radical students from Beijing. On December 22, this came to a head at the newspapers' offices, where more than 2,000 people gathered to protest the shutdown. When one of the student militants attempted to make a speech, the crowd beat him badly. The next day another crowd of equal size destroyed a student propaganda truck that broadcast slogans over a loudspeaker. At yet another confrontation at the newspaper offices on December 25, an angry crowd overturned a propaganda van, resulting in one death and eight severe injuries. The incident crystallized popular resentment against student radicals, especially those from the north, and on January 2 two alliances, one of workers, one of students, formed out of those who opposed the closing of the paper. In response, students who supported the closing of the paper formed an alliance of their own. In the final two weeks of December the floodgates opened, and rebel organizations were formed in workplaces across the city—both in factories and within the provincial and city government offices. As 1966 drew to a close, Guangzhou was showing signs of the same developments that were already far advanced in Shanghai and Nanjing.

Nanning.   Guangxi's provincial capital was much smaller than Nanjing and Guangzhou. Its urban population was close to 411,000, with 153,000 industrial workers and staff.[18] There were only 38 middle schools, with an enrollment of close to 23,000, and fewer than 2,000 college students.[19] It had a large and active student rebel movement, but worker rebels did not begin to mobilize until December.[20] Rebels were able to extract a series of apologies from local officials, but they had not yet undermined their authority or disrupted public order even in ways that approached Guangzhou. The first alliance of Red Guards was formed on August 25. Their activities had the approval of the city authorities, who gave them favorable coverage in local newspapers. During September and October, the Red Guard movement was given a boost by more than 32,000 militant students who visited Nanning from elsewhere. The most influential of these were roughly one thousand Beijing Red Guards who arrived as part of 91 delegations. Their activities escalated levels of violence against the victims of home searches and struggle sessions. Their attacks soon turned against top officials in the provincial and city leadership.

The first rebel confrontation with party authorities was on September 9, when a group of Red Guards staged a sit-in protest at the offices of the Provincial Party Committee to denounce its "reactionary line."[21] In response to the threat, party and government departments, factories, and neighborhoods began to form Scarlet Guards to protect against the marauding students. These groups were active until early November, when they were dissolved after being denounced at the October Party Conference. The first citywide student rebel alliance was founded near the end of September, and in the coming weeks no fewer than 5 more large rebel alliances appeared. The first direct challenge to the provincial and city leadership was an October 19 wall poster that accused them of carrying out the bourgeois reactionary line by suppressing the student movement. The tide quickly turned, and the rebel movement gained energy. Large rebel rallies were held near the end of October, denouncing the provincial and city authorities. Many top officials attended, making conciliatory speeches. On November 1, rebels assembled at the city government offices to demand that heads of work teams be turned over to them.

On November 22, the first alliance of worker rebels was established at a mass meeting held at the Provincial Party headquarters. Several provincial leaders gave speeches. One week later, the provincial leaders told cadres and staff in party and government organs that they had the right to form their own rebel groups, and they spread rapidly. In early December, the worker rebel alliance was expanded, reorganized, and renamed. Large mass meetings to denounce the provincial and city authorities were held in mid-December, with top officials giving contrite and apologetic speeches. At the end of December, workers in the railway system and public bus lines formed rebel alliances and denounced the local authorities. The authority of Nanning's leaders was rapidly evaporating, but public order had not yet deteriorated to the extent it had in Shanghai, Nanjing, or Guangzhou.

Prefecture-Level Cities

The prefecture-level cities were directly under the jurisdiction of provincial governments. Excluding provincial capitals, they had an average urban population of 350,594 and 121,100 salaried workers. The three cities described here—Qiqihaer, Qingdao, and Wuzhou—range from the large to the relatively small.[22] Each of them had robust rebel movements, but by the end of the year none of them were as large, active, or threatening as the ones in the provincial capitals I have just described.

Qiqihaer. This city in China's northernmost province of Heilongjiang ·had an urban population of 957,068 and a state-sector workforce of

151,013.[23] The city's 57 middle schools had 37,369 students in their lower divisions, and 6,654 in high school. Two college-level institutes taught courses in industrial technology, and had a total enrollment of 1,498.[24] The city's rebel movement forced the replacement of the local party leadership surprisingly early, an accomplishment that appeared to satisfy the rebels and stabilize party authority in the city.[25] On August 6 the first rebel challenge to the municipal party committee appeared in the form of a wall poster put up at the party headquarters by students from the local machinery institute. It charged that the work teams sent to their institute had committed errors of political line. In mid-August, the city's party committee learned that students in that institute had seized the school's party secretary and other officials, subjecting them to violent and humiliating struggle sessions. An official sent to the school by the Qiqihaer Party Committee failed to convince them to stop, and it then issued a directive prohibiting similar rebel actions. When, on August 16, close to 700 students and others from the school paraded their party secretary in the streets, they were surrounded and blocked by workers from nearby factories, who broke up their procession. This became known as the "August 16 incident."

Shortly afterwards, the students at the machinery institute, defying the city authorities, pushed aside their school's party leadership and set up their own committee to run the Cultural Revolution. Days later, more than 300 rebels from the provincial capital's Harbin Industrial Institute disrupted a mass meeting underway at a local factory. They denounced the city's Party Secretary and other leaders. They then invaded nearby city district offices and subjected one of its Deputy Party Secretaries to a struggle session, charging that the city authorities were suppressing the student movement. On August 23, like-minded student rebels from local colleges formed a broad alliance to coordinate their actions. The next day they held a mass rally at which one of the city's Party Secretaries was forced to announce the dismissal of several district officials, after which they were subjected to humiliating struggle sessions.

Shortly afterwards the first worker rebel organization was formed. Rebel groups spread to other factories near the end of August and began to protest the suppression of the student movement, and rebel cadres in the city's party and government organs organized against their superiors. Rebels seized several members of the city's top leadership and paraded them around the city on August 28. The next day the Heilongjiang provincial authorities stepped in to remove Qiqihaer's First Party Secretary from his post. At a mass meeting shortly afterwards in the city government's assembly hall, the deposed party secretary was denounced for his alleged political crimes. The city's Cultural Revolution Committee was reorganized to cooperate more closely with local rebels. Attacks on leading officials continued, and on September 23 the remaining Secretaries on the Qiqihaer Party Committee all resigned.

With the city's government already completely paralyzed by the end of September, Beijing sent in an official to stabilize the situation. The former Mayor was denounced at a mass rally, and on October 1 the first citywide alliance of rebel students was established. In early October, emissaries from Beijing met with rebel leaders to calm the situation, and a new temporary party leadership was established near the middle of the month. Near the end of October, the city's new leaders convened a mass rally of rebels and denounced the "bourgeois reactionary line" carried out by their predecessors.

This unusually rapid overthrow of the city's leaders appears to have satisfied local rebels and stabilized the city until the year's end. In other city annals, the months of November and December mark an upsurge of rebel activity and often increasingly serious disruptions of local governments. In Qiqihaer, however, little appears to have happened during these two months. In November, the student rebels divided into two opposed factions, causing the collapse of an earlier alliance, but there are no reports of further confrontations with the city's political leadership through the end of 1966.

Qingdao.   This large seaport on Shandong Province's south coast had an urban population of 850,000 and a workforce of 366,718 workers and staff.[26] The city had 175 middle schools with a total enrollment of 88,187, but only 2,987 students were enrolled in 3 university-level institutions.[27] The city had a large and active student rebel movement, and it engaged in spirited attacks on the city's party leadership, but by the end of the year they had not seriously undermined the city authorities.[28] The first Red Guard protest at the offices of the Qingdao Party Committee was on August 24, when students from Qingdao Medical College demanded the removal of one of their school's Deputy Party Secretaries. The next day, workers confronted militant Red Guards on the streets. In response, a group of students, blaming the workers' action on the local authorities, invaded the offices of the Qingdao Party Committee. The city's leaders reacted by issuing a directive that called upon all workers and cadres to respect the student activists and not to attack or debate with them. Unappeased, an alliance of rebel students from various colleges denounced the Qingdao Party Committee for conspiring to incite violence against the student movement.

Near the end of August more than a thousand student rebels from Beijing and the Shandong provincial capital of Ji'nan arrived to support attacks on the Qingdao party authorities. On August 28, the provincial party committee ordered Qingdao's Party Secretary to go to various colleges and make a self-criticism. When he did so the next day he was subjected to a mass criticism meeting, forced to wear a dunce cap on which was written "counterrevolutionary oppressor of the revolutionary student movement," and to wear a signboard that stated, "I am a counterrevolutionary." On August 31, the Shandong Provincial Party Committee, trying to placate the students, removed him and appointed an acting Party Secretary for the city.

The next day workers and other citizens rallied at the gates of the Qingdao Party Committee. They demanded that the city's Party Secretary be restored to his post, and that the student rebels be severely punished. Later that day more than 100,000 city residents demonstrated in the streets in support, and an estimated 40,000 held sit-in protests at the party headquarters and the city's assembly hall. On September 4, the Beijing authorities weighed in to defuse the situation, and ordered a halt to the quarrels between workers and students. Mao concluded that the local authorities were inciting workers to oppose the student movement, and he ordered the publication of a central party directive on September 11 that forbade the incitement of workers to oppose student rebels.[29] Days later, Qingdao's student rebels formed their first citywide alliance. With the publication of Mao's directive, rebel workers from several factories went to university campuses to declare their support for the students.

The firing of Qingdao's Party Secretary, and the firm suppression of the controversy surrounding him, appeared to take the steam out of further rebel attacks on the Qingdao Party leadership. Not until October 13 was there another reported protest at the city's party headquarters, when a delegation of more than a thousand university students, returning by train from Beijing, went there to demonstrate. In late October, the city government estimated that there were more than 490 separate Red Guard groups in the city, with close to 23,600 members. Despite occasional disturbances, the reshuffled Qingdao party leadership continued to operate normally, holding regular conferences through the end of the year. Worker rebels had yet to form a cross-city coalition and did not yet play a significant role in local events. Having been firmly rebuked by Mao in early September, citizen countermobilization in defense of the local authorities disappeared, and there is no mention of worker Scarlet Guards.

Wuzhou.   This city in Guangxi Province had an urban population of 118,120 and an industrial workforce of 39,514. Ten middle schools had 8,300 students in the junior divisions and 1,204 in high school. There was no significant population of college students.[30] The first challenge to the city's leaders came from a group of rebel students from Guilin, another prefecture-level city in Guangxi, in early September, when they vowed to throw Wuzhou into "great disorder."[31] When the Guilin rebels traveled to schools and workplaces around the city, they were met by Scarlet Guards and local Red Guards, who strongly objected to their message. The Guilin rebels denounced this as "suppressing the masses," and some local activists began to agree. Officials in the city government put up wall posters denouncing outside agitators.

The tide started to turn when more than 700 local students returned from Beijing in mid-October and formed a rebel group that denounced the Wuzhou Party Committee for suppressing the students. Responding to the October Party Conference in Beijing, the Wuzhou Party Committee issued a self-criticism on October 23. The rebel students pushed their advantage and organized a series of mass meetings to denounce the city's leaders. They denounced Scarlet Guards as tools of the "bourgeois reactionary line." Responding to this turn of events, and recognizing the implications of the October Party Conference, the Scarlet Guards disbanded in November. Many of them distanced themselves from their superiors and their earlier actions. They formed new rebel organizations that attacked local officials, demanding that they step down from their posts. Until the end of December, however, there was no broad rebel alliance opposed to the Wuzhou Party Committee. Through the end of the year there were no reported seizures of city leaders or invasions of government offices.

County-Level Cities

County-level cities, directly below prefectures or prefecture-level cities in the national hierarchy, averaged 169,400 urban residents and 40,800 salaried workers. The three that are described here—Shijiazhuang, Anshun, and Beihai—were even less disrupted than the larger cities, and their rebel insurgencies appeared very late.[32]

Shijiazhuang.   This city in central Hebei Province was also the seat of Shijiazhuang Prefecture. It had 643,000 urban residents and 156,800 salaried employees, 91,300 of whom were industrial workers.[33] Its 19 middle schools had 14,909 students in their lower divisions and 2,681 in their high school divisions. There were also 5,253 students in 3 university-level institutions.[34] The rebels targeted both prefecture and city governments.[35] The first wall poster to challenge the local authorities appeared very early, August 12, when students from a local university called on all students to "bombard the city party committee." At the end of August, Red Guards demanded to be let into government office buildings to read wall posters put up by their staff, but the city officials refused. They next day they broke into the building and occupied the premises, forcing government staff out of their offices. The first citywide alliance of Red Guards was formed on September 10, but the first alliance of rebel students did not appear until more than one month later, on October 25.

The first group of worker rebels did not appear until early December. A clash between worker factions occurred at a textile mill on December 5, injuring more than 300 employees and causing considerable damage. This incident led to the formation of a citywide coalition of worker rebels on December 8. Just over one week later, two separate alliances of student and worker rebels declared their intention to "bombard" the city authorities. The first reported invasion of a government office was on December 25, when university students occupied the offices of the party newspaper, *Shijiazhuang Daily*. At this point in time, rebel groups began to form within party and government offices: 19 rebel groups in the prefecture's party offices established an alliance in December.

The accounts for Shijiazhuang portray a rebel movement that developed much more slowly than in the larger cities. Unlike in some of the larger cities, there were no reported seizures of top officials and no reported invasions of government offices until the newspaper's editorial offices were occupied near the end of the year. There was no citywide alliance of worker rebels until mid-December, and the primary activities of rebel workers were limited to workplace clashes with workers who were loyal to the factory officials. As 1966 came to an end, Shijiazhuang's rebels were only beginning to gather strength.

Anshun.   This small city in Guizhou Province, which served as the seat of Anshun Prefecture, had only 78,422 urban residents, two middle schools, and no universities.[36] During August students began to denounce the actions of work teams sent into their schools.[37] Red Guard organizations appeared, and the local authorities tried to keep ahead of their demands. On September 6, the city authorities organized a mass meeting attended by a reported 30,000 students, workers, and cadres, at which the leaders of work teams were denounced and subjected to struggle sessions.

Perhaps recognizing that militant students would be less threatening if they left the city, in early October the city's Party Committee began sending delegations of local Red Guards to Beijing and elsewhere at the city's expense, and the majority of local students soon left. This had the effect of stabilizing the political situation until students returned from their travels in November, having been radicalized by their experiences and inspired by the directives of the October Party Conference. Eventually, in late December, the prefecture and city authorities were finally faced with rebel groups that called for "kicking aside" local leaders. Top leaders of both the prefecture and the city were seized and subjected to violent treatment. By the very end of 1966, local leaders had lost the ability to protect themselves. While the accounts describe aggressive student groups, there is no evidence of coordination or organizational capacity among them. There is no mention of any citywide alliance of student or worker rebels through the end of the year, and there is no mention of any activities by worker rebels.

Beihai.   This small port city on the Gulf of Tonkin is located on the southern coast of Guangxi Province. It had an urban population of 48,400, a salaried workforce of only 11,484, and 3,187 students enrolled in 12 middle schools, only 495 of whom were high school students.[38] The local rebel movement was very slow to develop, and the Beihai Party Committee was fully in charge of local events until the very end of December.[39] Red Guards emerged in middle schools with official encouragement and cooperated with work teams sent to purge the ranks of the teachers and principals in the summer. Remarkably, these work teams were not withdrawn until mid-October, two and a half months after they were denounced by Mao and withdrawn in Beijing and other cities.

The first challenge to the city's party committee was by rebel students from Beijing. On September 1, a small contingent put up a wall poster that called for "bombarding" the Beihai Party Committee, which in response immediately put up wall posters attacking the Beijing students. Scarlet Guards were quickly set up in party and government organs, factories and other workplaces. At the end of September, hundreds of local student activists left for Beijing, and there were no challenges to Beihai's leaders until the students began to return in late December. The first wall poster composed by local high school students calling for "bombarding" the Beihai Party Committee did not appear until December 22. In response, city officials quickly issued an apology for carrying out the "bourgeois reactionary line," and later that week they went further, ordering cadres at all levels to support rebel organizations then being formed among workers, teachers, students, and cadres. On the very last day of 1966, an alliance of 16 rebel organizations denounced the local People's Congress as unrepresentative, and they disrupted the session then underway. This was the first recorded rebel attack on a party-government organ in Beihai, where a rebel insurgency had barely emerged by the end of 1966.

Urbanized Counties

China's counties were primarily rural, and their urban settlements employed an average of only 6,433 salaried workers. The remaining county residents lived in villages organized as collective farms, and their political activities during this early period, if any, were focused on the villages or small rural towns that served as their headquarters. The counties, however, are enormously varied. Some contain relatively large urban settlements. The top quintile in terms of urbanization had urban populations that averaged 60,312 (an urbanization rate of 15 percent) and 13,073 salaried workers. We should expect that rebel movements developed more rapidly in the more urbanized counties than in the least urbanized, and perhaps that there would be little if any rebel activity during this period in the most agrarian counties. To provide a concrete sense of these differences, I will describe events in several counties in the most urbanized quintile and the least urbanized two quintiles.[40]

Ankang.   The seat of a prefecture with the same name in southern Shaanxi Province, Ankang County had a relatively large urban population of 67,140 and an industrial workforce of roughly 4,500. The county had 8 middle schools with 3,462 students, but only one of the schools had an upper division, which had 646 high school students.[41] The local rebel movement grew during September, as student rebels from the provincial capital of Xi'an poured into Ankang.[42] The first local rebel organizations were formed on September 15 by Red Guards who returned from Xi'an, where they had observed rebel attacks on the provincial party committee. These rebels distanced themselves from the officially approved Red Guards, which they denounced as conservative. During this period rebel groups also began to form within the Ankang party and government offices. After the October Party Conference, the rebel movement grew and became more aggressive. The gates to the prefecture party offices were plastered with wall posters, and on October 15 the prefecture's leaders were forced to come outside to hear the students' denunciations. Rebel middle-school students invaded the county's party offices on November 12, and Ankang's first alliance of student rebels was established the next day. In late December workers finally began to form rebel groups, and on New Year's Day 1967, they established an alliance. Ankang's rebel movement had yet to seriously challenge the county authorities, and was just gaining momentum as the year ended.

Yulin.   Located in southeastern Guangxi Province, this county was also the seat of Yulin prefecture. It had 58,433 urban residents and 20,100 salaried workers. Its 11 middle schools had 10,134 students.[43] The first student attack on local authorities was on September 7, when a group of 500 high school students invaded the prefecture headquarters, forcing their way into the building and holding struggle sessions against a number of office workers.[44] In response to invasions of the prefecture offices, officials in the party and government organs formed Scarlet Guards, as did cadres in the county government offices. The first student rebel organizations formed in late September, and they proliferated in the coming weeks.

Fortunately for local authorities, student rebels began hopping trains to Beijing in late September. The government encouraged this by subsidizing student travel expenses. This temporarily quieted the local rebellion. However, when rebel students returned, they turned their fire onto the prefecture authorities. They initially targeted the head of the prefecture's Cultural Revolution Committee, forcing his removal in mid-December, and they subjected two prefecture officials on this committee to a public criticism and struggle session. On December 25 and 26 they convened mass meetings to denounce the "bourgeois reactionary line" of the prefecture's party committee. In attendance were more than 10,000 people: cadres from the offices under the prefecture and county government, workers and cadres from factories and mines, and Red Guards from the local schools. The prefecture's top official gave a self-criticism and was denounced on the stage, and several other leaders were denounced and interrogated. There was, as of yet, no mention of any worker rebel organizations.

Zengcheng.   Located in Guangdong's heavily populated Pearl River Delta, Zengcheng had an urban population of 42,453 and 11,377 salaried employees. It had 6 junior middle schools with an enrollment of 3,353, and two high schools with an enrollment of only 476.[45] The first wall poster to attack the county authorities, authored by Red Guards at the local high school, appeared on September 7, and set off a sharp backlash.[46] Cadres attending a conference in the county seat reacted strongly, charging that opposition to the county party committee was tantamount to opposing Chairman Mao. A number of them wrote wall posters denouncing the rebel students and demanded that they be punished. But the students refused, and instead distributed handbills charging that party committee had organized attacks on the Red Guards. Alarmed by the charge, the county's leaders convened an urgent cadre meeting and ordered a halt to counterattacks against the students.

Despite this incident, local Red Guards gave Zengcheng's leaders little trouble over the next two months, largely because the authorities organized delegations of student activists to travel to Beijing at government expense in September and October. The students returned radicalized, however, and the rebel movement grew during December. By the end of the year more than 100 rebel groups had formed with a total membership of more than 6,000. They formed in schools and factories, and also in the government's own offices. According to the chroniclers of these events, the "vast majority" of cadres, staff, and workers joined rebel groups in late December, fearing that if they failed to do so they would be considered "waverers" and suffer discrimination. Despite the rapid formation of rebel groups, the year ended in Zengcheng without any reported attacks on the county offices, no seizures of officials, and no alliances among the many small rebel groups that had formed in the county.

Agrarian Counties

The counties in the least urbanized two quintiles contained an average of only 3,693 urban residents (an urbanization rate of 5.8 percent) and 2,130 salaried workers. Often relatively remote, and with tiny populations of students and workers, rebel activity in these agrarian counties was even slower to develop, and in many cases was virtually nonexistent.

Shanglin.   Located near the geographic center of Guangxi Province, Shanglin had an urban population of 7,871 in 1966, and just over 5,000 salaried workers and staff, many of whom lived on collective farms. The county's 7 middle schools had 2,375 students enrolled in their lower divisions, and only 231 in high school.[47] After independent student organizations appeared in late September, county officials organized Scarlet Guards within the county offices to defend against office invasions.[48] This proved to be unnecessary, because student activists soon began to travel with the assistance of local authorities. In October, the county sent three delegations of Red Guards to Beijing to participate in the large mass rallies on Tiananmen Square. Perceiving new opportunities for travel, rebel groups formed in workplaces and nearby villages and demanded that the county government also fund their travel. Recognizing that potential rebels would be less troublesome if they left the county, the authorities allocated large sums of money to pay for the trips.

Left unmolested, the county authorities continued to issue directives about the conduct of the Cultural Revolution, and they held major government meetings in the county seat well into the last half of December. Trouble did not appear until the last days of December, and not from students, but from rebel cadres. A group of rebels who worked in the county offices demanded that the county's leaders make a self-criticism for their earlier loyalty investigations of teachers and students, which in their view was a clear case of the "bourgeois reactionary line." On December 30, at a mass meeting held in the county's one movie theater, the county magistrate gave a speech apologizing for errors committed earlier in the Cultural Revolution and rescinded the verdicts against those persecuted during July and August. Several rebel cadres stood up to make further accusations, and the meeting fell into bedlam and dispersed. The last activity for the year was an intriguing order issued by the county government for all firearms in the possession of cadres and staff to be turned over to the bureau of public security for safekeeping.

Zichang.   Located in a remote region in northern Shaanxi province, Zichang had an urban population of 5,970 and a salaried workforce that numbered only in the hundreds. The county had only two middle schools, one of which had an upper division, with a total of 935 students.[49] Red Guards appeared in late August and attacked remnants of feudalism and capitalism, including violent actions against private food stall vendors in the county seat.[50] At the end of October Red Guards began traveling to Beijing to attend mass rallies in Tiananmen Square. The first rebel organization was formed after some of these students returned to Zichang at the end of November. Rebels also appeared among the staff of the county's radio station, cultural center, and government offices. At the end of December there were 79 small rebel groups in the county. They had a range of viewpoints and constantly disagreed with one another. On December 23 rebel students dragged members of their high school's work team back to their school to denounce them for carrying out the bourgeois reactionary line—an action that was common in provincial capitals three months earlier. They destroyed the files compiled during the school's loyalty investigations, and the school's Party Secretary and the head and members of the work team were seized and subjected to violent public interrogations. By the end of the year the rebels had yet to form an alliance, they had yet to invade and occupy party and government offices, and they had yet to challenge the county's leaders.

Zhang.   Located in southern Gansu Province, Zhang County had a nonagricultural population of close to 2,000 and almost no salaried employees outside of the party and government offices. The county's one middle school had only 290 students, 28 of whom took high school instruction.[51] The county authorities organized local political activities, un-challenged, until the end of the year.[52] The first Red Guard group is mentioned on December 8, when the Zhang County Party Committee gave them permission to travel to Beijing. During the last week of December, county officials were making travel arrangements for local students and planning their itinerary. While on their trip to Beijing students from the Zhang County Middle School formed a rebel organization that would eventually target the county authorities after their return home early the next year. Given the tiny student numbers it is hard to imagine them as a serious challenge. Until the end of 1966 there was no hint of a local rebel movement.

There is a vast gulf between the massive upheavals that shook Shanghai and Nanjing to their foundations in November and December and the modest Red Guard and rebel activity in the agrarian counties. The popular insurgencies in Shanghai and Nanjing developed early, they were large, well organized, and effectively reduced local political authorities to complete impotence by the end of the year. In both cities, large popular mobilizations of Scarlet Guards served only to further destabilize public order and undermine local authorities. The insurgencies in other cities that we have described had not progressed this far by the end of December, although in some cases they appeared to be heading toward a similar outcome. Most of the other cities had just begun to deal with rebel insurgencies in the last weeks of the year. Qingdao and Qiqihaer faced serious disruptions early in the autumn, but interventions by higher-level authorities to reshuffle the local leadership in response to rebel demands stabilized government authority and slowed the further development of rebel insurgencies. Red Guards appeared virtually everywhere, but as we move from provincial capitals down through smaller cities, and from urbanized counties to agrarian ones, student rebels were smaller in numbers, less well organized, less likely to form city or county-wide coalitions, less likely to invade party and government offices, and less likely to seize leading officials for struggle sessions. If they did any of these things, it was not until the following year. Outside of the large cities, worker rebels were less likely to appear, and where they did, they rarely formed coalitions. Outside the large cities, we are also less likely to observe large and well-organized Scarlet Guard groups that confronted rebel forces and undermined public order. And we are less likely to find that the authority of local officials was seriously undermined, even if they faced challenges from local rebels.

By any comparative standard, however, these developments still reflect a remarkable nationwide level of popular political mobilization. This is especially noteworthy given the complete lack of independent political activity in China prior to the summer of 1966. There were student Red Guards even in the most remote rural counties by the end of 1966, and rebel groups were beginning to appear even there. Yet outside of the major cities, student and worker rebels had yet to seriously disrupt local governments or show a capacity for coordinated political action. Despite a remarkable overall level of popular political activity, the insurgencies in existence by the end of 1966 were far too modest to account for the extraordinary wave of power seizures that toppled local governments across China during the first weeks of 1967. More importantly, as we shall see, the fragmented and disorganized character of rebel insurgencies presaged the struggles that would follow from the power seizures and drive the much larger and more violent conflicts that developed during 1967 and persisted well into 1968.

4

THE IMPLOSION OF THE PARTY-STATE

THE NEXT PHASE OF CHINA'S POLITICAL upheaval was initiated by spectacular developments in Shanghai during the first week of 1967. The mobilization of two massive and antagonistic alliances of workers—the Workers' General Headquarters and the Scarlet Guards—paralyzed the city at the end of December. The Scarlet Guards, frustrated by their demands for equal recognition with rebel workers, turned against the Shanghai authorities. Cadres within the city's party and government offices, including some ranking officials, were rapidly forming rebel groups of their own in opposition to Shanghai's Mayor and First Party Secretary. Street fighting between factions began during the last days of December and escalated in early January. Masses of workers loyal to the two alliances left their jobs for rallies and street confrontations. Railway traffic was interrupted and the port and dockyards were paralyzed. Factories were idled and parts of the electrical grid shut down. Deliveries of coal for heating and cooking were interrupted and supplies of staple foods dwindled. Workers demanded and received cash from beleaguered officials. As balances dwindled in the bank accounts of state enterprises and offices, residents swarmed to retail outlets, causing runs on scarce consumer goods. Citizens rushed to withdraw their savings from banks, and public transportation was paralyzed.[1]

Officials in Beijing who had earlier warned of the risks of worker rebellion had been proven correct, but they were not vindicated by these events. Instead, it was up to Mao and his followers to ensure that their movement

would accomplish more than simply throw China into disarray. Their so-
lution was a power seizure by rebel forces on January 6, which overthrew the
Mayor, the First Party Secretary, and the vast majority of the city's ranking
officials. The power seizure was led and organized by the Maoist radical
Zhang Chunqiao, who in November had signed the agreement legitimating
Shanghai's new alliance of worker rebels. Zhang returned to Shanghai on
January 4, and working with cadre rebels inside the party apparatus and
leaders of the Workers' General Headquarters, he pulled together a coali-
tion to overthrow Shanghai's government, placing himself in charge.

At a mass rally attended by more than 100,000 on the city's main public
square, Zhang's coalition declared victory for the rebel movement. They
ordered all workers to return to their posts, and relayed Mao's denunciation of the Scarlet Guards. Relying on workers' militias and troops in the
local garrison, they acted quickly to restore factory production, transportation links, and public order. They denounced the disruption of the city's
public order as a plot devised by underhanded party officials to save themselves by luring workers to make demands for workplace benefits and cash.
Some days later they would mark their revolution by renaming the city's
government the "Shanghai Commune," a label that was eventually aban-
doned in favor of "Revolutionary Committee."[2] This signaled a new form
of governance by cadre rebels and the leaders of popular insurgencies.

Mao viewed the Shanghai events as a victorious conclusion to the rebel
campaign. He issued a congratulatory telegram showering the Shanghai
rebels with praise; it was published nationwide and read out on radio broadcasts on January 12.[3] This made clear to rebel groups throughout the
country that the overthrow of local governments was not only acceptable,
but encouraged. The response elsewhere in China was initially slow, as the
implications of Shanghai's example sunk in. Prior to Mao's declaration of
support on January 12, only 8 other localities reported power seizures.[4] The
pace sped up on January 12, and over the next 10 days, no fewer than 75
cities and counties reported one.[5]

The power seizures turned into a tidal wave after January 22, 1967. On
that day the national media, going beyond praise for Shanghai, urged rebels
nationwide to seize government power. Several articles on the first page of
that day's *People's Daily* called on rebels to overthrow local leaders and seize
power. The title of the authoritative front-page editorial captures the tone:

Table 4.1. Rebel Power Seizures, by Month and Jurisdiction Level
(cumulative percentages)

Month	Provincial Capitals*	Prefecture-Level Cities**	County-Level Cities**	Counties	Overall
December 1966	0	0	0	0.04	0.04
January 1967	86.2	70.2	67.0	46.7	48.5
February	89.7	89.5	81.8	68.3	69.6
March	89.7	91.2	85.2	76.4	77.3
April	89.7	91.2	86.4	78.0	78.9
May	89.7	91.2	86.4	79.0	79.7
Number of Jurisdictions	29	57	88	2,072	2,246

Notes: *Includes Beijing city; **Excludes provincial capitals.

"Proletarian revolutionaries, join together and seize power from capitalist power holders!" A second article informed rebels that the essence of rebellion is nothing less than the seizure of power.[6] These articles were reprinted in regional newspapers and read out on local radio broadcasts.

These pronouncements set off a surge of power seizures across China's cities and deep into the countryside. By the end of January, only 9 *days* after January 22, a total of 1,090 local governments were overthrown— just under half of all cities and counties in the entire country. By the end of February, the number reached 1,563, and by the end of March, 1,736. A few months later there were confirmed power seizures in 80 percent of all cities and counties. Table 4.1 charts the remarkably rapid spread of power seizures, and it reveals a top-down pattern, with provincial capitals falling first, followed by other cities and after some delay, rural counties. Despite the small size of the urban populations of rural counties, their frequently remote locations, and their much smaller numbers of students and workers, almost half of all county governments were already overthrown in January, and more than 75 percent had been overthrown by the end of March.

Figure 4.1 shows in more detail the explosive impact of the January 22 call for power seizures, drawing on the subgroup of localities that reported the exact date. The dates underneath each bar represent the last day of each period. The first bar on the left represents the power seizures that occurred

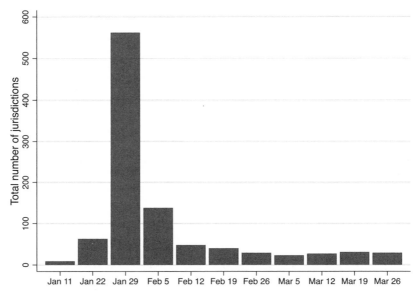

Figure 4.1. Number of Local Power Seizures, by Week, January–March 1967
(N = 1,033)

before Mao's January 12 congratulatory telegram and its praise for the Shanghai events. The second bar represents the power seizures that occurred over the next 11 days, up to the January 22 declarations. From that point forward each bar represents one-week increments. In the first week after January 22 local governments fell with remarkable speed. Among the 1,033 power seizures in this subgroup that would occur through March 26, well over half (563) occurred during this first week. After this initial surge, the weekly numbers subsided and settled into a constant pattern. By the end of March, 93 percent of all recorded power seizures whose exact date is known had already taken place.

Local Rebellions and the Timing of Power Seizures

The rapid spread of power seizures contrasts sharply with the slow spread and limited development of regional rebellions. By the end of 1966 popular insurgencies had yet to develop very far, and still had little impact outside of China's major cities. Recall the trends noted earlier: the first reported seizures of at least one party-state official occurred in fewer than half of county-level cities and fewer than 40 percent of counties by the end of December. The first reported rebel invasion of party and government offices occurred in only 26 percent of county-level cities and only 11 percent in counties by the end of December. Virtually the same percentages were recorded for the first reported rebel coalition.

How seriously were local authorities undermined by rebel insurgencies prior to power seizures? Local annals frequently refer to a situation where local governments were so disrupted that they were no longer able to function. The common term for this is that governments were "paralyzed" *(tanhuan)*. This term was used to describe the condition of local governments at some point in time in 1,415 out of 2,246 local annals—63 percent of the total (see Table 4.2). It is possible that some annals did not use this term where it was warranted. It is also possible that the term was not used because local authorities were never seriously undermined. The percentages reported in Table 4.2 refer only to those localities where "paralysis" was reported, and to the *timing* of the paralysis of local governments.

Only 30 percent of provincial capitals that reported an inability to govern had reached this point by the end of December. As previously described, Shanghai and Nanjing were among them, but Guangzhou and Nanning were not. Less than one quarter of other cities, and 19 percent of counties, reported a state of paralysis by the end of December. Yet government paralysis spread very rapidly during January 1967. By the end of that month the governments of almost all provincial capitals were reportedly paralyzed,

Table 4.2.   Timing of Reports that Local Government is "Paralyzed," by Jurisdiction Level (cumulative percentage of reports)

Month	Provincial Capitals#	Prefecture-level Cities*	County-level Cities*	Counties	Overall
September 1966	5.0	2.6	1.7	1.9	2.0
October	15.0	10.3	6.9	4.2	4.7
November	20.0	15.4	13.8	8.2	8.8
December	30.0	23.1	22.4	18.9	19.4
January 1967	95.0	61.5	77.6	65.1	65.9
February	100	89.7	94.8	88.4	88.3
March	100	92.3	96.5	94.8	94.9
Number of reports	20	39	58	1,298	1,415

Notes: #Excludes Beijing; *Excludes provincial capitals.

as well as the vast majority of other cities and counties. By the end of March, the percentages ranged from 92 to 100 percent.

Even under the extreme assumption that a state of paralysis existed only in localities whose annals used that term, it is clear that something quite extraordinary happened in January—but what, exactly? Did slowly developing and still limited rebel insurgencies suddenly scale up, become highly organized, and overthrow local governments over the next few weeks? Did small and poorly organized rebel factions arbitrarily declare a power seizure during one of their periodic office invasions? Or did something else happen to simultaneously overthrow local authorities and paralyze local government capacity?

Figure 4.2 provides a broader perspective on the timing of power seizures relative to indicators of rebel activity. The trend lines are averages for all cities and counties, but unlike Table 4.2 it traces the cumulative percentages of *all* 2,246 cities and counties, by month, that reported each type of event. The trend lines for seizures of officials, rebel coalitions and the paralysis of local government show that only very small percentages of all jurisdictions reported each type of event by December 1966. The most com-

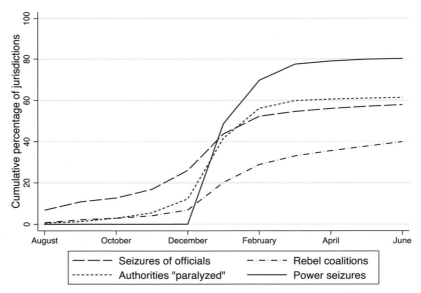

Figure 4.2. Indicators of Rebel Activity, by Month, August 1966–June 1967 (N = 2,246)

monly reported event was the seizure of a local leader—still well below 30 percent of local governments. Rebel coalitions and government paralysis both remained around 10 percent. In January 1967, the trend lines for each move upward more rapidly, but the line for power seizures shoots past all of them during January and February and stays well above all three other indicators of rebel insurgencies thereafter.

Hints about the relationship of prior rebel activity to power seizures are evident in the subset of the most detailed of local narratives. When was the first seizure of a local leader by rebels relative to the date of a power seizure? There were 420 annals that reported the exact date of both events. Slightly more than half of all seizures of government leaders occur before the day of a power seizure, but in the remaining localities the first seizure of a local leader occurred only on the day of a power seizure or afterwards. In this subgroup of localities, the median date for the seizure of an official was only 10 days before the power seizure.

When was the first report of the formation of a rebel coalition relative to a power seizure? There were 415 annals that reported the exact date of both events. In only 42 percent of these localities were rebel coalitions reported before the day of the power seizure, and in close to 30 percent of the others the first rebel coalition was reported on the day of the power seizure itself—which suggests that rebel coalitions were often formed only for the purposes of seizing power. This conclusion is reinforced by the fact that the median date of the first report of a rebel coalition in this subgroup of cases is the *same day* as the power seizure.

A final hint can be found in reports of local government paralysis. Of the 368 cases where the date of both government paralysis and the power seizure is known, only 13 percent report paralysis *before* the day of the power seizure. This suggests that the paralysis of most local governments—unlike Shanghai and Nanjing—was in fact a *consequence* of power seizures rather than a precursor.

Power seizures, in other words, occurred far more widely, and far more rapidly, than indicators of the strength and impact of rebel insurgencies would have predicted. This is true even if we assume that seizures of officials, rebel alliances, and government paralysis were reported less fully than local power seizures. Essentially, there were far more power seizures, occurring far earlier, than what we would expect if they were the product of rebel insurgencies based on popular rebellions.

The Spread of Power Seizures

Although there is a puzzling lack of connection between popular rebellion and power seizures, there is a clear relationship between the timing of power seizures at different levels of the national government hierarchy. Power seizures spread in a top-down pattern. This was already indicated by Table 4.1, which showed that power seizures spread first in the provincial capitals, later in other cities, and later still in the counties. The top-down pattern was in fact tighter and more systematic than these aggregate figures suggest. Within each province, prefecture-level cities and prefectures overwhelmingly experienced power seizures only after their provincial capital. Within prefectures, county-level cities and counties overwhelmingly experienced power seizures only after their prefecture. Power seizures occurred in a top-down cascade that radiated downward through the lines of the national bureaucratic hierarchy.

We have seen that January 22 was the starting point for the rapidly spreading wave of power seizures. It was also the starting point for a downward cascade of power seizures within the state's bureaucratic hierarchy. Before January 22, power seizures occurred more or less randomly across regions and levels of the bureaucratic hierarchy. Afterwards, a clear top-down pattern takes hold. Before January 22 the majority of power seizures occur *before* a power seizure at the immediately higher jurisdiction. In the subset of 1,110 cases where the exact dates are known, 63 percent of city and county power seizures before January 22 occurred before a power seizure over the province; 67 percent of prefecture power seizures occurred before their province; and 47 percent of county power seizures occurred before their prefecture. After January 22, the pattern is reversed: only 15 percent of counties and 17 percent of prefectures seized power before their province, and only 18 percent of counties before their prefecture.

In this top-down pattern, distance did not matter. The distance of prefecture-level cities from provincial capitals, and the distance of counties from their prefecture capitals, did not have an impact on the likelihood or timing of a power seizure. Table 4.3 divides jurisdictions into five quintiles by distance from the next higher level in the bureaucratic hierarchy, among the subset of cases where the date of the power seizure is known. The second column shows the average distance from the immediately higher jurisdiction in the government hierarchy, and ranges from localities that

Table 4.3.   Prevalence and Timing of Power Seizures, by Distance from Superior Jurisdiction

Quintile (by distance)	Average Distance from Superior Jurisdiction (miles)	Percent with Reported Power Seizures	Median Date of Reported Power Seizures
1	6.6	77.3	January 27
2	23.5	78.2	January 28
3	35.2	82.1	January 28
4	49.7	81.5	January 29
5	174.6	81.0	January 28
Total	41.9	81.2	January 28

Notes: N = 1,110. Source for distances: China Data Center (2005).

are very close (an average of 6.6 miles) to those that are very distant (an average of 174.6 miles). There is no relationship between distance and either the percentage of jurisdictions that experienced a power seizure or the median date at which a power seizure took place. Whatever the pressures generated by a power seizure at the immediately higher level of government, and whomever these pressures acted upon, it was just as strong where the higher-level jurisdiction was distant as when it was nearby.

The apparent lack of connection between the strength of popular insurgencies and power seizures is accompanied by clear signs that power seizures diffused in a top-down fashion within the bureaucratic structures of this centralized dictatorship. What political process generated this pattern? These patterns raise a fundamental question: what, exactly, *was* a "power seizure"? Who seized power, and what was it that spurred them to do so when they did, creating such a clear top-down pattern? These questions are especially puzzling because of the extraordinarily rapid spread of power seizures, representing the virtual collapse of what had been a disciplined and highly centralized state structure.

Who Seized Power?

Who, if not rebel students and workers, generated the rapid wave of power seizures across China? I have already described rebellions by party and government cadres against their own superiors. These rebellions got underway much later than the student and worker rebellions, and they only became a major force near the end of 1966. In cities like Shanghai and Nanjing, which had very large and highly disruptive popular insurgencies well before the end of 1966, rebellions by party-state cadres appeared during December and critically undermined local governments from within. In large cities with sizable popular insurgencies, cadre rebels cooperated with worker and student rebels in overthrowing their superiors and declaring new organs of power. In one typical example, the January power seizure from the Zhejiang provincial authorities was carried out jointly by an alliance of 30 mass organizations together with an alliance of cadre rebels known as the "Allied Command of Revolutionary Rebels in the Provincial Organs."[7] But the influence of cadre rebels was much greater outside the large cities. In smaller cities and counties, as we shall see, these rebel bureaucrats actually organized and led power seizures. They sometimes cooperated with relatively small groups of students or workers, if there were any in existence, but they frequently seized power unilaterally. Only through reference to the political action of rebel bureaucrats can we account for the remarkably rapid spread of power seizures across China, and in particular their top-down spread within the national bureaucratic hierarchy.

It seems counterintuitive that cadres would act to undermine the very structures to which their vested interests were intimately tied. This ran entirely counter to their presumed group interests. Yet the motives for rebel bureaucrats, on closer examination, are not hard to understand. In the summer of 1966 they were already mobilized into loyalty campaigns in which selected individuals at all ranks were stripped of their posts and denounced. During these initial months, the vast majority of party and government functionaries sought to demonstrate unquestionable loyalty to their superiors, who coordinated these loyalty campaigns. As rebel movements among students gathered momentum in September and October, some of them actively participated in Scarlet Guard groups that were founded explicitly to protect their offices and especially their superiors from rebel attacks. After the end of the October Party Conference, however, the loyalty investigations conducted by local governments were denounced, and official efforts to restrict the student movement and coordinate countermobilization—in particular the Scarlet Guards—were declared to be severe political errors.

In this altered context, it appeared increasingly likely that leading officials at all levels would lose their posts. Subordinates in party and government offices who had previously supported their superiors actively, especially those who had been active in Scarlet Guard organizations, found it necessary to distance themselves from their superiors and show sympathy for the rebel movement. In provincial capitals and other large cities, cadres began to form rebel groups of their own, and they found it in their interest to cooperate actively with student and worker rebels who were preparing to seize power. Only in this way could party and government officials hope to avoid becoming victims of the escalating campaign.

In the small cities and counties, there was little threat from popular insurgencies, which were small and weak, and in many remote localities practically nonexistent. Cadre rebels in these localities were spurred to seize power by news of a power seizure at the immediately higher level in the bureaucratic hierarchy. If they failed to follow suit, they risked being deposed by rebels at higher levels who had seized power before them. And they risked being preempted by other local cadres contemplating their own power seizure, or by a sudden office invasion by a small group of student or worker rebels who might declare themselves in charge. Under such rapidly shifting circumstances, the only way to control your own fate was to act quickly before others did so.

Before substantiating this analysis with examples drawn from the most detailed local accounts, we should take note of the size, distribution, and characteristics of this crucial group. China in the mid-1960s was a highly organized and centralized dictatorship. Two intertwined hierarchies reached from the capital to the grass roots. The central government presided directly over 29 province-level jurisdictions, which in turn presided over a hierarchy of more than 200 prefectures, close to 170 cities, and more than 2,100 rural counties, each of which was directly subordinate to a unit at the immediately higher level.[8] Paralleling the government hierarchy was a network of party committees whose personnel overlapped with and controlled government agencies at each level. On the eve of the Cultural Revolution, there were 2.4 million full-time party and government functionaries in these two hierarchies. Close to 300,000 were full-time party functionaries in 4,400 party committees and related offices. The remaining 2.1 million staffed government offices, and more than 80 percent of them were party members organized into 117,000 party branches.[9] Communication within this hierarchy was highly effective. Officials were woven into a national network that spanned levels in the hierarchy, and that promoted discipline within local agencies.

No occupational group in China had a more direct interest in the course and outcomes of political campaigns, especially if they took the form of a loyalty investigation. No group enjoyed more privileges in this centrally planned economy. As an interest group, party-state cadres had enormous vested interests in the preservation of a system in which they held a highly favorable position. But their positions as individuals were not secure. More than any other group, the loyalty of party-state officials was monitored, and significant numbers were periodically found wanting and were sanctioned. Throughout the 1950s and as recently as 1965 there had been periodic loyalty campaigns, during each of which significant numbers of cadres lost their positions in disgrace, and in some cases were expelled from the cities or sent to labor camps. Survival in such a hierarchy required vigilance to ensure that one's loyalty did not come under suspicion. There was no alternative form of employment, and no palatable exit option. Cadres lacked personal assets or business interests that could support a post-bureaucratic career. They could not resign to take up employment in a private sector or independent public institutions. They could not initiate a transfer to another location or workplace.

Finally, the distribution of cadres across government jurisdictions ensured that they were an important political force in virtually every locality in the country. While this may seem obvious, it is less obvious that they comprised a far higher percentage of the nonagricultural labor force in China's vast rural hinterland, where their political influence was thereby magnified. In Table 4.4 we can see the enormous differences between cities and counties in both the numbers of cadres and their relative weight in the nonagricultural workforce. Cadre numbers were largest in the provincial capitals, where they averaged more than 50,000. But the provincial capitals had massive nonagricultural workforces, so at the median, cadres as a group were only 9 percent of the total. The ratios were similar in cities of all sizes. But in the counties, the median number of cadres relative to workers and staff was 34 percent, one third the size of the total salaried workforce.[10] This means that in half of all counties, the number of cadres was more than 34 percent of the salaried workforce. In the least urbanized counties, the ratio was even more heavily weighted in favor of the cadres. The median county in terms of urbanization has an urban population that is 6.2 percent of the total. In counties below that level of urbanization cadres actually outnumber other nonagricultural workers by a ratio of 1.4 to 1. This indi-

Table 4.4.   Demographic Features of Local Jurisdictions, 1966

Jurisdiction Level	Average Population	Average Urban Population	Percent Urban	Average No. Cadres	Average No. Workers	Median Cadre-Worker Ratio	N
Provincial Capitals*	1,446,620	1,260,528	76.6	54,964	476,436	.09	29
Prefecture-Level Cities**	542,895	350,594	66.5	14,242	121,130	.11	57
County-Level Cities**	241,688	132,513	61.4	3,981	40,859	.09	88
Counties	307,417	22,497	13.0	1,760	6,430	.34	2,072
Valid N	2,241	2,236	2,235	2,084	2,157	2,013	

Notes: * Includes urban Beijing; **Excludes provincial capitals.

cates that it is precisely where the populations of workers and students were small that the relative numbers of party and government functionaries were high—and by extension, that they would be the main force behind power seizures.

The Rebellion of the Cadres

This reasoning is borne out by the most detailed available accounts of power seizures. Published local annals for the cities routinely mention cadre rebels and describe their participation in power seizures alongside worker and student groups. Published annals for the counties and small cities sometimes mention their existence, but provide little detail about their activities or motives. Fortunately, we have access to highly detailed internal investigation reports for Guangxi Province, and they shed considerable light on the cadre rebellions. These materials describe a late but very rapid spread of cadre rebellions. Only 33 percent of all cities and counties in the province reported active cadre rebels by the end of November, but the number reached 60 percent by the end of December 1966, and 98 percent by the end of January 1967.[11]

The intrabureaucratic rebellion emerged slowly, after some delay. The October Party Conference was a crucial turning point and signaled the imminent end of local leaders' strategies to contain rebel insurgencies. Held in Beijing in mid-October and attended by thousands of officials from

across the country, the meeting's purpose was to "clarify thinking" about
the Cultural Revolution. The key event was Chen Boda's speech of October 16, in which he denounced local leaders' efforts to restrict the scope
of the rebellion and specifically repudiated mass organizations whose purpose was to protect power holders. Chen declared that these and other efforts represented a "bourgeois reactionary line" *(zichan jieji fandong luxian)*
that was anti-party, anti-socialist, and anti-Mao. He called for all such actions to cease, and for student rebels to target leaders who carried out this
reactionary line. Chen's speech was issued nationwide as the key document
to come out of the October meetings.[12]

Local accounts in Guangxi mention the October Conference as causing
a major shift in local politics, and some specifically mention Chen's speech.[13]
When the meeting's decisions were relayed to lower levels, they signaled to
all who had been targeted in loyalty campaigns directed by party officials
that their punishments might be overturned. More importantly, however,
they signaled to all who had cooperated loyally with their leaders that they
had to reconsider their position, because they were now exposed as collaborators in an erroneous political line. Should their leaders fall from power,
loyal subordinates would fall along with them. As the implications of the
October Party Conference sank in, cadres throughout China rapidly re-
evaluated their stances.

The rebellion began in the Guangxi provincial party and government
offices shortly after the October meetings. Accounts from various provincial departments mention independent rebel groups later that month, and
they are mentioned with increasing frequency in November and December.
By the end of 1966, virtually all of the departments in the provincial party
and government headquarters harbored rebel organizations with names
similar to those adopted by student and worker groups. By January 1967,
these internal rebellions appear to have become nearly universal in provincial agencies.[14]

After Beijing's early December directive authorizing the formation of
rebel groups among workers, Nanning's Municipal Party Secretary informed local office personnel that this authorization applied to them as
well. Rebel organizations and small fighting groups soon mobilized within
the city's bureaucracy. In mid-December, the cadre rebels held a large
meeting of all functionaries in the city's administration to hear their leaders'

self-criticisms. The following week they joined with student and worker rebels in staging a mass struggle session against the city's top officials.[15]

Scarlet Guards in the party and government organs fell apart rapidly after October. In Qinzhou Prefecture, they were disbanded shortly after October and cadres and staff began to form their own independent rebel organizations.[16] In Lingui County the Scarlet Guards rapidly disappeared as cadres and staff reportedly "rushed" to establish autonomous rebel groups. By the end of November, in the 29 offices and departments in the county administration there were more than 50 small fighting groups, with a membership of 520 out of the county's 883 cadres and staff.[17] Fusui County had more than 80 rebel organizations at this point in time, with 22 of them in various party and government offices, including the organization department, the party committee's staff office, and propaganda department. The rebel leaders were ordinary cadres, political instructors, and press correspondents.[18] In Tiandong County, cadres and staff in the party and government offices organized a range of small fighting groups and one cross-department alliance, the "Rebel Headquarters" *(zaofan silingbu)*, which had more than 100 members. Led by cadres from the Public Security Bureau, the Discipline Inspection Commission, and the courts, it took the lead in a rebellion against their own superiors.[19] In Pubei County, the Scarlet Guards, instead of disbanding, turned on their masters, simply changing their name and rebranding themselves as rebel organizations devoted to repudiating the bourgeois reactionary line.[20]

In Qinzhou County, ordinary cadres in the county office and trade union formed a rebel brigade of more than 400 individuals who had fallen under suspicion in recent loyalty investigations. They agitated to overturn their cases and held struggle sessions against the county officials who had organized the campaign that victimized them.[21] Cadre "fighting groups" became common in Lingchuan County in November 1966. In December, they formed an alliance across the departments under the county's party committee. Cadres formed a separate rebel alliance in the offices under the county government. They held struggle sessions against the county's Party Secretary, Vice-Secretaries, County Magistrate, and Vice Magistrate. Not satisfied with repudiating the current leaders, they traveled to the headquarters of Hechi Prefecture to seize the county's previous Party Secretary, who recently had been promoted to a higher post there, and subjected him to struggle sessions. The cadre rebels charged that the county's Party Secretary and the Chief Judge were "historical counterrevolutionaries," leading eventually to the Judge's suicide in January 1967.[22]

By late December, cadre rebels began to claim authority over the conduct of the local Cultural Revolution. Rebels in the offices of Yulin Prefecture pushed the official Cultural Revolution Committees aside and elected new ones.[23] In Lingshan County, cadres in the county offices formed new committees to "bombard" the county's Party Secretary and other leaders. They put up wall posters, held struggle sessions, and formed an alliance of the many small fighting groups in the county offices.[24]

Party leaders found it increasingly difficult to control regularly scheduled meetings. Near the end of December, the Guangxi provincial authorities, hoping to stem the spiraling loss of their authority, ordered party secretaries to apologize to rebels for conducting a bourgeois reactionary line. In Mengshan County, party leaders convened such a meeting, speaking to an assembly of some 2,000. On the second day, the head of the county's rural department stood up to denounce them. He revealed incriminating information about wrongdoing that the county's Party Secretary had failed to mention, and he called for his removal. The meeting broke up in disarray. On January 6, this beleaguered Party Secretary convened another meeting to repeat his self-criticism to an even larger audience. Shortly after the meeting began he and other officials were kicked off the stage, and they lost control of the proceedings. Cadre rebels in the county offices held struggle sessions against members of the county party committee and the heads of all 27 county departments. They were paraded through the streets and their homes were searched.[25] During December the leaders of Lingshan, Hepu, Wuming, Qinzhou, and Pubei Counties all lost control of regularly scheduled party congresses, which were taken over by cadre rebels who subjected them to struggle sessions and called for their removal.[26]

A series of interviews with five long-retired officials in Zouping County, Shandong, shed further light on the type of cadre rebellions described in the Guangxi Province materials.[27] Fifty miles from the provincial capital of Ji'nan, Zouping had 9,461 urban residents, 1,262 cadres, and only 1 high school in 1966.[28] All of the interviewees were junior staff members in the county headquarters at the time, and all were active in rebel groups. It was clear during the course of the interviews that the vast majority of cadres in the county seat were active in rebel groups, and that they played pivotal role in the conflicts of the period.

One cadre worked in the planning office of the county government and led a rebel group of office staff. According to him, rebel groups formed based on the structure of the party branches in party and government departments. Each party branch formed its own fighting group, and frequently the party branch secretaries ended up as rebel leaders. In this sense, the party organization turned back upon its own leaders, and the party's own organizational structure facilitated an internal rebellion. His group was formed in December 1966, after they sent delegates to Beijing and found that there was already widespread rebellion within party and government offices in the nation's capital.[29] When the delegates returned from Beijing and reported what they had learned, they immediately organized their rebel group.

A second cadre worked in the county industrial bureau, where he was the leader of a rebel group that included some 30 of the 40 cadres. The only cadres who were excluded were those who were department or section heads. According to his recollection, those who were most active in the rebellion against the county's leaders were political activists who were already influential and trusted by leaders prior to the Cultural Revolution. In this sense, the leaders' favored subordinates were among the key organizers of the rebellion.

The Role of Cadres in Power Seizures

What role did cadre rebels play in power seizures? In Guangxi, there were growing rebellions within party and government organs at each level of government by December 1966. These rebellions became larger and more militant in response to the publicity about Shanghai. After a coalition of rebels seized power over Guangxi Province on January 23, power seizures spread rapidly to cities, prefectures, and counties in the province. The narrative accounts make clear that cadre rebels were active at all levels of government, but they played a much more central role in rural prefectures and counties. In the provincial capital of Nanning and the prefecture-level cities of Guilin, Liuzhou, and Wuzhou, cadre rebels formed alliances with student and worker groups that had been active in late 1966. In the rural prefectures with headquarters in small towns, and especially in counties, cadre rebels played a dominant role, and in most counties, they seized power unilaterally with little attention to student and worker rebels, who were much less formidable than in the large cities.

In Nanning, there were separate power seizures in each of the government headquarters located in the city: Guangxi Province, Nanning Municipality, and Nanning Prefecture. Within the Guangxi provincial offices there were a series of separate power seizures during the third week of January. The cadres that seized power were not department or bureau heads. The highest ranking of the rebel leaders—in roughly half of the offices— were section chiefs or bureau vice heads. The remaining rebel leaders were primarily ordinary cadres, personal aides, or office staff. They displaced the top officials in their units—bureau and department heads—who were forced to yield control to their subordinates. The cadre rebels aligned themselves with coalitions of workers and students and participated in the power seizure over Guangxi Province on January 23.[30] In the Nanning Municipal offices, a large cadre rebel alliance joined a simultaneous power seizure over the provincial and municipal authorities as part of a larger alliance known as the "Grand Rebel Army" *(zaofan dajun),* whose main force was a group of rebel workers. On the day of the power seizure the cadre rebels elected new leaders for their departments.[31]

In the Nanning Prefecture offices, a rebel group within the party committee office issued an urgent communiqué on January 23 and called together rebels from various administrative departments for discussions. Along with rebels from five other departments, they issued a call for an immediate power seizure. On January 24, delegates from the prefecture offices met to plan a power seizure. Some argued for immediate action: if they did not move immediately, worker and student rebels might seize power first, making things "difficult to manage." On January 25, they held a mass meeting of more than one thousand prefectural cadres to denounce all of the party Secretaries and Vice-Secretaries, who were all expelled from their posts.[32] Unlike their colleagues in Guangxi Province and Nanning Municipality, cadre rebels in Nanning Prefecture seized power unilaterally, without any participation by students or workers.[33]

Guilin was another large city with militant student and worker alliances in the fall of 1966. Guilin was the seat of Guilin Prefecture, but it also had a separate city administration. The cadre rebels in the city administration acted as partners in power seizures carried out with large student and worker alliances. Their "Revolutionary Rebel Regiment of Staff and Cadres in the City Administration," established on December 10, eventually joined students and workers in seizing control of Guilin's city administration on January 24.[34] As in Nanning, the cadre rebels in Guilin were simply part of an alliance in which they were outnumbered by much larger groups of rebel students and workers, and with whom they cooperated in seizing power.

In the offices of Guilin Prefecture, however, cadre rebels played a much more central role. On January 24, they formed an alliance across departments and aligned themselves with other rebels. Late that evening they called together the leaders of their alliance and decided to move forward immediately with a power seizure before other rebels could do so. Shortly after midnight they placed the entire leadership of the prefecture under house arrest and issued a proclamation that they were now in charge.[35]

Narratives for the city of Liuzhou describe a central role for cadre rebels. Like Guilin, Liuzhou was the administrative seat for a large prefecture. The prefecture administered 11 counties, and Liuzhou City had separate party and government offices. Rebels in several city and prefecture departments declared power seizures within their own offices after the January 12 *People's Daily* editorial praising Shanghai, and the departmental power seizures accelerated in response to the January 22 articles in the same newspaper. The leader of one of the main rebel groups, an aide in the party committee office, called together rebel leaders from other city departments to discuss an alliance, and they planned for a power seizure on January 25. They belatedly realized, however, that they had forgotten to include representatives from rebels in the prefecture government. They were unaware of the fact that delegates from 29 rebel groups in the prefecture's party and government organs were simultaneously meeting to prepare a power seizure. The prefecture cadres learned that cadres in other offices were discussing their own power seizures, so the group decided immediately to proclaim a power seizure and forced the prefecture's leading cadres to sign an agreement to hand over power. The power seizures in city and prefecture therefore proceeded simultaneously without coordination, and with no involvement by worker and student rebels.[36]

In Yulin Prefecture, a rural jurisdiction of 8 counties, cadre rebels declared a unilateral power seizure explicitly in order to preempt a power seizure by an alliance of rebel workers. On January 18, a group of worker

rebels based in the prefecture's official trade union formed a "power seizure committee." Rebels in the prefecture headquarters hurriedly pushed
through their own power seizure to prevent this "outside group" from doing
so. On January 24, they issued a proclamation and summoned the Party
Secretary and Prefecture Head to a mass meeting of all cadres, and removed
them from office.[37] Cadres in Bose Prefecture, by contrast, included students and workers in their alliance. There were two rebel alliances in the
prefecture offices, and they formed a power seizure committee composed
of leaders from 16 rebel groups. On January 25, they called together 69
rebel groups for a power seizure rally on the premises of the prefecture,
taking control of the building.[38]

The accounts of province, city, and prefecture power seizures indicate
that it was primarily in the large cities that alliances of student and worker
rebels played an important role, but in each case, they were joined by alliances of cadre rebels, who frequently acted as coordinators. In some of the
cities and in the more rural prefectures, however, the narratives make clear
that cadre rebels were instrumental in organizing local power seizures,
sometimes choosing to include workers and student groups, sometimes not.

Below the prefectures and prefecture-level cities in Guangxi were 82
counties and county-level cities, almost all of which experienced power seizures. There were three basic patterns in accounts of these power seizures.
In the first, cadre rebels are described as seizing power unilaterally, without
any mention of student or workers. In the second, cadre rebels voluntarily
included students and workers in alliances that they organized. In the third,
cadre rebels unilaterally seized power precisely in order to avert the possibility that outside groups might do so, or in order to preempt rival cadre
rebels.

Examples of first pattern, in which cadre rebels seized power without
any mention of mass organizations, are Bose, Beiliu, Wuming, Dongxing,
and Lingshan Counties. In Bose, two large alliances of cadre rebels took
the lead: one was headed by a cadre in the party committee staff office, the
other by a cadre in the planning committee. The members of their power
seizure committee, which moved on January 27, were all ordinary cadres.[39]
In Beiliu, cadres formed a power seizure committee on January 26, the day
after they were informed that the cadres in the Yulin Prefecture offices had
done so. The rebel leaders all held lower-level staff positions.[40] Cadres in
the Wuming county headquarters seized power on January 26, under the

leadership of a clerk in the county court.[41] In Dongxing, the power seizure was carried out entirely by rebels in the county offices, after hearing news of the provincial power seizure.[42] Although Lingshan had a large and active student Red Guard movement, the power seizure there was coordinated by cadre rebels in the county offices. In mid-January, they selected a cadre from the bureau of public security as their leader, and seized power from their superiors.[43]

Examples of the second pattern, in which cadres cooperated with outside rebels, are Fusui and Pubei Counties. In Fusui, a cadre in the organization department and an investigator from the discipline inspection office led the effort. Formally declaring their power seizure on February 1, the 30-person power seizure committee included ordinary cadres, staff, technicians, workers, teachers, and students.[44] In Pubei County, the leader of a rebel alliance in the county administration, a staff member in the county party office, convened meetings of more than 90 rebel leaders from across the county to discuss a power seizure, and a separate meeting for rebels within the county administration, culminating in a power seizure.[45]

The third pattern was more common: cadre rebels seized power due to the imminent threat of an attempted power seizure by an outside group, or by rival cadre rebels. Imminent threats by outside groups or rival rebels are mentioned in the accounts from Guiping, Chongzuo, Qinzhou, Gongcheng, Laibin, and Lingui Counties. In Guiping, cadre rebels, worried that student Red Guards would soon act, seized power over the county in anticipation.[46] In Chongzuo, Red Guards led by a high school student joined together with a group of worker rebels to seize power in several county offices. This spurred cadre rebels to seize power the same day over their own offices, and they quickly formed a committee to seize overall power in the county two days later.[47] In Qinzhou, cadre rebels rushed to seize power ahead of a rebel alliance led by a high school Red Guard, but they failed to do so before the students acted. The cadres nonetheless declared their own power seizure, setting off controversy between the two sides.[48] In Gongcheng, two rival groups in the county administration planned separately to seize power, prompting one of them to act preemptively, sparking strong protests by the excluded cadre rebels.[49] In Laibin, cadre rebels were spurred to action by a proclamation by student Red Guards that they intended to seize power. They held an urgent a late-night meeting and seized power the next morning.[50]

The mere possibility that outside groups *might* eventually attempt to seize power appears to have been enough to spur cadre rebels to seize power in Tiandong, Luzhai, and Lingyun Counties. In Tiandong, cadre rebels noted that the inclusion of student and worker rebels in the provincial power seizure had created confused lines of authority, making it very difficult for them to conduct business. This argument was enough to spur them to seize power in the absence of any imminent moves by student or worker groups.[51] In Luzhai, cadres were spurred into action by news of the power seizure in Liuzhou Prefecture. Cadres who had observed the power seizure in Liuzhou rushed back and argued that failing to act quickly would risk power seizures by others—they seized power two days later.[52] In Lingyun, cadre rebels planning their power seizure disagreed about the severity of the county Party Secretary's errors, delaying their planned action. After a delay of several days, the head of the county People's Armed Department personally convened a separate power seizure committee, arguing that if the cadres did not act immediately outside groups might invade the county offices and take over. They proceeded to seize power a few days later.[53]

In Guangxi Province, the top-down pattern of power seizures was very pronounced. On January 23, one day after Beijing's urgent call for power seizures, there were simultaneous power seizures over the province and its capital city (Nanning). One prefecture experienced a power seizure on the same day. By January 26, three days later, all 12 prefectures and prefecture-level cities had experienced a power seizure, along with 19 counties. By January 31, power seizures had spread to all but 17 of the 82 counties and county-level cities. Only 7 county-level jurisdictions had yet to experience a power seizure by the end of February; two of these would have power seizures in early March, and five would never have one. Guangxi displayed a top-down pattern almost perfectly, as power seizures spread rapidly from higher- to lower-level jurisdictions. There were simultaneous power seizures in different levels of the hierarchy on 8 occasions, but none occurred prior to one at the immediately higher level.

State Collapse as a Cascading Process

The cascade of power seizures was not the product of popular rebellion. In fact, most power seizures were either organized by or unilaterally carried out by government functionaries who worked in party and government agencies. The speed with which they spread, and the clear top-down pattern, are indicators of internal political processes within the structures of the party-state. In this sense, the collapse of civilian political authority in this vast political hierarchy was more an "inside-out" than a "bottom-up" process.

As they spread downward in the hierarchy, power seizures are more accurately described as a series of internal political coups—with varying degrees of popular participation—where government functionaries turned against their own superiors. Given the central political role of cadres, who enjoyed high status and privilege in this political system, one might legitimately question whether this was a "real" rebellion. As we shall see, power seizures carried out unilaterally by cadres were later vulnerable to accusations that they were "fake," nothing more than palace coups. Whatever one's view on this issue of interpretation, these rebellions were undeniably very real in their consequences. They marked the collapse of civilian political authority across much of the country, and in most regions paved the way for another 18 months of factional conflict and political violence.

Two decades later, similarly organized communist regimes collapsed rapidly and unexpectedly across Eastern Europe. In response, social scientists began to question prevailing theories of revolution, which seemed unable to predict such events or adequately explain them in retrospect.[54] One response was renewed attention to threshold and critical mass models of collective behavior, which emphasize the interdependencies of individual decisions that shift propensities of individuals to participate in collective action.[55] Applied to protests in these settings, these models explained sudden escalations in protest as a function of information flows or social networks.[56]

These analyses appeared, at least implicitly, to treat the collapse of a regime as a function of the scale of popular protest. State-centered theories of revolution, by contrast, insist that the impact of mass mobilization is highly contingent on the prior existence of structural weaknesses that make regimes vulnerable to mass mobilization from below. Especially important are prior cleavages among ruling elites or organizational weaknesses of the state apparatus.[57] These theories emphasize preexisting conditions—the organization of state authority, fiscal strains, or pressures emanating from the international system. They leave unexamined the internal politics of state structures during the course of the events whose outcomes they seek to explain. Popular challenges are assumed to place pressures on states: strong states are more likely to withstand them, while structurally flawed states are more vulnerable. How and why states unravel remains unexamined, and is assumed to follow from initial structural circumstances.

What emerges from our examination of China in early 1967 is a state-centered analysis that applies dynamic models of collective behavior to the individuals who are agents of the party-state. These state-centered processes, however, do not depend on structural flaws or preexisting cleavages in state structures. In fact, the same features that lent these political structures their extraordinary discipline and mobilizational capacity—their unitary structure and close monitoring of agents—in fact promoted the movement-like behavior of state agents.

Dynamic models of social action view the decisions of actors as interdependent—they are influenced by choices reflected in the prior actions of relevant others. Threshold and critical mass theories emphasize the interdependencies of individual choices that shift group behavior in ways that do not reflect the average or aggregate fixed preferences of individuals in a social category. These ideas also motivate familiar diffusion models of political events. The rate at which strikes, riots, or protests spread across time and space is not affected solely by fixed structural features indicating group motives or capacity to act. There is a dynamic temporal dimension that indicates mutual influence. A period of heightened protest activity emerges through "imitation, comparison, the transfer of forms and themes of protest from one sector to another."[58] There is typically a wave-like pattern in which the influence of prior actions by others eventually diminishes over time.[59]

Diffusion models are fundamentally about two processes: the first is how information is transmitted. Actors can be influenced by the actions of others only if they learn of them, and the mechanisms fall into two broad types—relational and nonrelational.[60] Relational mechanisms of transmission operate through either local or distant social networks or formal organizations.[61] Nonrelational mechanisms operate among actors who are not connected through networks or formal organizations—information is transmitted through the mass media.[62] For present purposes the question of how information is transmitted is not much of a puzzle. The actors described were awash in information transmitted via mass media that were uniform throughout the country and through the formal bureaucratic hierarchy of the state. There were, in addition, face-to-face social networks created by the travel of Red Guards across the country and the constant participation of cadres in meetings at different levels in the government hierarchy.

Of much greater relevance to our present case is the second preoccupation of diffusion models—how actors evaluate the information they receive, and how and why they act on it. In some analyses of collective action and protest, the prior occurrence of a type of protest event signals the vulnerability of authorities to a challenge, and the likelihood that a similar challenge of their own might be successful, something that affects the propensity to act.[63] In other analyses, what is transmitted is information about effective techniques of organization or strategies of protest, which are subsequently imitated by similarly motivated actors.[64]

Most diffusion models appear to assume that the preferences of actors are given—individuals' propensity to act on these shared preferences shifts in response to the actions of others. In this case, however, what shifts is not the propensity to act on political preferences. Instead, we observe a shift in political preferences. In a trivial sense, of course, the preferences of individual cadres are stable—they want to survive the upheaval. What shifts decisively, however, are the choices they make and the political orientations that they adopt in pursuit of this end. Active or passive support of one's superiors shifts toward criticism and eventually open rebellion. The shift is especially pronounced in the case of the Scarlet Guards, many of whom reversed course and became among the most active and effective critics of their superiors after having defended them for many weeks. As the political context shifted, they had the most urgent reasons to turn against their superiors.

In my analysis, I have portrayed a top-down process of diffusion, essentially a form of collective behavior by party-state cadres. Rebellions among the cadres grew in response to signals emanating from Beijing in the wake of the October Party Conference. This signaled to all cadres in the hierarchy that the actions of their superiors were viewed in Beijing as manifestations of a "bourgeois reactionary line." The next shift in the national political context was the favorable publicity given to the Shanghai power seizure in early January, which stimulated internal rebellions by cadres, culminating in the January 22 call for rebels to seize power in imitation of Shanghai. This touched off a top-down wave of power seizures across the country, one that was accelerated by a power seizure at the immediately higher level in the bureaucratic hierarchy. When a power seizure occurred in a province or a prefecture above a local government jurisdiction, this immediately placed pressures on local cadres to act and ensure an opportunity to control their own fate.

I have built up this portrayal through a close examination of selected local narrative accounts of cadre rebellion and power seizures, along with an examination of broad descriptive patterns in the data set. Is such a pattern reflected systematically in the data set as a whole? Elsewhere, the analysis presented here has been evaluated more rigorously with event history models, applied to the entire data set that predicts the timing of local power seizures.[65] Here I will summarize the results of that analysis.

The model estimates conform closely to my descriptive analysis. Overall, the cities experienced power seizures before the counties. However, power seizures were not delayed by either distance from the next higher level of government or by the percentage of cadres in the nonagricultural labor force. In other words, distant counties with small, cadre-dominant workforces did not experience power seizures later than less remote and more urbanized counties closer to administrative centers. The top-down pressures that spurred power seizures operated uniformly across lower-level jurisdictions.

The crucial test of the idea that power seizures spread in a top-down cascade is the contrast in the impact of a power seizure at the next higher level of government in the periods before and after January 22. Earlier (Figure 4.1) we saw that power seizures spread slowly before January 22, but accelerated rapidly in response to signals from Beijing issued on that day. Event history models confirm that this decisively altered the dynamics of power seizures. In the period prior to January 22, power seizures were more likely in a locality if one occurred nearby at the same level in the government hierarchy.[66] But a power seizure in the immediately higher level of government had no discernible impact. During this initial period, in other words, relatively familiar diffusion mechanisms were evident, with nearby events influencing local politics in a manner often observed in other political settings.

After January 22, top-down influences within the state hierarchy overwhelmed local influences, and the earlier pattern was reversed. After this date, the probability that a locality would experience a power seizure was highest immediately after a power seizure at the next higher level of government. The influence of power seizures in nearby localities at the same level was no longer measurable. The difference across periods is portrayed graphically in Figure 4.3, which illustrates the interaction between time period and a higher-level power seizure. The dashed line traces the impact of a higher-level power seizure before January 22. It is almost flat, indicating that there is no discernible impact on the predicted time to a local power seizure.

After January 22, the predicted time to a local power seizure is shortest immediately after a higher-level power seizure, and it rises steadily thereafter. One day after a higher-level power seizure, the predicted time to a local power seizure is one month. If a local power seizure has not occurred after one month, the predicted time grows to roughly two months. If a local power seizure has not occurred within two months, the predicted time to power seizure grows to 5 months. Essentially, if a local power seizure has not occurred within two months of a higher-level power seizure, it is highly

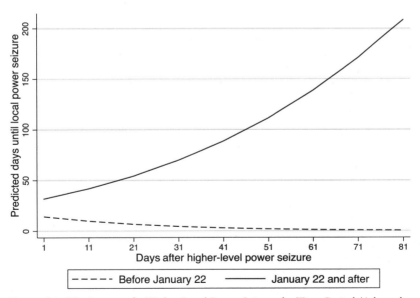

Figure 4.3. The Impact of a Higher-Level Power Seizure, by Time Period (Adapted with permission from Walder and Lu, "The Dynamics of Collapse in an Authoritarian Regime: China in 1967," *American Journal of Sociology* 122, no. 4 (January 2017): 1144–82, figure 4. © by The University of Chicago.)

unlikely that one will ever occur. In other words, the probability of a local power seizure is highest immediately after one at the next higher level. The notion that power seizures spread in a top-down cascade as cadre rebels responded to power seizures in higher-level jurisdictions is reinforced and in fact clarified by the application of event history models to the data set as a whole.

It is hard to avoid the observation that this otherwise disciplined and centralized state hierarchy unraveled as collective behavior among the state's own agents unfolded in a distinctly bureaucratic pattern. In a manner of speaking, the state bureaucracy destroyed itself, as cadres at all levels turned against their own superiors. This was not interest group behavior, but instead a cascading series of acts by individuals of the kind posited in threshold and critical mass models of collective behavior. Interest group behavior, to be sure, was evident at certain points in time. The Scarlet Guard mobilization that was designed to protect bureaucrats and their offices from invasions by outside rebel groups is a clear example. However, the cascading defections of cadres initiated in the wake of the October Party Conference marked an end to this instance of interest group politics, initiating a dynamic process that undermined state structures in a growing wave. The process culminated in the celebrated Shanghai power seizure, and was accelerated by Beijing's January 22 declarations, creating pressures that spurred cadres to overthrow their superiors and effectively destroy structures of civilian authority across the country.

The rapid and extensive spread of power seizures went far beyond what could be accounted for by local popular insurgencies, which had not previously advanced very far outside provincial capitals and large cities. Somewhat paradoxically, the rapid spread of power seizures outside the large cities was due primarily to internal rebellions by party-state cadres. In large cities with active and threatening popular insurgencies, cadre rebels cooperated with student and worker rebels, took part in power seizure alliances, and helped to coordinate the takeover of power. In regions without significant insurgencies, cadre rebels took the lead in organizing power seizures, or they seized power unilaterally, often ignoring local student and worker rebel movements, if there were any. It is impossible to explain the speed and extensive reach of the wave of power seizures, not to mention their distinctive top-down pattern of diffusion, without reference to the activities of rebels within the structure of the party-state.

This wave of power seizures represented the collapse of China's civilian state. Party organizations were decapitated and they no longer functioned. A variety of new actors, representing a range of students, workers, and cadre rebels, laid claim to government authority, and they now had to defend these claims. Rebels who were left out of power seizures, or preempted by rivals, typically refused to recognize these claims, and immediately contested them. Cadres had played a central role in the destruction of party-state structures to which their group interests were closely tied. The axis of conflict was about to shift fundamentally, and the most destructive and violent phase of this political upheaval was about to begin.

5
THE FORMATION OF FACTIONS

THE WAVE OF POWER SEIZURES altered political relationships across China. New factional identities would soon form in response to power seizures, and violent warfare between these factions would become the primary story of the Cultural Revolution well into 1968. As detailed in this book's Chapter 1, the initial wave of research on this period speculated that these factional divisions were somehow a continuation of the conflicts prior to the wave of power seizures. In other words, these were disputes between the defenders of the party system and their challengers—as exemplified in the conflicts between rebel alliances and Scarlet Guards in the streets of Nanjing and Shanghai in late 1966. From this perspective, the conflicts were a contest between those with interests tied to the status quo and those who pursued grievances against it.

Previously we uncovered one major problem with this interpretation. Party-state cadres, whose interests were more closely tied to the status quo than any other, were a major force in the overthrow of local governments, and they were themselves frequently divided against one another. Here I will address another aspect of this interpretation—the designation of factions as "radical" and "conservative," with presumably different political orientations toward the status quo. The lynchpin of the argument was that these preferences were presumably expressed in a faction's stance toward military units dispatched to enforce order. Factions that supported the efforts of military units were deemed "conservative" because they appeared to yearn for the restoration of order. Factions that continued to resist military units were deemed "radical," because they stubbornly opposed the restoration of order and wanted to keep their rebellion alive.

My alternative explanation does not presume that the foundation for the factions can be found in the social and political positions of activists prior to the fall of local governments. Instead, they emerged through an observable series of path-dependent interactions among rival rebel groups and military units that intervened in the wake of power seizures. The factions, in other words, did not express collective orientations that were fixed by the social or political categories of their individual members. Instead, they emerged out of contingent interactions among rebel groups and military units in a defined period of time—they were the product of the joint actions of two or more actors.

After an initial period of ambiguity and uncertainty that affected all parties, factional identities emerged around a central axis—orientation toward local military control. This did not express a general orientation toward the restoration of political order, but instead a rebel faction's position relative to specific actions taken by military officers during this formative period. Factional orientation toward military control, in other words, expressed preferences toward the restoration of order *on what terms*. This is a fundamentally different portrayal of what these factional conflicts were actually about.

The Roots of Rebel Divisions

The origins of the ubiquitous splits that emerged in rebel movements early in 1967 are already visible in the wave of power seizures. Rebel movements were everywhere highly fragmented and had a pronounced "cellular" quality. This was essentially an extreme version of bloc recruitment, a pattern often observed in the study of social movements that achieve scale by mobilizing blocks of adherents who are tied to one another in smaller organizations or social networks.[1] Although bloc recruitment facilitates rapid growth of an insurgency, it also lends itself readily to fragmentation and division.[2]

Rebel groups initially formed within the organizational structures of places of work or study; within administrative offices, workshops, academic departments; and even within communist party branches. The evidence for this cellular structure is overwhelming. Student rebels organized based on sections within their entry classes and academic departments. At Peking University in October 1966, there were a reported 92 different student "fighting groups" with close to 3,000 members, which were aligned with 3 broad rebel alliances. In the months that followed, 358 different "fighting groups" authored essays in the university's factional newspapers. At nearby People's University, there were no fewer than 196 separate rebel fighting groups.[3] In large cities, power seizures were carried out by alliances that contained scores of different rebel groups from schools, factories, and government agencies. In Zhejiang, the provincial power seizure was carried out by a coalition of more than 30 rebel organizations, including a coalition of cadre rebels. Each of these coalitions were in turn aggregations of smaller blocs.[4] Guangdong's power seizure was carried out by a coalition of more than 20 separate rebel alliances.[5] The fragmentation was evident even within single government offices. The executive office of the Communist Party Committee of Guangxi, for example, had no fewer than 8 small fighting groups among its staff on the eve of the provincial power seizure.[6] The fragmentation was equally evident in rural counties. The local party history for Zhenyuan County, Guizhou, stated that in early 1967, "all manner of rebel organizations sprouted like bamboo shoots after the spring rains, forming in each of the offices of all of the government divisions." The account went on to list by name more than 50 different rebel groups distributed across government departments and enterprises, which were evenly divided into two broader alliances.[7] In December 1966, Lingui County had more than 50 rebel fighting groups in the county's 29 administrative departments; in Fusui County there were more than 80 rebel fighting groups, 22 of them within the county's own headquarters.[8]

This fragmented and cellular pattern of bloc mobilization played a central role in the later emergence of factions, and its impact was felt at the point of power seizures. We have seen that power seizures spread rapidly in a cascade-like pattern, even though there was little evidence of prior rebel coalitions outside the largest cities in immediately preceding weeks. Most rebel coalitions were hastily pulled together for the purpose of seizing power. Coalitions had little prior history of cooperation, and the leaders of the smaller fighting groups often were unfamiliar with one another.

The sheer number of rebel groups, and the speed with which power seizures were carried out, meant that it was virtually impossible to include all rebel groups, or even a majority of them, in a government power seizure. Significant numbers inevitably were excluded. Sometimes this exclusion was intentional, such as when different groups competed to seize power first. Sometimes the exclusions were due to disagreements among rebel leaders during negotiations to form power seizure coalitions. But inevitably there were significant numbers that were excluded from power seizures due simply to the fact that there were far too many to coordinate in a brief period of time. Pressures to act created by power seizures at the immediately higher level of government contributed to this pattern. The exclusion of rebels from power seizures contained the seeds of disputes that would eventually coalesce into more coherent factions.

Rival Rebels: Discord over Power Seizures

In virtually every case that I am able to detail, power seizures excluded significant numbers of rebel groups. They objected to their exclusion almost immediately, denouncing power seizures as "fake" or unrepresentative of the broader rebel movement. The problem was evident even in Shanghai's celebrated January 6 power seizure, which generated strident opposition from major rebel organizations. This opposition came from prominent rebels, not from former Scarlet Guards, who had tried to defend the Shanghai authorities before turning against them in late December.[9] After Beijing publicized a congratulatory telegram praising the rebel power seizure in the city on January 12, the massive Scarlet Guard movement simply collapsed, and they issued a public statement, "Begging Forgiveness from Chairman Mao," apologizing for their previous opposition to the Workers' General Headquarters. Instead, vociferous opposition to the Shanghai power seizure came from within the city's large and diverse rebel movement. The Workers' General Headquarters was a loose coalition of several large "regiments," each headed by a well-known rebel worker. Several of these regiments objected strongly when they perceived that they were being given a subordinate position in the new power structure. They protested that the new form of government was being planned without their participation, and they refused orders to merge into the Workers' General Headquarters. One of these worker regiments mobilized to challenge these arrangements and announced the formation of their own rival government.

Even more dramatic was militant opposition to the power seizure by the largest student rebel alliance, the Red Revolutionaries. These students had been the main force of the rebel movement long before workers belatedly joined in near the end of November, and they protested the fact that they were now excluded from a significant share of power. They noted that Zhang Chunqiao, the senior official who coordinated the power seizure and who was now the head of the new government, was a ranking member of the former Shanghai Party Committee, and that he was now suppressing rebel activity and was forcing workers back to work. To them this looked suspiciously like the suppression of their mass movement. At a January 27 meeting, they detained Zhang Chunqiao and his deputy Yao Wenyuan and held them for two hours, trying to extract an apology for using troops to suppress rebels. After the two were freed without making any concessions, the Red Revolutionaries kidnapped one of their top aides and held him on the Fudan University campus. After Zhang dispatched troops to free the aide, the students distributed wall posters and handbills across the city attacking Zhang for suppressing the student rebellion.

The January 26 power seizure in Nanjing also generated strong opposition from a disaffected wing of the city's large rebel movement.[10] The provincial and city governments had become paralyzed after the emergence of street fighting between Scarlet Guards and worker rebels in late December. After Mao's approval for the power seizures in Shanghai became evident in early January, Nanjing's large Scarlet Guard alliance, like Shanghai's, simply collapsed, and they were no longer active in local politics. Their last mass action was in the street fighting of January 3. Jiangsu's First Party Secretary sent an urgent telegram to Beijing on January 22, reporting that the provincial party committee could no longer function, and he and other top provincial and city leaders were taken into custody by rebels. Concerned that the city was spiraling out of control with no end in sight, Zhou Enlai contacted rebel leaders and urged them to seize power. Rebel leaders met from January 22 to 24 to plan a power seizure, but discord emerged at the meeting. The leaders of several key groups objected to the balance of power on the power seizure committee and the "absence of democracy" in the meetings. In protest, one of the city's most celebrated rebel leaders, the head of a large student alliance, withdrew from the negotiations, and others joined him. The power seizure went forward without them shortly after midnight on January 25.

Noting the split in the city's rebel movement, Zhou Enlai hesitated to signal his approval, and instead summoned representatives of the two sides to negotiate in Beijing. Encouraged by this, the rebels who were excluded from the power seizure went on the attack and denounced it. In response, the rebels who seized power charged that opposition to their power seizure amounted to counterrevolution. The fact that negotiations were ongoing in Beijing provoked battles on the streets of Nanjing, as leaders on each side sought to strengthen their claims by weakening the other side. There were 8 violent street confrontations during the weeks that negotiations were underway. Not surprisingly, the Beijing negotiations failed to bring the two sides together. Jiangsu and the provincial capital of Nanjing were placed under military control on March 5, and the struggle between the pro- and anti-power seizure rebels dominated the region's politics well into 1968.

A similar sequence of events unfolded around the January 22 power seizure in Guangzhou.[11] During the preparatory meeting to establish a power seizure alliance on January 21, disagreements emerged over tactics and timing. Several leaders of large rebel alliances argued that a power seizure was premature—preparations for a broad-based alliance of rebel organizations had only just begun, and unity needed to be established before making such an important move. The leaders of other rebel groups, however, argued that they should act immediately, and that unity would come from the struggle to seize and consolidate power. Failing to forge an agreement, the leaders of a large portion of Guangzhou's rebel movement withdrew from the negotiations. The remaining rebels proceeded to seize power the next day.

Provincial leaders, realizing that resistance was futile, welcomed the rebels and negotiated an agreement whereby they would continue to occupy their posts but would for the time being work under rebel supervision. The rebels that had withdrawn from the power seizure negotiations were already unhappy that they had been left behind, but now they seized upon the fact that Guangzhou's top officials were not forced to step down from their posts. They denounced the power seizure as "fake" and began a propaganda campaign that denounced it as a fraud for excluding large swaths of Guangzhou's rebel movement, while permitting revisionist officials to stay on the job. Several violent clashes between the rival rebel groups soon occurred, and after an attempted "counter power seizure" on January 25, the rhetoric hardened the differences between the two sides.

These divisions would define factional conflicts in Guangzhou for months to come.[12]

In Guangxi's provincial capital of Nanning, the splits did not originate from rivalries between rebels included and excluded from power seizures.[13] Instead, the rebel alliance broke apart after its power seizure. Simultaneous power seizures over both Guangxi Province and Nanning City on January 23 were carried out by a broad alliance of cadre, worker, and student rebels. However, the alliance quickly fell apart over the behavior of its leaders and by controversies over which rebel groups had more genuine rebel credentials. The rebel group that dominated the coalition refused to accept former Scarlet Guards who had eventually turned against their superiors, and they denounced them and others as conservatives who had initially defended local authorities. Other rebel groups in the coalition objected to the lack of consultation with other rebel leaders about these actions. This split the rebel coalition, and those who withdrew formed rival alliances. In late February this new rebel alliance dispatched more than a thousand activists in 50 trucks to attack the power seizure committee's headquarters. This split Nanning's rebel movement into two antagonistic camps, and each side moved to consolidate its position and reorganize its forces, campaigning against one another in wall posters and handbills.

A range of different event sequences led to similar outcomes at the subprovincial level. Minor variations on this theme are described in detailed accounts from three Guangxi Prefectures—Yulin, Bose, and Guilin. The January 24 power seizure in Yulin, which was carried out by cadre rebels in the prefecture administration, fell apart because of a rivalry between cadres who seized power and an alliance of worker rebels who were left out. The excluded rebels immediately denounced it as "fake." They called together other rebels from close to fifty small rebel groups, and on January 29 they invaded the prefecture's administrative offices to seize power. The power seizure committee collapsed, and on February 8, the workers' alliance declared a second power seizure.[14]

The power seizure in Bose Prefecture fell apart even though cadre rebels had included a broad range of outside rebel groups. Cadres in the prefecture offices coordinated the power seizure by reaching out to student and worker rebels, and pulled together an alliance of 69 small rebel organizations. The next day, 13 rebel groups that had been excluded from the power seizure sent representatives to protest. The power seizure committee charged that the challenge was a "conspiracy to overthrow the power sei-zure," declared the group's handbills "counterrevolutionary," and seized more than 20 leaders of the rebel opposition for humiliating public struggle sessions, placing them under arrest. After widespread protests about these actions, the power seizure committee made a public apology and released the prisoners, but the divisions remained.[15]

The power seizure in Guilin Prefecture fell apart primarily due to divi-sions among cadre rebels in the prefecture offices. The power seizure was coordinated by an alliance of cadre rebels who pulled together a coalition that included student Red Guards and worker rebels. The problem was that almost every one of the offices in the prefecture party and government ad-ministration had at least two active groups of cadre rebels, and the power seizure had been carried out hurriedly, without pulling together a broad alliance across the prefecture offices. The excluded groups objected. More-over, the rebels in the power seizure committee themselves fell into disagree-ments, and those who felt that their views were being ignored began to dissent as well. Both began to argue that the power seizure was carried out without sufficient consultation. Some of those who spoke out were pres-sured, followed, and detained, deepening local antagonisms.[16]

Further variations on this theme were evident at the county level. In Tiandong County, rebels in the county's security bureau had hurriedly organized a power seizure on January 26, precisely in order to prevent outside rebels from doing so. The excluded outside groups, including some cadre rebels, objected. They denounced the power seizure as unrepresenta-tive, and in violation of Beijing's directives. They refused to acknowledge its authority, and commenced a wall poster campaign that denounced the power seizure as a "counterrevolutionary" act by a small group of conspirators. A second power seizure was declared a week later by a larger alliance.[17]

In Gongcheng County, cadre rebels decided to push ahead with a power seizure on January 28 and only afterwards build up a broader coalition of local rebel groups. Predictably, the excluded rebels objected immediately, and vigorous debate ensued. Widespread resistance paralyzed the power sei-zure committee within days.[18] In Wuxuan and Luzhai counties, power seizures led by cadre rebels were immediately denounced as "palace coups" and "fake power seizures" by rebel groups excluded from the act, and both sides mobilized to defend their positions.[19] In Lingshan County, after a power seizure organized by cadre rebels, student and worker rebels barged into their first meeting and denounced the power seizure, subjecting its leaders to struggle sessions and putting dunce caps on their heads. The action split local rebels.[20] Opposition to the power seizure in Lingui County was expressed at the very moment that it was being carried out. A rival rebel group crashed the meeting where cadre rebels were planning a power seizure, and immediately denounced it as "fake." Their main objection was that the alliance's leaders included cadres who had been Scarlet Guards before turning against their superiors. The power seizure committee counterattacked.[21]

These case descriptions illustrate the local processes that generated divisions in rebel movements precipitated by power seizures. These splits appear to have been almost universal, but they had yet to coalesce into two clearly defined and relatively coherent factions. This would come later, and a key event in crystallizing coherent factions was the intervention of military units that were ordered to support local power seizures.

The Problem of Rebel Power

These narratives make painfully clear that rebels who seized power lacked the ability to enforce their claims—whether they were coalitions of popular insurgents and cadre rebels or cadre rebels who acted alone. Without the ability to legitimately use force against challengers, political power would remain contested and unenforceable. Anticipating this fact, near the end of January, shortly after the call for rebels to seize power, Mao ordered military support for the rebels who responded to this call. Troops were ordered to support "genuine leftists" who had seized power from local governments.[22] From this point forward local political conflicts pivoted away from attacks on local party-state authorities to a new issue: the consolidation of a power seizure. For the first time in the Cultural Revolution, army units were thrust into the middle of civilian political conflicts.

Military intervention was intended to consolidate rebel power in the manner that was achieved successfully in Shanghai. The order for military support had two objectives. On the one hand, military units were to ensure that rebel insurgents were able to unseat incumbent party and government leaders. On the other hand, they were also to ensure that the political upheaval did not throw public order and China's planned economy into disarray.[23] The potential economic damage was magnified by the fact that government agencies played a central coordinating role in all economic activity—industrial, agricultural, and commercial. Much more than in a market economy, the paralysis of government agencies would have a large and immediate economic impact. The tension between these two objectives—consolidating rebel power while stabilizing local order—became evident as the armed forces sought to fulfil their mission.

This tension was exacerbated by conflicting political priorities among the surviving national leaders under Mao Zedong. The civilian radicals who supplanted veteran party leaders in the initial Beijing purges, and upon whom Mao relied to launch the Cultural Revolution, were overwhelmingly preoccupied with ensuring that genuine "leftists" replaced local leaders that they suspected of revisionism. Zhou Enlai, however, along with many veteran military commanders, was more preoccupied with ensuring that the disorders did not undermine the planned economy, public order, and national security (the United States was escalating the Vietnam War on China's southern border). Mao Zedong sought to modulate the conflict between these two objectives, shifting back and forth in the months to come between support for rebellion and for the military's consolidation of order. The shifting directives from Beijing served to crystallize and harden local factional conflicts.

The orders, issued to the People's Liberation Army (PLA) on January 28, were broad and vague. As a "proletarian revolutionary army," the PLA should stand on the side of the "revolutionary masses of the left" and serve as "an instrument of proletarian dictatorship." Previously the PLA was forbidden from interfering with rebel insurgencies but now, the document declared, the only question is on which side the PLA stands. Military officers were told to "resolutely support the genuine revolutionary left," but they were also ordered to "resolutely oppose rightists and counterrevolutionaries and counterrevolutionary organizations" and to "take necessary measures against them." One clearly stated task was to "safeguard production and normal work." What were military commanders to conclude if local rebels persisted in activities that disrupted "production and normal work"? What if rebels resisted military units when they proceeded to carry out their orders? The juxtaposition of these prohibitions, and the order to "resolutely oppose rightists and counterrevolutionaries" and "take necessary measures against them," seemed to suggest a firm hand in dealing with persistently disruptive rebels.[24] This required soldiers to make political judgments in the field, without clear guidelines; inevitably, it forced military officers to choose winners and losers in active rebel disputes over power seizures.

The Reach of Military Intervention

Systematic and widespread military intervention was facilitated by China's deeply intertwined civilian and military hierarchies. Regional forces were dispersed around the country in 29 military districts *(jun diqu)*, which were divided into subdistricts *(jun fen diqu)*. Military districts were largely coterminous with provinces; military sub-districts with prefectures. They had detachments of troops on local bases. Below the prefectures were Garrison Commands *(weishu qu)* in large cities, and People's Armed Departments *(renmin wuzhuang bu)* in counties and smaller cities. People's Armed Departments did not have full-time troops, but they led local militias *(min bing)* consisting of reserve forces with stockpiles of light weapons. Separate "main force" combat units were not tied to government jurisdictions. There were 36 army corps under the command of 13 large Military Regions *(jun qu)*. These forces were jointly under the Military Region headquarters and the Central Military Commission. They included mainline infantry forces, as well as specialized armored, artillery, air force, and (along the coast) naval divisions. Detachments from these forces could be called upon for domestic political tasks as needed, and they were indeed called upon repeatedly in the months to come.[25]

The structure and distribution of army units facilitated widespread military intervention to "support the left." Figure 5.1 traces the cumulative percentage of cities and counties, by month, of local intervention by military units.[26] Military intervention was extensive and rapid, reaching the vast majority of local jurisdictions by March. The military had intervened in 90 percent of all cities by April. Counties lagged somewhat behind, but reached 80 percent by May. The coverage of "military support" was remarkably complete. The armed forces made their presence felt almost everywhere but their impact, as we shall see, was very different from the intentions of political figures in Beijing.

The Military's Dilemma

The near ubiquity of splits among local rebels over the power seizures presented dilemmas for military units as they tried to carry out their orders.

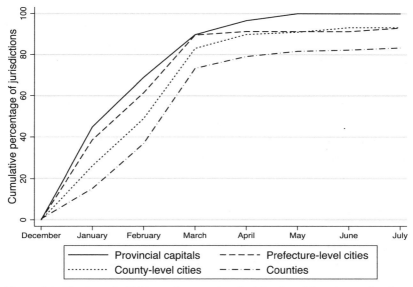

Figure 5.1. The Spread of Military Intervention, by Month and Jurisdiction Level, December 1966–July 1967 (N = 2,246)

Where rebels were already divided against one another—a nearly universal situation—each side looked to the armed forces to support their respective claims. If military officers supported the claims of those who had declared a power seizure (as implied in their orders), they immediately earned the opposition of rebels who contested that power seizure. This could place the armed forces in a virtual alliance with one faction, which warmly applauded the military's stance. It also turned rebels who opposed power seizures into opponents of military intervention—not as a matter of political principle, but because the army did not support their side.

Even if military forces initially tried to maintain strict neutrality in local factional rivalries, they could inadvertently become entangled in them *because* of their neutrality. Rebels who had seized power viewed a neutral stance as a failure to support their legitimate claims—essentially a stance of nonrecognition. They also suspected that a neutral stance implicitly credited the claims of rival rebels. A noncommittal stance was applauded by groups opposed to the power seizure, because it essentially refused to acknowledge the claims of those who had seized power.

When in these circumstances military units tried to maintain the normal operations of factories, public services, and local infrastructure, they often met with resistance. When they moved to impose control over radio stations, train depots, courts, banks, post offices and public security organs, rebel groups that controlled them frequently resisted, clashing with soldiers, and this deepened their antagonism with the military. The fragmented nature of rebel coalitions made these kinds of conflicts more likely. There was little apparent prior preparation by rebel groups to establish a unified and consistent position regarding military intervention. If a rebel fighting group in charge of a bank or a railway station got into a confrontation with an army unit, other rebels in the coalition could be pulled into conflict with local commanders.

When military units met with rebel opposition, they had to decide how to respond. Even when they declared neutrality in local rebel rivalries, they still were forced to defend themselves when rebels resisted their moves to exercise control over local installations that were crucial to maintaining public order and the operations of the planned economy. In some regions military units responded with arrests and the banning of entire rebel groups.

Provinces, Cities, and Prefectures

Acts of resistance by rebels to army actions—and army responses—are evident in local annals. There were 122 reported confrontations with army units initiated by rebel groups during the first four months of 1967. There is even more evidence during this period of the suppression of rebel groups by either the armed forces or by those who claimed to have seized power. There were only 12 such reported events in January 1967, but there were 181 in February and March. It is likely that there were many similar actions in other jurisdictions that were not reported in local annals.

These developments were especially clear in provincial capitals. In Nanjing, after February negotiations conducted in Beijing failed to reconcile the divided rebels, Jiangsu Province was put under military control in early March.[27] Troops from the Jiangsu Military District moved into Nanjing and other major cities. When they tried to take over key communication, transportation, and other sites, they met with resistance from rebels that had carried out the power seizure in those units. The troops responded with arrests of hundreds of rebels who forcibly resisted military control. The rebels who had carried out the power seizure referred to this as the "March Suppression." These rebels viewed military control as an overthrow of their legitimate power seizure, while the rebels who had objected to the power seizure saw the army's moves as a vindication of their claims, and applauded the army's actions. The arrests became a major political issue for that wing of the rebel movement, and reinforced their view that the army was there to suppress legitimate rebels.

In Guangzhou, violent confrontations over the power seizure occurred within days of the event, and the rebels who carried it out charged that their opponents were counterrevolutionaries.[28] In late January, troops from the military district moved in to take control of key sites in the city. They were under strict orders to take a neutral stance, and not dislodge the rebel groups. Although one wing of the rebel movement had declared a power seizure over the provincial and municipal administrations, rival rebels still controlled a number of units across the city. When, in early February, rebels affiliated with the power seizure attacked the radio station to dislodge rebels opposed to the power seizure, the troops on site helped them to repel the invaders. This convinced the rebels who had seized power that the army did not support their claims, and they staged a mass protest at the military region headquarters, invading the building, putting up wall posters, cutting telegraph lines, and detaining several officers. Finally, Guangdong was put under military control in mid-March, and the armed forces quickly moved to suppress the rebels in the power seizure alliance who had resisted them with force. In actions later called the "March Black Wind," close to 1,200 rebels were arrested, more than 16,000 rebels were registered as members of "reactionary organizations," and several rebel alliances that were part of the power seizure were banned as illegal. The exercise of military control in Guangzhou turned the military region's forces into virtual allies of one wing of the rebel movement, despite their initial intention to remain neutral. A similar sequence of events occurred in Wuhan.[29]

Patterns in provincial capitals were replicated at the sub-provincial level, although the military's entanglement in local rebel rivalries came about in a variety of different ways. In the northern Jiangsu prefecture of Xuzhou, the armed forces became deeply involved in local factional politics, despite their recognition of the power seizure and its rapid move to certify it as a revolutionary committee.[30] While preparing to certify the power seizure as a revolutionary committee, some of the rebel groups in the coalition chafed at military authority, and wanted a leading role that was independent of army tutelage. When the leaders of one rebel group criticized the army's moves, its leaders were arrested and the organization banned. When other rebel leaders charged that the punishments were excessive, they too were arrested and banned. By mid-March the army had banned 34 rebel groups, arrested close to 150 leaders, and placed several thousand rebels "under supervision." Some rebel groups complied with the army's authority reluctantly, but others enthusiastically approved of the army's moves. This divided the rebels who initially were allies in the power seizure into two antagonistic groups, now defined by their different responses to the army's actions as it prepared to certify a new regional government.

Counties

In the cities, military control usually took place in the context of large and diverse rebel coalitions. In counties rebel movements were smaller, and cadre rebels in the county administration played a dominant role in power seizures. We have already seen that disagreements over power seizures were almost as common in counties as in the large cities. In counties, however, the local People's Armed Department (PAD) played a much more direct role in sorting out factional disputes, and they insinuated themselves more deeply into local politics.

The head of the county PAD almost invariably was a member of the county's party leadership, though rarely among the top-ranking members. In many cases the PAD head had only recently been appointed to the post on the eve of the Cultural Revolution.[31] The January 28 orders regarding military support for power seizures essentially made local PAD heads the only members of a county's leadership that were immune from overthrow, and in fact turned them into arbiters of local disputes among rebels. They were initially the only figures with any authority to make decisions and enforce them. Rebel groups turned to the PAD to support their respective positions in disputes about power seizures. When the PAD threw its support behind one group of local rebels, the rebels whose claims they denied invariably claimed that they had a conservative bias against "genuine" rebels. While they were obviously vulnerable to such a claim, the head of the local PAD faced the same dilemmas as PLA units did in larger jurisdictions. They may well have preferred cadre rebels over others, but they usually faced a choice between rival groups of cadre rebels, and their actions as described in historical accounts indicate that their decisions depended on a range of contingent events. Like military units elsewhere, they often vacillated and shifted support from one group to another, trying to forge a coalition that would stabilize the locality.

In Cangwu County, Guangxi, the PAD set up a "support the left" office even before the power seizure by a large rebel alliance. When a rebel alliance within the county administration refused to acknowledge the power seizure and appealed to the PAD for support, they counseled the cadre rebels that the power seizure was indeed legitimate and in accord with Beijing's policies. The cadre rebels persisted in their objections, and conducted a campaign against the power seizure that prevented it from exercising power. In the interim, the PAD head set up a production command post. The propaganda war between the two rebel groups continued, while the PAD continued to administer the county. Gradually the PAD's attitude toward the original power seizure cooled, and they convinced several key leaders to withdraw from the power seizure alliance and join together with the dissident cadre rebels. Under the PAD's direction, they formed a new alliance, which made them backers of one party to the evolving conflict.[32]

Shortly after Beiliu County's power seizure, the PAD was thrust into the middle of rebel disputes. The power seizure was carried out by cadre rebels in the county offices. To prevent paralysis, the PAD moved in on February 5 to set up a command center. A week later certain rebels in the public security system and other county departments declared that a local rebel organization contained "bad elements" and was counterrevolutionary. They banned it and seized two of its leaders. The PAD tried to defuse the situation, stating that mass organizations could not arbitrarily be declared counterrevolutionary. The rebels on the power seizure committee split over the PAD's stance, and those who disagreed withdrew from the power seizure and formed a rival alliance. The power seizure committee promptly collapsed, leaving the PAD's command center as the only effective authority in the county. Shortly thereafter, the rebel alliance whose "counterrevolutionary" label had been disputed by the PAD, counterattacked against its primary accusers, invading their offices and imprisoning their leaders. The PAD approved of the action, which drew them into support for one side in Beiliu's ongoing factional struggles.[33]

The head of Lingyun County's PAD directly orchestrated a power seizure. Near the end of January, cadre rebels in the county administration met to elect a power seizure committee, but they disagreed about how to treat the county's Party Secretary, delaying their deliberations. The head of the county PAD argued that a delay might permit outside rebels to seize power first, and he worked with one of the rebel groups to form a new power seizure committee. These rebels carried out the act under the PAD's guidance, and the entire county leadership was deposed. Immediately afterwards the PAD distributed arms to the militia and led a parade through the streets to demonstrate support. In subsequent months, rebels who had been excluded from the power seizure charged that it was little more than a military coup and a unilateral power grab by the PAD.[34]

Foundations of Emergent Factions

All of these examples illustrate interactions between military officers and rebel groups whose outcomes were contingent on the joint actions of two parties. Military officers were forced to assess a local political situation and make judgments about which course of action would facilitate the successful fulfillment of their assigned task. They did not automatically support a group that had declared a power seizure, and often tried to remain neutral. Their stances toward a local group—whether or not it had seized power—depended on the reaction of that group toward them. They often tried initially to remain neutral, and could be drawn reluctantly into an alignment with one wing of the divided rebel forces. They often hesitated to choose sides, and could switch their support from one group to another in reaction to local developments. They would decisively respond when rebel groups resisted them by force, arresting leaders and banning organizations—an action that could create irreversible schisms with one wing of the rebel movement, while drawing their rivals into a tighter alignment with the military. Rebel groups, for their part, responded to military units primarily based on whether they perceived that their actions supported their stance in local disputes. This was true whether they had seized power or had been excluded from the power seizure. The eventual alignment of rebel factions for and against military units was the contingent outcome of these interactions. The emerging political orientations—who ended up on which side—were the product of joint actions by two parties, not the expression of interests defined unilaterally before the period of interest.

There was an undeniable random element in determining which rebels ended up on which side of emerging factional divisions. But the mechanisms that created the divisions and aligned rebel groups for and against the military are observable and lend themselves readily to explanation. An interesting feature of these processes is that a wide variety of local interactions all lead toward a single outcome—factions aligned with, and against, military forces. This is an example of a "robust" multi-level process: collective-level outcomes are not dependent on the specific form of micro-level processes.[35] In these instances, the formation of factions with different orientations to military control did not depend on the specific sequence of interaction between rebels and soldiers. It did not matter which side the army supported; how they came to this decision; which rebels seized power first, or which were left out. All of these interactions converged on a single outcome: factions with opposed preferences regarding military control.

The processes that are described here are an example of what Tilly defined as "category formation" in collective conflicts, which generate foundations for political identities—ways to identify oneself and one's allies in distinction from others. These categories form the basis for "stories" that the resulting groups tell about themselves and others—in this case, narratives about the correct or incorrect actions of other rebel groups, and the correct or incorrect actions of local military commanders.[36] Conflict processes of this sort bring previously unrelated individuals into closer association, based on their shared antagonism toward military units and their favored rebel groups.[37] As conflict grows, the ties that bind these individuals together strengthen.[38]

In terms of social networks, the emerging pattern of relationships among rebel groups and military units represent a realignment of local social ties based on "structural equivalence"—the occupation of equivalent positions in local networks that create common interests among individuals or small groups that previously had no ties with one another.[39] The collapse of local governments in the wake of power seizures, and of the formally organized networks of local party organizations, sorted rebels who were included in and excluded from power seizures into structurally equivalent positions. Rebels who were excluded from power seizures found themselves with one attribute in common: their exclusion from, and opposition to, power seizures. As political interactions evolved in the wake of military intervention, new political categories emerged that became the basis for factional identities—rebels whose claims were supported by the military, and those whose claims were not.

This was the context in which highly fragmented rebel movements began to cohere for the first time into more solidary and self-conscious factions. The fragmentation due to the ubiquitous pattern of bloc recruitment began to reverse itself. In many regions, under the right circumstances, this resulted in much more disciplined and coherent factions that would later develop specialized combat units. Power seizures served as a catalyst for closer alignment among the smaller rebel groups included in power seizures, as they drew together to defend their claims against rival rebels. Disparate rebel groups that were excluded from power seizures also drew together to press their claims and protest their exclusion. The interventions of military actors crystallized these emerging new factions, often inadvertently, and their actions hardened these emerging new identities and further promoted their internal solidarity and discipline.

As each side sought to draw others who were in structurally equivalent positions into tighter alignment, they also began to recruit other citizens who were not previously aligned with rebel factions into their fold. These were, in a sense, rival local governments in formation, in a situation of deeply contested sovereignty. For the first time each side began to settle on a single name for their emerging alliances, and they began to develop narratives about local conflicts that portrayed their rivals in a negative light, while justifying their own past actions and present stances. These narratives were expressed in petitions sent to higher authorities, in handbills and wall posters issued locally, and in some regions by periodically published bulletins and news sheets. These processes account for the somewhat anomalous growth of factional rivalries after power seizures and military intervention—widespread combat between rebel factions developed only afterwards in most regions of China.

These were the structural bases and interactive processes that generated the political identities that would spawn factional warfare in many Chinese regions. We now turn to the process of consolidating larger and more coherent political factions, and the emergence of organized violence between them.

6

THE EMERGENCE OF FACTIONAL WARFARE

DISPUTES AMONG REBELS IN THE WAKE of power seizures were ubiquitous. They were an inevitable product of the fragmented and cellular structure of rebel insurgencies, and of the rapid downward diffusion of power seizures in the national political hierarchy. In localities where a new structure of political authority was created quickly and certified by Beijing—as in Shanghai—these disputes were unlikely to coalesce into large and antagonistic factional alliances, and factional warfare was unlikely to emerge. When a new structure of power—a "revolutionary committee"—received the direct sanction of Beijing, military units defused opposition relatively quickly in support of new structures of political power.

In the vast majority of Chinese provinces, however, a revolutionary committee certified by Beijing would not be established for well over a year. These regions were instead placed under military control, forcing military officers to operate on their own. They intervened in the midst of festering rebel disputes, and they inevitably inserted themselves into the middle of local conflicts. The initial impact of military intervention was to shift the axes of local conflicts from disputes among rebels over the power seizure to stances of support or opposition to military authority. These were new factions, defined by a rebel group's initial position relative to local power seizures, and by their evolving relationships with military units.

Figure 6.1 traces the emergence of factions relative to power seizures and military intervention.[1] Military intervention reached almost everywhere by

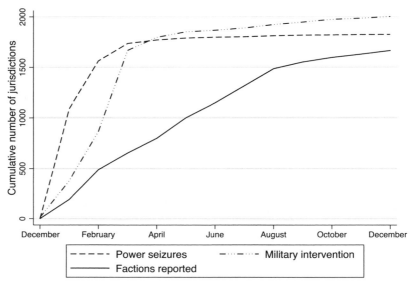

Figure 6.1. The Formation of Factions Relative to Power Seizures and Military Intervention, December 1966—December 1967

March 1967, even localities that had not experienced a power seizure. Factional divisions continued to develop into the summer of 1967, eventually becoming almost as prevalent as military intervention. Very few localities (2.5 percent) reported factions prior to the calendar month that a power seizure occurred. Only 19 percent reported factions prior to military intervention. The median month for a reported power seizure was January, for military intervention March, and for the development of opposed factions April. This pattern is what one would expect if military intervention crystallized nascent factional divisions.

Factional conflict did not develop everywhere—it was reported only in two thirds (67 percent) of all localities. There were many more regions where there were power seizures (81 percent), military intervention (93 percent), or both (76 percent). How close was the statistical association between power seizures, military intervention, and the formation of factions? Figure 6.2 displays the results of a simple event history analysis of the emergence of factions. The trend lines display estimated probabilities that factions form, conditional only on the *prior* occurrence of a local power seizure, military intervention, or both. All other potentially important variables

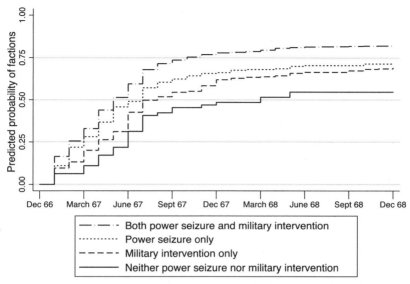

Figure 6.2. Kaplan-Meier Probabilities for the Formation of Factions

are ignored, in particular regional political developments, which become increasingly important over time. The trend lines show that localities that experienced both power seizures and military intervention developed opposed factions faster and more extensively than localities that experienced neither. Localities that experienced *either* a power seizure *or* military intervention alone generated factions at roughly the same pace. But they did so more slowly and less extensively than localities that experienced both, and more rapidly and extensively than localities that experienced neither.[2]

Explaining the Emergence of Factional Warfare

Clearly, military intervention did not curtail the development of factions, and appears instead to have contributed to its development. But this falls well short of a satisfying explanation for the development of violent factional warfare. We need to examine more closely the timing of signals emanating from Beijing, which decisively influenced the actions of both military units and rebel groups during the periods when factional identities solidified and their violent antagonisms first emerged.

The first and most important of these signals was a drastic reversal in the military's orders in early April 1967, which prevented local army units from taking direct action against rebel groups that opposed their decisions. A simple interpretation of this reversal is that this altered political opportunity structures to permit dissident rebels to pursue their objections to the decisions of military commanders. But such an interpretation would miss an equally important consequence. If military units were no longer able to suppress rebel opposition, and if dissident rebels now seized the opportunity to organize and mobilize to press their claims, rebels who benefited from and supported the recent decisions of military officers were now *compelled* to mobilize to *defend* their stances, and in particular to defend the armed forces. The reversal of the orders under which military units operated hastened the formation of factions and eventually served to generate violent warfare between them, unrestrained by military units.

The reasons for this reversal are well understood. Radical figures in Beijing, who had supported and steered rebel movements in late 1966 and had helped to orchestrate regional power seizures in Shanghai and elsewhere, became alarmed about the actions of military units during February and March. They began to suspect that the army was bringing the Cultural Revolution to a premature end without fundamental transformations of the kind they felt they had achieved in Shanghai. These same radical figures were willing to rely on military force to suppress opposition to revolutionary committees that had their approval. Zhang Chunqiao, who now headed Shanghai's Revolutionary Committee, openly acknowledged this when he said that anyone who challenged his seizure of power "would automatically be labeled a counterrevolutionary and arrested."[3] Similar suppressions of rebel opposition to provincial power seizures occurred in Heilongjiang, Guizhou, Shandong, and Shanxi, the other provinces where new revolutionary committees were approved between January and March 1967. There was little elite disagreement in Beijing about these outcomes. Mao and his radical associates viewed them as victories for their movement, while Zhou Enlai welcomed this as a restoration of order and the end to disruptions of the planned economy.[4]

Disagreements arose over the remaining 23 provinces where a revolutionary committee had yet to be approved. There were two common reasons for this delay. First, there was no local leader acceptable to Mao and his radical subordinates and also deemed sufficiently senior to head an entire province. Second, rebel alliances were too deeply and evenly divided to forge an agreement to support new arrangements. After a frenetic early effort to resolve the disputes that had already broken out over provincial power seizures, Beijing placed one province after another under military control.[5]

Although the Central Cultural Revolution Group, staffed by younger radical figures, had become a powerful force in Beijing by this point in time, Zhou Enlai convened and chaired the group's meetings and still wielded the surviving machinery of government. Zhou was an active proponent of power seizures as a means to restore a rapidly deteriorating economy and public order, and he urged rebels in Nanjing, Guangzhou, and elsewhere to seize power shortly after the events in Shanghai.[6] Suspicious of Zhou's motives, Beijing radicals were also disturbed by trends in the provinces that were placed under military control. They were initially sympathetic to charges by the large rebel alliances left out of the power seizures in Guangdong and Jiangsu—that the power seizures were "fake."[7]

Reports from some provinces reinforced their suspicion that the armed forces were suppressing genuine rebels. In Sichuan, two large rebel organizations laid siege to the headquarters of the Chengdu Military Region for one week, and in response the commander ordered the arrest of tens of thousands of rebels across the province. An unarmed student was shot and killed while demonstrating at an army post in Inner Mongolia, and 169 rebel protesters were killed and 179 wounded during a confrontation in Xining, the capital of Qinghai province.[8] Hunan's provincial capital of Changsha was placed under martial law in early February, and local troops suppressed a large rebel organization that had attacked an army command post, arresting some 10,000 rebels.[9] These events bred suspicion that regional military commanders were hostile to rebels and were prematurely shutting down an insurgency that was to bring about China's political transformation.

Developments in Beijing intensified worries about the political sympathies of army commanders. An angry confrontation at a leadership meeting in mid-February pitted senior PLA marshals against radical members of the Central Cultural Revolution Group. Several marshals angrily denounced them for attacking veteran revolutionaries and throwing China into chaos. Mao was informed of the confrontation and responded by ordering the marshals to step down from their posts. The incident was publicized to rebel organizations across the country, who expressed outrage over this "anti-Mao" incident and the attempts of certain military leaders to suppress their movement.[10] The strident propaganda campaign against senior military figures signaled to rebels across the country that military authorities could legitimately be opposed, and that there was support for such opposition in Beijing.

These developments culminated in an abrupt reversal of the army's orders. The initial directive had given them the authority to act decisively against "counterrevolutionary" organizations. Two directives from Beijing drastically reformulated these orders on April 1. They prohibited military units from condemning any rebel organization as "counterrevolutionary." All rebel groups previously banned were to be recognized as legitimate, and their arrested members were to be released from prison and exonerated. In the future, rebels who challenged army units must be treated leniently through "education" and "criticism." Attacks on military units no longer justified arrests, and no actions were to be taken against rebels for opposing the military. It was now absolutely forbidden to use armed force against mass organizations.[11] The new orders were accompanied by arrests of army officers in regions where some of the worst suppression campaigns had been carried out.[12] These punishments signaled to the military officers that failure to adhere to the new orders could have severe personal consequences.

The new orders tied the hands of PLA units and undermined the authority of local PAD commanders. Rebels who had initially opposed them, and who had been the objects of suppression, were able to reassert their opposition and mobilize to contest the initial actions of army officers and the local PAD. Certain senior officials in Beijing encouraged resistance to the army. In a meeting with rebels from Shandong Province near the end of April, one leader asserted that local PAD commanders "are nothing more than local cadres who wear a military uniform."[13] Local PAD officers were later prohibited from mobilizing rural militias to stabilize their control, ensuring that the impact of these directives would reach into rural counties.[14]

The impact of this reversal is clearly reflected in local annals. Figure 6.3 traces the reported actions of rebels and military or government authorities from January 1967 to December 1968. The dashed line traces actions by military or government authorities to repress rebel activity. The spike in repression in February and March of 1967 reflects the initial intervention of the armed forces and the arrests that followed in some regions. The impact of the new April orders was immediate. Repression against rebels

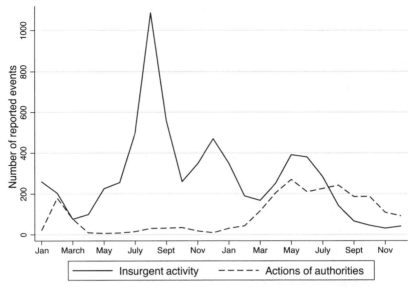

Figure 6.3. Monthly Counts, Insurgent Activity and Acts of Repression by Authorities, 1967–1968

disappeared almost entirely until the end of the year. The solid line traces the number of reported actions by rebel groups—their attacks on civilian or military compounds, or violent clashes between rebel factions. The trend line is almost the inverse of that for repression—rebel mobilization accelerated rapidly after April 1967 and reached its height the following summer before subsiding, but rebel activity persisted at high levels into mid-1968, before finally ebbing in response to elevated levels of repression.

The upsurge in rebel activity does not indicate a simple story of political opportunity. It also represents the mobilization of rebel factions that *supported* military forces and fought to defend military control in a context where the armed forces were forbidden from directly intervening—this is what factional clashes were about. The curtailment of repression represented not merely an opportunity for anti-army rebels to mobilize—it compelled pro-army rebels to defend their sponsors and themselves.

Redrawing the Lines of Conflict

The army's new orders undercut their ability to enforce their decisions, and in some cases even to defend themselves. They were forced to release

from prison rebels they had previously arrested and to permit them to rebuild their banned organizations, although in some regions they delayed
doing so, further stoking rebel animosity. After their release, these rebel
leaders pulled together increasingly coherent rebel organizations, which
adopted an intensified hostility to the armed forces. There was, however,
an additional consequence. Rebels who had cooperated with the armed
forces and who felt that the army's intervention favored their side in local
disputes, *also* became the targets of rebel factions now making a comeback.

New factional identities were forged and reinforced as resurgent rebel
factions denounced the army's actions and their rebel supporters. Denunciation of military units and their commanders was intended to de-legitimize
rival rebel groups. If the army's actions were politically reactionary, then
the rebel groups who cooperated with and benefited from the army's previous moves could be portrayed as "conservative" collaborators with army
units opposed to the Cultural Revolution. These charges left their opponents with little choice but to minimize the army's errors and defend their
earlier actions. In defending the army, they drew on the fact that Lin Biao,
the commander of China's armed forces, had risen to the nation's second-
highest position at the outset of the Cultural Revolution as Mao's "closest
comrade-in-arms" and designated successor. This stance implied that the
previous charges against their rivals were justified—those who opposed the
People's Liberation Army in their mission to "support the left" had committed grave political errors. The anti-army rebels, on the other hand, portrayed themselves as the only genuine rebel force. The comeback by the
suppressed rebels sharpened and intensified earlier divisions over power seizures, driving one wing of the rebel movement into a closer and mutually
supportive relationship with the armed forces, and the other wing into intensified hostility to both the military and their rebel rivals.

The rhetoric generated by this confrontation made it appear that the
anti-army rebels were more radical than their rivals. Their position was not
radical in the sense that they sought more thoroughgoing change in the
status quo ante. Instead, it was radical only in the sense that they refused
to accept the legitimacy of the army's actions and opposed the re-imposition
of political order on the army's terms. Resurgent anti-army rebels con-
sciously cultivated the idea that they were suppressed precisely because
they were the only genuine revolutionary force. In their view, the supportive
relationship that rival rebels developed with the military showed that they

lacked revolutionary spirit, and were aligning themselves with forces inimical to the Cultural Revolution. This impression was reinforced in the months to come as resurgent rebel factions pressed their campaigns against the army, actions that made them a disruptive force. Early analyses of these factional divisions adopted the labels "conservative" and "radical" to describe these splits, and saw them as expressing inherent political orientations of the leaders and members of the two wings of the rebel movement.[15] These analyses suggested that there were orientations inherent in the two groups that were fixed beforehand. But these political orientations were the *product* of the interactions that split rebels in early 1967, not their cause.

The contingent and interactive construction of factional orientations is also evident in the shifting reaction of radical figures in the Central Cultural Revolution Group to the developing splits among provincial rebels. As we have seen, power seizures in Guangzhou and Nanjing were carried out by one wing of the local rebel movement, while excluding a number of large and prominent rebel groups. In both places the rebels who were left out loudly denounced the power seizures as "fake." Beijing radicals initially supported the cause of these excluded rebels, in large part because they suspected that the power seizures were part of an expedient effort simply to restore order. At that point in time the excluded rebels could be viewed as "radical." In supporting their opposition to the power seizures, radical figures in Beijing hoped to keep the spirit of rebellion alive and ensure that power seizures were genuine.

As *pro*–power seizure rebels in these two provinces became antagonistic to army units that imposed military control without certifying their power seizure, and as rebels opposed to the power seizures became more supportive of the armed forces, the Beijing radicals shifted their support from one rebel faction to another. Their initial concern had been that regional power seizures had to be broadly representative of rebel forces. By April, however, their primary concern was to push back against the army. The *anti*-army rebels, who had earlier carried out power seizures in Guangzhou and Nanjing initially denounced as "fake," now became their preferred rebel force, because they now clashed with army units. In this context, *they* now appeared to be the "radical" force. In subsequent months, the Beijing radicals developed supportive relationships with anti-army rebels and steered their activities through liaison personnel that were stationed in the provincial capitals. In other words, even in the perception of Beijing politicians who tried to steer the direction of the rebel insurgencies, the definition of "radical" and "conservative" was malleable and entirely context-dependent.[16]

The Formation of Regional Alliances

To this point I have described local political processes that laid the foundations for factional antagonisms. This implicitly treated local jurisdictions as developing factions in parallel, relatively independently of events in nearby regions, as a product of contingent and intensely local sequences of events. The factional warfare that followed, however, increasingly involved coordinated action among like-minded factions across the boundaries of counties and cities. As local clashes escalated, factions sought allies and reinforcement outside local political boundaries. By 1968, as we will see, the largest and most violent final battles were between regionally defined factions that drew upon fighters across entire prefectures.

On what basis did cross-regional alliances form? How did local rebels choose allies in another jurisdiction? Factions frequently aligned with one another based on their occupation of equivalent positions vis-à-vis local military authorities. So long as there was a unified military command structure in a military district or subdistrict, local rebels sought out allies who shared the same orientation toward the military.

Factional alignments within military districts were driven by the need for allies outside one's own city or county. When factions crystallized in the provincial capital that were defined by attitudes toward the provincial power seizure and the army's actions, rebels in equivalent positions at lower levels pledged allegiance accordingly. In Guangdong Province, for example, when the rebels who were suppressed by the military rebounded in April and May, they formed a new alliance that was hostile to the army's actions; it eventually became known as Red Flag. Their opponents, who had originally objected to their exclusion from the January power seizure and who denounced it as "fake" (because it left the entire provincial leadership in place), came to be known as East Wind. They favored military control because it refused to acknowledge the legitimacy of the power seizure. East Wind therefore defended the army's earlier actions, and in so doing defended their own claims to legitimacy as a genuine rebel force.[17]

After these factions crystallized in the provincial capital, they were soon replicated at lower levels. Rebel groups in cities and counties aligned themselves with structurally equivalent groups at higher levels. In prefectures, cities, and counties across Guangdong, rebel groups whose claims had been favored by the army's intervention—and who as a consequence were favorable to the army's local role, aligned themselves with East Wind. Rebel groups who dissented from local settlements imposed by the armed forces aligned themselves with Red Flag. It did not matter which rebel faction had benefited most from the army's decisions. It did not matter whether the faction favored by the local armed forces had seized power or had objected to the power seizure. It did not matter whether those who seized power were cadre rebels or whether the cadre rebels had objected to a more broad-based power seizure. What mattered was who was satisfied with the local political settlement as determined by military units. If you were satisfied, which meant that you were not opposed to the army's actions since January, you aligned yourself politically with East Wind. To do otherwise would undercut your own position. If you were dissatisfied with the results of military control and objected to the army's local role, you aligned yourself with Red Flag and appealed to similarly identified factions for support. These province-wide political alliances were based on the structurally equivalent positions of actors across levels of government. The political affiliations were rooted in factional divisions that had structural parallels across jurisdictions.

One example among many that could be cited is Haifeng County, located on the Guangdong coastline midway between Hong Kong and Shantou. Rebel cadres declared a power seizure in the county in late January 1967, and with the support of the People's Armed Department they proceeded to consolidate their control in the name of a rebel alliance known as the "Left Committee" *(zuo wei)*. Rebels left out of these arrangements formed a separate alliance known as the "People's Headquarters" *(ren zong)*, and a violent rivalry followed. At the end of March regular PLA troops moved into the county and established a Military Control Committee and a production command headquarters dominated by the Left Committee. In April, after some preliminary clashes with People's Headquarters rebels, they declared the alliance a counterrevolutionary organization and arrested its leaders. After the April shift of the army's general orders the People's Headquarters made a comeback and began to reassert itself. In response, the Left Committee mobilized militia forces, obtained automatic rifles and machine guns, and staged two massacres of their poorly armed opponents in late August and early September. The two assaults left 91 dead and more than 3,000 wounded. The massacre alarmed officials in Beijing and the Guangzhou Military Region, and the local Military Control Committee was dissolved. The PLA troops stationed in Haifeng were blamed for the incident, and they were transferred out and replaced by a new unit.[18]

After the massacres, many activists in the Left Committee alliance quit and joined the People's Headquarters, which soon changed its name to Red Flag to identify with provincial factions that opposed military control forces. The remaining leaders of the Left Committee maintained control over the production command headquarters, but they changed their name to East Wind, reaffirming their alignment with provincial military authorities. The two sides identified themselves with province-wide factions by adopting the names of the corresponding factions in the provincial capital of Guangzhou.[19]

This pattern was replicated in many provinces, and identification of allies by lower-level actors was made easier by the colloquial labels given to the province-level factions. In most of Jiangsu province and especially in the region surrounding its capital of Nanjing, the pro-power seizure (and anti-army) factional alliance was known colloquially as the "good faction" (hao pai)—the power seizure was "good." The anti–power seizure (and pro-army) faction was known as the "crap" or "stinks faction" (pi pai)—the power seizure "stinks."[20] Rebel factions in neighboring Anhui Province adopted the same nicknames.[21]

In Guangxi, the crystallization of factional alliances is particularly well documented. The province's First Party Secretary, Wei Guoqing, was also the political commissar of the Guangxi Military District. He had been targeted by rebels as Guangxi's "number one capitalist roader" and as the mastermind behind Guangxi's "bourgeois reactionary line." He was kidnapped and held hostage for a period in January and was subjected to violent struggle sessions. The rebel alliance that seized power in Nanning in January 1967 saw his overthrow as one of their major accomplishments, but like rebels elsewhere they soon split into factions over representation in the provincial power seizure committee. Given the deepening divisions between rebel factions and their inability to unite, Guangxi was put under military control in March.[22]

Military control placed Wei Guoqing in charge of Guangxi's armed forces as political commissar of the Guangxi Military District.[23] Many rebels in the provincial capital vehemently opposed the decision to leave him in charge, and organized mass rallies to call for his overthrow. Other rebels in the capital accepted Beijing's decision, and supported Wei. The decision split the rebel alliances in Nanning. Under Wei's direction production command posts were formed in cities and counties. These temporary organs of power were a first step toward establishing a permanent revolutionary committee. As military control was enforced across Guangxi, certain wings of local rebel movements were incorporated into them, and others were opposed. The splits among local rebels derived from their original stances regarding the local power seizure and their reaction to the army's local decisions.

Opposition to military control under Wei Guoqing in the provincial capital coalesced into the "April 22" faction (named after large and dramatic protests in Nanning on that date), after which a delegation travelled to Beijing to plead the local rebels' case. Shortly afterward, the April 22 faction expressed their support for Wu Jinnan, the third-ranking official in Guangxi's party leadership. In line with the new April orders to military units, Wu had criticized Wei Guoqing for the continuing suppression of rebels opposed to military control. Across the province, local factions took opposite sides for or against Wei and Wu based on their support or opposition to local military control.[24] Rebels who had cooperated with PLA or PAD forces adopted the name Allied Command, while those opposed to local settlements took the name April 22. By June these identities had spread across the province, leading to province-wide factional conflict between rebel groups pledging allegiance to rival party leaders in Guangxi.

By July 1967 these factional identities had spread across the province. Factional conflict had developed in 95 percent of Guangxi's eighty-six cities and counties. Rebels opposed to local military control had adopted the name "April 22" in 77 percent of these localities, while rebels that supported military control had adopted the name "Allied Command" in 85 percent of them. By the end of 1967, these labels had been adopted by opposed factions in almost every city and county in the province.[25] At the local level, this often left the PAD commander as the head of the Allied Command faction. It would be a daunting task to try to identify one of these factions as more favorable to the status quo than another—each pledged allegiance to a different provincial leader.

These alignments grew rapidly, for reasons that are easy to specify. Rebel groups locked in violent rivalries needed outside allies. The support was mutual: factions in cities and prefecture capitals could call upon allied factions in nearby counties, and factions in rural counties, in turn, could call on help from allies in nearby cities or counties. There was a structural foundation for these factions, but the relevant structures were not the static ones defined by the relative positions of individuals and groups in prior structures of power and privilege. Party and government cadres, the pillars of the status quo ante, had rebelled against their own superiors and in many cases organized power seizures. Cadre rebels were themselves divided into opposed factions. Rebel students and workers, who had united in the late-1966 movements to overthrow incumbent party and government authorities, also divided into factions according to their positions vis-à-vis the recent power seizures. The antagonisms that resulted led, after the intervention of armed forces, to new structures of power, in which some rebel factions had the support of military units while others' claims went unrecognized. Factions formed in local jurisdictions, and eventually across local jurisdictions within provinces, based on the location of groups in structurally equivalent positions in these evolving structures of power and conflict. The ability of opposed rebel factions to identify with one another along these lines, and to form alliances with rebels across jurisdictions, boosted the organizational capacity of both sides in their growing confrontations.

The Upsurge of Collective Violence

The rebels liberated by the new restraints placed on the armed forces proceeded to build more coherent organizations to press their grievances. In many cases serious charges had been lodged against them that would have serious repercussions if their opponents prevailed and the army remained to preside over a local revolutionary committee. As rebels mounted campaigns to undermine the armed forces and force the removal or transfer of local army commanders, antagonisms deepened. These rebels could anticipate that if military officers they had antagonized presided over a final political settlement, they would likely suffer harsh retribution. Their offensives against the armed forces also threatened the rival wing of the rebel movement that had aligned itself with the military. Confrontations between the two sides intensified in May and spilled out into armed clashes. Al-

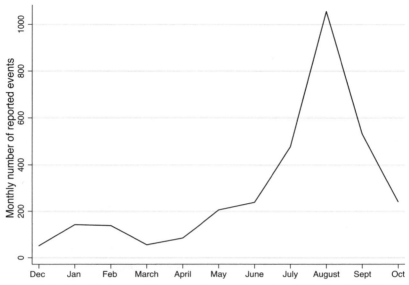

Figure 6.4. Monthly Count of Insurgent Events, December 1966–October 1967

though the armed forces were now forbidden from using force against rebel opponents, the other wing of the rebel movement was not. This drove local armed forces and pro-army rebels into closer collaboration, and the weapons that military units were forbidden to use against rebels found their way into the possession of pro-army factions. This set off local arms races, as anti-army rebels raided arms depots and military installations to seize weapons and defend themselves.

The anti-army rebels regrouped and rebuilt their organizations during April and May. Figure 6.4 traces the trajectory of rebel activity from December 1966 to October 1967. It displays monthly counts for the 3,321 insurgent actions reported during this period—violent confrontations between rebel factions, rebel confrontations with military units, and rebel attacks on government installations. The most common reported type of rebel activity was a violent factional confrontation (1,950 events), well above the numbers for confrontations with military units (950) and attacks on government installations (351). The initial conflicts that emerged in response to power seizures and military intervention are evident in January and February, and the army's suppression of rebel opposition is reflected in the decline in rebel activity in March. By May insurgent conflicts rise

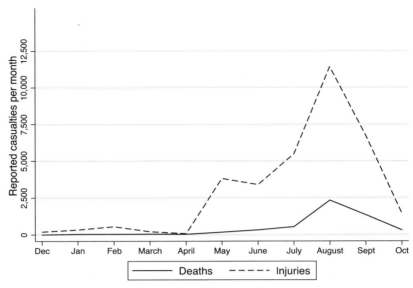

Figure 6.5. Casualties Due to Insurgent Events, by Month, December 1966–
October 1967

rapidly, as the impact of the army's new April orders was felt. The upward
trend accelerates in July and into August, when there were more than one
thousand reported insurgent conflicts, the highest monthly count during
this entire period of upheaval.

The striking overall rise in collective violence is apparent in Figure 6.5,
which traces monthly totals of casualties reported in connection with the
events tracked in Figure 6.4. Aggregate numbers suggest that the factional
battles became larger and more violent, as factions obtained weapons and
formed specialized brigades of fighters. These trends are clear in comparisons of the first quarter of 1967 (January–March) with the third quarter
(July–September). In the first quarter of 1967, there were a total of 337 violent events; during the third quarter, there were 2,065, a 6-fold increase.
Casualty counts, however, grew much faster. During the first quarter of
1967, 1,084 injuries were reported; during the third quarter, there were
23,606, a 22-fold increase. The number of reported deaths increased at an
even faster rate. During the first quarter of 1967 there were a total of 113
reported deaths; during the third quarter, there were 4,210, a 37-fold
increase.

Although levels of violence were rising, overall casualty rates remained modest. In the first quarter of 1967 there were 3 reported injuries per violent event, and only 1 death for every three events. By the third quarter, there were 11 reported injuries and 2 deaths per event. These are large increases, but still modest casualty counts. Until late July, street fighters relied primarily on clubs, spears, and rocks thrown or propelled by slingshots. Even at the height of the collective violence in August 1967, when firearms and heavy weaponry first spread among combatants, the number of casualties remained relatively low. These were not trained and committed fighters and they did not yet appear willing to risk life and limb during confrontations. The events referred to in local annals as armed battles *(wudou)* during the summer of 1967 were not yet the larger and more dangerous affairs described by that term in 1968.

A more comprehensive and perhaps representative view is provided by summary data compiled for individual regions. The annals for the Hebei provincial capital of Shijiazhuang stated that there were 132 violent clashes between rebel factions in the city from May to July 1967—around 3 clashes every 2 days. They generated a reported total of 10 deaths, 536 serious injuries, and 1,918 minor wounds—an average of 1 death for every 14 events, and 4.1 serious injuries per event.[26] Summary figures of this kind capture the large numbers of small clashes between rebel factions that often went unmentioned in local annals, which tended to report only the largest and most dramatic clashes. They remind us that while violent clashes were increasingly common, large-scale combat was still rare.

Explaining the Summer Upsurge

Despite these caveats, it is clear that there was an upsurge in violent conflict in August 1967 and a sudden drop shortly afterwards. How can we explain this? Once again, signals emanating from Beijing shaped the pace and direction of local insurgencies. The April reversal in the army's orders strengthened the hand of rebel factions antagonistic to military control. They rebuilt their forces in May and June and mobilized to challenge rival rebels who had developed a more supportive relationship with the armed forces. As these antagonisms and related violent clashes gradually increased, a sudden and dramatic shift emanating from Beijing intensified the violence. Central propaganda organs suddenly called for rebels to "drag out a handful of capitalist roaders in the army"—openly sanctioning direct attacks on army units. This was coupled with a directive originating with Mao himself in mid-July that called for arms to be distributed to genuine rebel factions.[27] This was a dramatic signal to anti-army rebels, and for the first time it gave factions on both sides access to arms with which to wage their battles.

The frustration of radical figures in Beijing with the actions of the armed forces had persisted since the April shift in the army's orders. Many regional commanders initially delayed the release of arrested rebels, and the reversal of verdicts on their organizations. After finally complying with their new orders, they were perceived—justifiably—to favor the rebel factions that were favorably inclined to them.[28] This frustration came to a head after dramatic events in Wuhan near the end of July that were condemned as an attempted rebellion by regional military forces—the "July 20 Incident."

The Wuhan events followed from a series of unusually aggressive actions by regional military forces. Initially, events under military control in Wuhan followed the pattern in other regions—rebel forces who claimed to have seized power resisted military control and were suppressed, while rival rebels applauded the army's actions. Shortly afterwards, however, frictions developed between the military command and the other rebel faction, and the army suppressed the other wing of the rebel movement as well. Both wings of the divided rebel movement began a comeback after the reversal of the army's orders in April, and in response local military commanders sponsored a new mass organization that strongly supported the military forces. Known as the "Million Heroes" *(baiwan yingxiong)*, the membership and organizational foundations of this resurgent group resembled the Scarlet Guard organizations that had earlier defended party authorities. The Million Heroes grew rapidly and waged a violent campaign against the now-united rebels, and had them on the verge of total defeat in early July. Alarmed by these developments, Mao sent the Minister of Public Security along with a radical member of the Central Cultural Revolution Group (Wang Li) to negotiate an end to the hostilities, save the rebel forces from extinction, and force the Million Heroes to stand down. Mao secretly arrived at a state guest compound to monitor the negotiations and sanction the anticipated cease-fire agreement.[29]

Events there took an unexpected turn when leaders of the Million Heroes refused to believe that Mao's emissaries represented his actual views. Angered by their apparent hostility to their organization, militants from the group, along with soldiers from supportive military units, stormed the guest compound where they were staying and took the two emissaries from Beijing hostage. They did not realize that Mao Zedong was staying in a nearby villa. Fearful for Mao's safety and unsure of the intentions of the local military commanders, Mao's security detail rushed him to board a flight to Shanghai in the middle of the night.[30]

Beijing immediately denounced the events of July 20 as a "counterrevolutionary rebellion" and an attempted military coup. Wang Li, the captive emissary from the Central Cultural Revolution Group, who was beaten in captivity and suffered a broken leg, was flown back to Beijing to a hero's welcome that was publicized nationwide. The Million Heroes was condemned as a reactionary organization and quickly collapsed. Wuhan's army commanders were summoned to Beijing, stripped of their posts, and physically abused in denunciation meetings.[31] Beijing radicals called for rebels to defend themselves with armed force. Mao ordered the distribution of arms to "leftist" rebel forces.[32] *Red Flag* magazine, the authoritative mouthpiece of the Central Cultural Revolution Group, published an editorial on August 1 that called for the "dragging out" of "capitalist roaders" in the army.[33] Anti-army rebels mounted major offensives against local commanders. They obtained arms for their offensive, as did rebels friendly to the local military.[34] The August upsurge of violence was the result.

Regional Violence

Descriptions of the rebel clashes that generated the largest reported death tolls during this period provide a concrete sense of these events at their most violent. Some of the most dramatic factional warfare was in Sichuan Province, where the February campaign of suppression against rebels who opposed the power seizure was particularly broad and harsh. After their release, these rebels reconstituted their forces and engaged factional rivals in armed clashes across the province. The casualty rates were inflated by seizures of military-grade weaponry from the armaments factories concentrated in the province. One of the first major battles was in Chengdu, the provincial capital, where, on May 6, more than 10,000 rebels from the two factions faced off at a large factory that produced military weaponry. The clash that day left 48 dead and 629 wounded.[35]

Elsewhere in Sichuan, in and around the large city of Chongqing, a major Yangzi River port and manufacturing center, the first battle in which each side used firearms took place at a diesel engine factory on July 8, leading to 9 deaths and the capture of more than 200. Military weaponry soon appeared in other clashes. Near the end of July each faction staged a series of raids on local armaments factories, seizing stores of weapons and ammunition in preparation for further clashes. A series of battles in nearby Rongchang County in the first week of August involved more than 600 fighters armed with machine guns, rifles, and hand grenades, leaving 78 dead. On August 3, rebels attacked a military launch in the Yangzi River with an antiaircraft gun, sinking it and killing 3 soldiers who were on board. Two days later, rebels deployed tanks, antiaircraft guns, and machine guns in a battle at a local machine tool factory, leaving 22 dead.

The continuing battles in the city would cut off shipping down the Yangzi River to Wuhan and Shanghai for almost 40 days. Rebels raided disabled ships and seized large shipments of consumer goods, medicine, cigarettes, and pork. Combatants from one of the city's shipyards outfitted 3 makeshift gunboats and attacked a number of factories and docks along the harbor on August 8, killing 24, injuring 129, and sinking 3 boats and damaging 12 others. On August 12 and 13, more than 500 rebel fighters engaged one another at a local machine-building plant, deploying a variety of military armaments and tanks, killing 10. Fighting at the Jialing River Bridge the next day left 11 dead. Fighting in the city's central district between the two largest factions from August 18 to 20 left over 100 dead; two days later a battle in a nearby district left 22 dead and scores wounded. Military officers in jeeps who drove into the area were fired upon; one was killed and 5 others were seriously wounded. A battle in suburban Tongliang County the next day left 35 dead and left a paper mill a smoking ruin. On August 28, a clash near a military installation in Chongqing involving more than 3,000 rebels left 40 dead. Fighting in one neighborhood engaged more than 1,000 fighters in a battle that left more than 100 dead.

During the August warfare in Chongqing, 157 of the 165 large industrial enterprises in the city were at least partially shut down, and 109 of them were completely closed. The documented death toll from these battles was close to 600. Alarmed that weaponry intended for the war effort in Vietnam was being seized for factional battles, Beijing issued an order on September 5 for regular army units to disarm the rebels, and the fighting in Chongqing quickly subsided.[36]

In Xiangtan, Hunan, similarly violent confrontations occurred, though on a smaller scale. Xiangtan was a county-level city 32 miles upriver from the provincial capital of Changsha, and 15 miles downriver from the prefecture-level city of Zhuzhou. The factional battles in Xiangtan drew on allies from both cities, who often arrived by boat. On July 10 and 11, some 1,000 rebels from two factions faced off in fighting that spread from a local boiler plant to the Xiangtan Hotel, leaving 3 dead and several hundred wounded. On August 11 and 13 local factions staged raids on local military arms depots, taking with them arms and ammunition. On August 12 one of the local factions rolled tanks into position at the main port on the Xiang River to deter reinforcements from Changsha by their opponent's allies. Several days later, a demonstration march by several thousand rebels through the streets of Xiangtan was blocked by their opponents, leading to a clash that left 2 dead and 12 wounded. After this, fighting intensified, leading to the closure of the city's steel plant and several mines, and rebels raided several military installations to seize arms. The fighting was temporarily quelled after regular army units were dispatched to cities in Hunan in mid-September. During this period the factional warfare in Xiangtan, waged on occasion with tanks, armored personnel carriers, and heavy artillery, generated 92 deaths and several hundred wounded.[37]

In Changzhou, a prefecture-level city in southern Jiangsu, midway between Nanjing and Shanghai, the first major armed clashes began on July 25 and lasted two days. Fought with knives, spears, and bottles of sulfuric acid, the clashes left 10 dead. The next major confrontations some weeks later involved more lethal weaponry. It began with one faction dynamiting the rail lines on September 11 to prevent the movement of rebel forces, cutting the line between Nanjing and Shanghai and alarming officials in Beijing. The clashes continued across several locations in the city until September 17, between factions armed with rifles and artillery pieces. The fighting did not subside until regular combat troops were dispatched to the city that afternoon. When the dust cleared, 83 were dead and 115 wounded. The rail line connecting Nanjing and Shanghai was cut for 11 days, postal service, telephone and telegraph service were interrupted for two weeks, and public transportation was shut down for 10 days.[38]

In Zaozhuang, a prefecture-level city in Shandong, the most violent incident during this period occurred at the local flour mill on July 26. Rebels from one of the mill's two factions captured 8 rebels from the other side and tortured one of them to death. In retaliation, their comrades mobilized militia forces from nearby collective farms, and more than 4,000 farmers, armed with rifles, marched into the city and surrounded the mill, touching off a battle that left 96 dead and 692 wounded.[39]

In Jinzhou City, Liaoning Province, several hundred fighters from one of the local factions invaded the arms depot of a local military academy and seized more than 300 rifles. When cadets from the school, who were allied with the opposing faction, discovered the theft in progress, they opened fire, and in the ensuing battle 21 were killed and 76 seriously wounded. According to the account, these were the largest casualties from any armed battle in Jinzhou during the entire period.[40]

High death tolls could also be generated in more remote rural counties, although sustained battles of the kind observed in Chongqing and other cities were rare. The largest recorded death toll for a county from a single battle during this period occurred in Gan County, around a bend in the Ganshui River from the county-level city of Ganzhou in Jiangxi Province. For several days beginning on June 29, armed rebels from Ganzhou and Gan County assembled there for a battle that left 178 dead and cut off river shipping. The fighting was quelled several days later only after the intervention of regular army troops.[41] In Sheng County, 83 miles southeast of Zhejiang's provincial capital of Hangzhou, factional warfare during the summer left 191 dead.[42] In Yongning County, just south of the Ningxia provincial capital of Yinchuan, more than 2,000 rebel fighters who were crammed into some 100 trucks tried to cross two bridges across the Yellow River on August 8, and they were met with rifle fire from 4,000 fighters from the opposed faction. The clash left 87 dead and hundreds wounded. Two smaller clashes in late August left 20 dead and 68 wounded. Regular PLA combat troops were dispatched to Yongning at the beginning of September to quell the fighting.[43] Battles during August in Tongshan County, a suburb of the northern Jiangsu prefecture-level city of Xuzhou, left 51 dead.[44]

Rebel confrontations with army units were less frequent and less perilous during this period. Rebel actions against army units and their commanding officers grew only modestly until July, and spiked in August. These were primarily mass demonstrations outside army compounds, or invasions of army compounds with the objective of seizing military officers, raiding arms stockpiles, or both. This would seem to be a particularly dangerous action, especially given the harsh measures employed by many army units against hostile rebels in February and March. But the army's April orders banned the use of armed force against the rebels, and throughout this period they appear largely to have abided by these restrictions. Of the 798 rebel actions against army units reported from April to October, there was an average of one death for every four events, and one injury per event. Fewer than 7 percent of the rebel confrontations with the armed forces during these seven months reported any deaths or injuries. When casualties were reported, they averaged 4 deaths and 17 injuries, well below the comparable estimates for armed factional battles. Clashes with army units would become much more dangerous in 1968, when soldiers were once again given the authority to use force, but during the high point of 1967, the toll from rebel confrontations with army units was still relatively low.

Invasions of military headquarters and arms depots during August were rarely resisted with armed force. A typical example is from Hanshou County, Hunan, where a rebel faction opposed to military control raided the headquarters of the People's Armed Department on August 25 and seized rifles and ammunition without incurring any casualties. Subsequent gunfights between factions in the county over the next two weeks generated 19 deaths and more than 30 wounded before the army was ordered to disarm civilian factions in early September.[45] After Beijing ordered that arms be recovered from local factions on September 5, local army units put up more spirited resistance to raids on arms depots. The deadliest recorded confrontation between a civilian faction and local armed forces during this period was in Laibin County, Guangxi, on September 6—the day after the army's new orders. More than 200 rebels from Liuzhou City staged a raid on suburban Laibin County's People's Armed Department to seize arms. In the ensuing conflict 17 were killed, 2 of them soldiers.[46] In Wanxian City, Sichuan, the largest single death toll from a civilian confrontation with military or security forces during this period did not come about due to the use of arms. During a June 3 invasion of the city's public security bureau, at that time under military control, hundreds of rebels rushed into the building, causing many to be crushed and trampled underfoot. Dozens were sent to local hospitals, and 31 of them eventually died.[47]

Toward the Rebuilding of Political Order

The upsurge of collective violence in the summer of 1967 was short-lived. Violent insurgent conflicts and related casualties dropped sharply after the August peak. The decline in collective violence had the same origins as the previous upsurge—a decisive shift in signals emanating from Beijing. The change in political direction became apparent through several different channels. It began in mid-August, when Mao became concerned about the nationwide upsurge of rebel attacks on local army units and made it known to his aides that calls to "drag out" army commanders was a mistake.[48] Soon thereafter he personally reassured besieged commanders of military regions that he fully supported them, and would not permit them to be overthrown.[49] Near the end of August Mao concluded that several of the younger radical members of the Central Cultural Revolution Group had "wrecked the Cultural Revolution" by encouraging attacks on the army. Within days they were charged with being secret agents and were placed under arrest along with several members of their staff. The purged traitors included Wang Li, the official who had been kidnapped by the Million Heroes in Wuhan and who had returned with a broken leg to a hero's welcome in Beijing in late July.[50]

This quickly reversed the signals being sent to regional rebels by senior figures in Beijing. Zhou Enlai, who met constantly with delegations of rebels from various provinces, stated in no uncertain terms that attacks on local military commanders would no longer be tolerated. More senior members of the Central Cultural Revolution Group, mindful of the purge of their younger colleagues, withdrew their backstage support for attacks on military commanders.[51] The shift in direction was made public and official by a September 5 directive that called on all factions to support the armed forces, emphasizing that they represented Chairman Mao. It denounced the seizure of military weaponry by rebel factions, and it also prohibited military units from distributing arms to their supporters. Local army units were ordered to retrieve weapons from rebels, who were ordered to turn in their weapons. If necessary, soldiers were given permission to defend themselves with armed force.[52] The new orders were rapidly disseminated through the military hierarchy. In some regions, the orders were read out over the telephone at the county level on the very same day that the orders were transmitted.[53]

This reversal, which was signaled through a variety of channels, decisively influenced the local insurgencies. By October the number of insurgent events and the number of casualties had dropped to the levels observed in June, prior to the summer upsurge (See Figure 6.4). Factional divisions were still deeply entrenched, and violent clashes continued, but for the time being on a reduced scale. Mao decided that it was time to resume the long-stalled effort to establish revolutionary committees in the many provinces that had been placed under military control. Zhou Enlai was put in charge of the effort, and he immediately began to negotiate cease fire agreements between deeply divided regional factions, and push for political settlements that would permit the formation of revolutionary committees. This would turn out to be a laborious and increasingly coercive process, carried out province by province. Delegations of representatives from rival rebel factions and local military units were summoned to Beijing and isolated for intensive negotiations.[54] There were still 22 provinces that remained under military control, and it would take another year before all of them had revolutionary committees. The greatest upsurge of collective violence, however, was yet to come.

7

THE DYNAMICS OF REGIONAL ESCALATION

THE REIMPOSITION OF order in the form of revolutionary committees spread gradually, province by province, beginning in late 1967, and continued throughout 1968. Mao himself set the process in motion in September 1967, when he complained about the slow progress of imposing provincial revolutionary committees, and called for the establishment of 10 new ones by February 1968.[1] As this effort spread, factional violence escalated even further, and it was concentrated in regions where military control had endured for long periods of time. Rebel factions in these regions appear to have fallen into an escalation trap. The longer that violent factional warfare raged on in a region, the more likely that the losers could expect severe retribution at the hands of their factional enemies. This fear was especially salient for factions that had fought long and hard against military control. This process drove the escalation of factional warfare during 1968, even as the number of regions with active insurgencies declined.

As the push to rebuild political order resumed, the pattern of rebel activity shifted in striking ways. As Beijing imposed political settlements backed by military units in one region after another during 1968, the overall level of insurgent activity declined steadily. Figure 7.1 traces the monthly count of all 7,976 reported events that indicated rebel activity during 1967 and 1968.[2] There is a sharp decline after the summer of 1967, and an eventual collapse after May–June 1968. There were twice as many reported in-

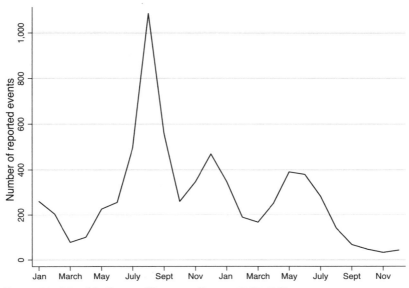

Figure 7.1. Monthly Count of Insurgent Events, 1967–1968

surgent events during the three violent months in the summer of 1967 (2,134) as there were in most violent three months in mid-1968 (1,054).

During this same period, however, the casualties generated by insurgent conflicts rose to unprecedented levels. Figure 7.2 traces the monthly number of deaths generated by the events displayed in Figure 7.1. As insurgent activity declined, violence intensified. The reported number of injuries and deaths was much higher in 1968. During the three-month peak in mid-1968, there were almost twice as many reported deaths as in the prior three-month peak in mid-1967 (8,049 versus 4,630).[3]

Increasing repression by the armed forces does not account for rising casualties from factional warfare. The impact of repression, as we shall see, was very large. The events examined here are actions by rebel insurgents, the vast majority of which are direct clashes between rebel factions. Factional violence intensified over time, and appears to have escalated as the end of rebel insurgencies approached.

How can we explain this pattern? To do so we need to reverse the customary emphasis of theories about political mobilization. These theories focus on the problem of how movements are initiated and sustained—how

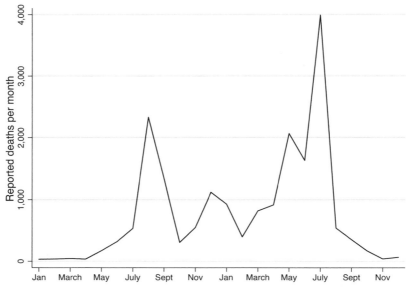

Figure 7.2. Monthly Count of Deaths Due to Insurgent Events, 1967–1968

they get underway, how they grow, and the factors that influence their relative success. This depends on the organizational capacity of groups, their
access to resources and how effectively they deploy them, opportunities provided by the political environment, and the effectiveness of tactics and
strategy. In other words, this familiar approach is essentially about how collective action emerges, and how it is sustained.[4]

In the present case the key to understanding the escalating intensity of
violence is to be found in examining *exit from* collective action, or how it
ends. The nature of these conflicts, and the structure of this political setting, meant that failing to prevail in factional warfare did not simply mean
a failure to win certain advantages. Much more importantly, there were
potentially severe costs to be borne by defeated rebel factions. The longer
and more violent the conflicts, the more severe were the likely costs of losing.
In one sense, of course, rising casualties from a smaller number of insurgent conflicts surely reflected the increasing scale and organizational co-
herence of rebel factions, and their growing access to military weaponry.
But an increased fighting capacity does not explain why rebel factions became so intensely motivated to prevail that they would be willing to bear

the much heavier casualties in the larger and more dangerous battles of 1968. The longer that local factional warfare continued without the prospect of an equitable political settlement, the greater the stakes for the participants and the more intense the collective violence as factions fought to avoid the consequences of losing.

Before pursuing this line of analysis, one needs to be clear about the ultimate objective of rebels who took different sides over the issue of military control. Once factions formed, why did anti-army rebels fight to press their claims, and why were their rebel opponents so adamant in defending the armed forces? For rebels opposed to military control, there was no prospect of an equitable settlement so long as the same military commanders remained in place to establish local revolutionary committees. This was especially true where struggles against military control had been long and violent. Narrative accounts indicate that anti-army rebels wanted local commanders to be reprimanded or removed. Continued resistance was a signal to higher authorities that local commanders had failed in their mission. The longer resistance continued, the greater the prospect that military commanders might be removed and replaced by ones with a more equitable stance toward local factions.

New army units transferred in from elsewhere might be more neutral in local conflicts, or even switch support from one faction to another. This did happen on occasion during the course of prolonged conflicts. In some regions, military units in nearby jurisdictions, or units from different branches of the military, were supportive of factions that were antagonistic to local military control.[5] In one particularly dramatic case, rebels whose resistance to military control had been supported by a regional People's Liberation Army (PLA) unit pleaded with that unit's commander to disobey transfer orders out of the province. As these rebels feared, the removal of this army unit led quickly to a harsh crackdown that crushed their resistance.[6] The prospect of harsh retribution spurred rebels opposed to local commanders to harden their resistance, which compelled pro-army rebel to defend their local sponsors.

There was an inherent zero-sum quality to the situation, making compromise more difficult. If new army commanders, or entirely new military units, were transferred in as replacements, rebels that had supported military control feared losing their backing or, even worse, the new commanders might side with their rivals. This zero-sum quality was further accentuated by the features of this single-party dictatorship and planned economy—there was literally no exit from the locality. Rebel activists could not migrate to other regions of China to escape punishment at the hands of their factional enemies. They would remain in the same communities and even in the same workplaces. Household registration and the rationing system for staple foods and consumer goods tied individuals to their local communities, making it impossible to leave. Job assignments were considered permanent, and switching to new workplaces (or schools) was virtually impossible.

The absence of an exit option from local settings ensured that defeated factions would return to their original places of work, under the control of their enemies. If one faction prevailed with military backing, the losers could anticipate a broad and enduring array of persecution. Aside from summary execution or prolonged imprisonment, one's opponents would now control a range of distributional questions, in particular the allocation of jobs and career opportunities. Because life chances in a planned economy were based on administrative decisions, the distributional outcomes of political conflict were particularly salient and the impact long lasting. Once violent factional warfare was entrenched, factions had strong motives to prevail, pushing at least for stalemate. The longer and more violent the factional conflicts, the more likely that losing would bring severe and prolonged retribution. In this setting, factional warfare, once prolonged beyond a certain point, became something of a trap. The combatants were compelled to fight to the bitter end, fearful of the potentially severe consequences of defeat.

The Political Geography of Escalation

Evidence for this explanation can be found in the political geography of escalation—where and when factional violence persisted for long periods, where it escalated over time, and where it did not. There was broad variation across China's provinces in how long factional conflict was sustained, and how it ended. Table 7.1 lists the dates of provincial power seizures (column a), the date that military control was imposed (column b), and the date that the province's revolutionary committee was formed (column c). The jurisdictions are ranked according to the length of time between the date of the provincial power seizure and the eventual formation of the revolutionary committee (listed in column d). Provinces that did not ex-

Table 7.1.   Provincial Power Seizures and Central Government Responses

Province-Level Jurisdiction	(a) Power Seizure (1967)	(b) Interim Military Control (1967)	(c) Revolutionary Committee	(d) Time Lag, (a) to (c)
Shandong	February 2	—	February 3, 1967	1 day
Shanghai	January 6	—	January 12,1967*	6 days
Heilongjiang	January 16	—	January 31, 1967	3 weeks
Guizhou	January 25	—	February 13, 1967	3 weeks
Shanxi	January 15	—	March 18, 1967	8 weeks
Beijing	None	—	April 20, 1967	—
Qinghai	January 29	May 8	August 12, 1967	7 months
Inner Mongolia	January 27	May 8	November 1, 1967	10 months
Tianjin	None	January 18	December 6, 1967	—
Jiangxi	January 26	February 23	January 5, 1968	12 months
Gansu	February 5	May 12	January 24, 1968	12 months
Henan	January 21	March 27	January 27, 1968	12 months
Hebei	January 23	May 10	February 3, 1968	13 months
Hubei	January 26	March 27	February 5, 1968	13 months
Guangdong	January 22	May 14	February 21, 1968	13 months
Jilin	January 18	April 17	March 6, 1968	14 months
Jiangsu	January 26	March 5	March 23, 1968	14 months
Zhejiang	January 18	March 15	March 24, 1968	14 months
Hunan	January 23	May 14	April 8, 1968	15 months
Ningxia	January 27	March 25	April 10, 1968	15 months
Anhui	January 26	March 27	April 18, 1968	15 months
Shaanxi	January 23	March 2	May 1, 1968	16 months
Liaoning	January 31	February 20	May 10, 1968	16 months
Sichuan	January 19	March 2	May 31, 1968	16 months
Yunnan	January 26	March 31	August 13, 1968	19 months
Fujian	None	May 11	August 14, 1968	—
Guangxi	January 23	March 12	August 26, 1968	19 months
Xinjiang	January 25	February 11	September 5, 1968	20 months
Tibet	February 5	March	September 5, 1968	20 months

*The Shanghai Commune was approved by Beijing on this date: it was reorganized and renamed as a Revolutionary Committee on February 5, 1967. Source: Provincial Annals.

perience a power seizure are ordered according to the date that their revolutionary committee was established.

The table shows a large contrast between the 6 provinces whose revolutionary committees were ratified in early 1967, and the remaining 23, which were instead placed under prolonged military control. Six revolutionary committees were quickly ratified by Beijing, and new governments were appointed, all headed by civilians who had expressed sympathy with the rebel cause.[7] In these regions it took an average of only 21 days for a provincial power seizure to be ratified as a revolutionary committee. In the remaining provinces, there was anywhere from 7 to 20 months before a revolutionary committee was ratified, and almost all of this period was under military control, an average well in excess of one year.

Prolonged periods under military control extended the duration of local factional warfare, because it was precisely the role of local military forces that was the fulcrum of factional conflict. Once a provincial revolutionary committee was formed, rebels in the provincial capital who were excluded from representation on these committees—rebels whose claims were denied—faced the impossible task of overturning a new government that had been personally approved by Mao himself. Once a revolutionary committee was ratified, rebel groups in the provincial capital were ordered to disband, and armed force could be freely deployed to quell any remaining dissent.

An early provincial settlement affected cities and counties within a province, almost all of which already had factional disagreements over power seizures. As elsewhere, local army units sought to impose order and adjudicate disputes in anticipation of a local revolutionary committee, but they did so in the name of a Mao-approved provincial government. The pacification of factional conflict in the provincial capital meant that there was little effective resistance to the new authorities, and no potential allies for disgruntled local rebels. This facilitated the ability to forge compromise and create revolutionary committees in the cities and counties below. If local troops imposed an inequitable settlement, the rebels that lost out would not achieve their objectives, but they would not face severe repression unless they resisted with violence. Exit from collective action imposed relatively few costs, even though the gains of inclusion in local revolutionary committees were foregone. In these settings, compromise or surrender was more likely than obdurate resistance. Half of the cities and counties in these provinces already had their own revolutionary committees by May 1967.

Beijing halted the approval of provincial power seizures after March 1967, and imposed one by fiat in the nation's capital in April. All but two of the remaining 23 provinces had to wait until the following year for ratification of a revolutionary committee. In the interim there was no legitimate civilian authority, only temporary military control, with a political settlement indefinitely postponed. Rebel conflicts in the provincial capital remained unresolved, with one faction adamantly opposed to military control and able to sustain an active insurgency. Here the ability of army units to forge a local compromise was hampered, and rebels whose claims were denied were much more likely to resist. So long as there was no political settlement in the provincial capital, local rebels were unlikely to curtail their resistance.

Figure 7.3 illustrates the resulting differences across provinces in the timing of local political settlements. The solid line represents provinces where revolutionary committees were approved by April 1967. It traces the cumulative percentage over time of localities within these provinces that had established their own revolutionary committees. In these regions, more than half of cities and counties established revolutionary committees by May 1967. The remaining provinces, which were placed indefinitely under military control, are represented by the dashed line. In these regions, almost no local revolutionary committees were established until the very end

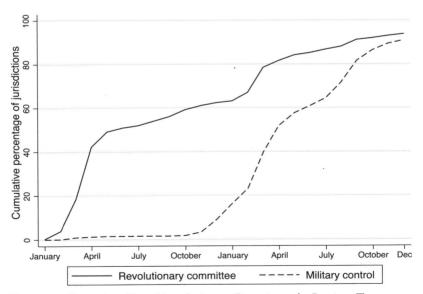

Figure 7.3. Formation of Local Revolutionary Committees, by Province Type, 1967–1968

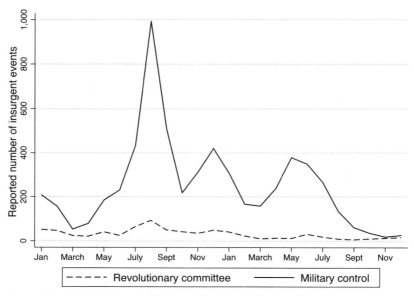

Figure 7.4. Monthly Count of Insurgent Events, by Province Type, 1967–1968

of 1967. After that point the push to establish revolutionary committees resumed, and not until May 1968 did more than half of these localities have one—the level achieved in the other provinces one year before. This meant that conditions for the development of violent factional warfare were far more prevalent and lasted far longer in provinces placed under military control. Such conditions, however, were by no means absent in the provinces that quickly established revolutionary committees. The upward trajectory of the solid line slowed markedly in May 1967, surely reflecting the April orders that restrained military units from using force against rebels, and that at the same time signaled that resistance to military control had supporters in Beijing.

Given these regional contrasts, we should expect to see large differences in the prevalence of factional conflict between these two regions. Figure 7.4 traces the monthly number of events that indicate any form of rebel activity throughout 1967 and 1968. The solid line represents provinces placed under military control, while the dashed line represents provinces with early revolutionary committees. Almost all of the factional conflict during these two years occurred in provinces placed under military control. This did not mean that there was no factional conflict in provinces with

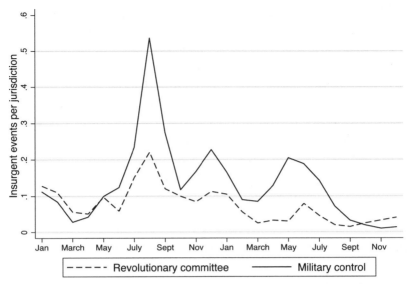

Figure 7.5. Rates of Insurgent Conflict, by Month and Province Type, 1967–1968

early revolutionary committees. We have seen that the establishment of local revolutionary committees in these regions slowed greatly after May 1967, so local military control persisted in many localities even in these provinces.

Figure 7.5 examines regional differences from a different angle—*rates* of factional conflict expressed as per-jurisdiction numbers of reported insurgent events. Here we see that rates of conflict were virtually identical in the two regions until May 1967, at which point conflict escalated sharply in provinces placed under military control. Thereafter the two lines had roughly parallel trajectories, with the same three peaks in activity in mid-1967, late 1967, and mid-1968. Rates of conflict were always substantially higher in the provinces placed under military control, and the differences were most pronounced during the peak periods, when rates of conflict were twice as high.

Regional Escalation

The creation of a province-level revolutionary committee facilitated the establishment of local revolutionary committees. But it did not immediately bring local factional warfare to an end. In fact, preparations for a provincial revolutionary committee was likely to have quite the opposite effect in provinces that had remained under military control for long periods. By signaling to local factions that a final political settlement was imminent, each side was likely to redouble their effort to fight to achieve at least a stalemate, if not a decisive victory. The localities where political settlements were delayed the longest, and where violent factional warfare had persisted, escalated the potential costs of losing. This is where the escalating violence of 1968 was concentrated.

As new revolutionary committees were established in rapid order during 1968, they took on an ominous character for factions opposed to military control. The provincial revolutionary committees established in early 1967 were headed by a civilian who had expressed sympathy for rebel movements. This second wave of revolutionary committees, by contrast, essentially formalized military control. Military commanders who had been attacked by anti-army rebels for many months generally remained to head the new revolutionary committees. Of the remaining 23 provincial-level revolutionary committees, 20 were PLA generals.[8] The core of the new revolutionary committee was almost always the officer previously placed in charge of military control. In Jiangsu Province, by 1970 the top official in almost every city and county was a military officer—all 13 prefectures, and 60 out of 68 counties.[9] In Guangdong, Liaoning, Shanxi, Yunnan, and Hubei, between 81 and 98 percent of all revolutionary committees above the county level were headed by PLA officers.[10] Some new revolutionary committees sought to achieve a balance by including representatives of both major factions; others strongly favored one faction at the expense of the other.[11] Rebel leaders rarely occupied positions of genuine authority. Those who had stubbornly resisted the formation of army-led revolutionary committees were typically pushed aside, and in some cases arrested, and replaced by more cooperative leaders from the same faction.[12] Deposed local officials who had been cast aside during power seizures were in a similar position—their placement in new structures of power as "revolutionary cadres" did not confer real power.[13]

The prospect that the same military officers who had long been stationed in your locality would remain as heads of a new government intensified the urgency of prevailing in local conflicts. Rebel factions aligned with local commanders fought to ensure that they were not removed and replaced,

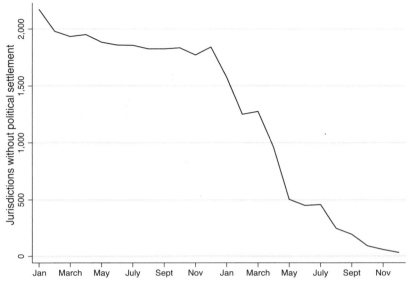

Figure 7.6. Number of Localities without a Political Settlement, by Month, 1967–1968

while their anti-army rivals fought to ensure that they would leave the locality. The approach of a final settlement compelled local rebels to fight hard to avoid the severe consequences of losing.

If we define local political settlements as a county or city where both a local and a provincial revolutionary committee has been established, we can chart their spread. For present purposes, we are interested in localities that were without a political settlement for the longest period of time. Figure 7.6 traces the decline in the number of these localities during 1967 and 1968. We see a slow decline throughout 1967, with a very rapid decline during 1968. It is in this rapidly diminishing number of localities without a political settlement that the most violent factional warfare should have occurred, with the highest levels of escalation occurring in the localities where warfare persisted the longest.

Figure 7.7 examines the number of deaths per insurgent event in the localities without a political settlement that are displayed in Figure 7.6. It shows a sharp and steady rise in the death rate over time, with the highest observed levels occurring in October 1968—when there remained only around 100 localities without a settlement. There were roughly 3 deaths

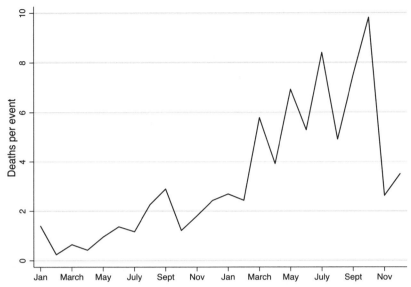

Figure 7.7. Deaths per Insurgent Event, by Month, in Localities without a Political Settlement, 1967–1968

per event in the peak of rebel violence in the summer of 1967, but a rapid and steady increase during 1968, finally reaching close to 10 deaths per event on the eve of the local rebel movement's extinction.

Although these descriptive patterns seem clear, a more convincing test of the argument requires a statistical model. The model would examine variation in the intensity of factional violence (number of deaths per month) across localities and over time. The descriptive data indicate that violence escalated primarily in provinces placed under military control, and that it intensified over time as the duration of unresolved conflicts increased. To test this idea, the model will divide provinces into two groups—those with early revolutionary committees, and those placed under military control. Within each of these two broad regions, the model would then examine differences in the intensity of violence according to the length of time that elapsed before the locality had a political settlement.

To examine the idea that violence intensified over time in regions without a political settlement, for each locality we calculate the duration in months between the first local intervention by military units and the month when both a provincial and local revolutionary committee were established (this corresponds to the definitions employed in Figures 7.6 and 7.7). The localities are divided into three groups of equal size, based on their time duration prior to a final political settlement: short, medium, and long. Each of the three groups are then examined separately for provinces that had early revolutionary committees and provinces that instead were placed under military control. This results in 6 different periods across the two types of provinces, with the periods before military intervention and after a political settlement as baseline periods.

Once these categories are defined, a regression model estimates differences across these periods of varied duration for evidence that longer durations exhibited higher death rates (deaths per month).[14] The regressions control for both local population (larger populations would likely generate larger insurgencies and more deaths per month) as well as the contrast between cities and counties (urban areas were able to mobilize larger numbers).

Because our outcome of interest is a count of deaths per month, the appropriate model is negative binomial estimation. In addition, because there is surely selectivity in whether a local account reports numbers of fatalities, the appropriate statistical model is a two-stage zero-inflated model. In the zero-inflated model, the cases where the dependent variable is zero (a month with no reported deaths) are modeled separately from non-zeroes. A first-stage equation predicts the likelihood that a locality will report no deaths for a given month. The second-stage equation estimates coefficients that are re-weighted and adjusted for the results of the first-stage model. In the first-stage model is a variable "length" that is the count of the number of Chinese characters that a local history devotes to the description of events. The reasoning is that longer descriptive accounts will be more likely to report details, in particular the number of casualties for each of the reported factional clashes. Length is essentially an indicator of the resources devoted to compiling local histories, and also of editorial decisions about how much detail to provide. Adjusting estimates for the length of accounts reduces the potential biases that may result from differences in the propensity of local accounts to report details.[15]

The results of this procedure are summarized in Figure 7.8, which reports differences in death rates across provinces and local durations of different length.[16] For readers unfamiliar with margin plots, the black dot is the point estimate for the predicted death rate in a certain period of time, and the brackets of equal length that are attached to each side of the point

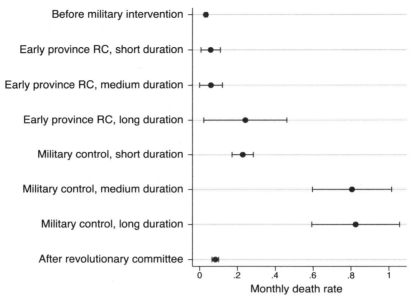

Figure 7.8. Intensity of Insurgent Conflict (Deaths per Month), by Province Type and Duration of Military Control

estimate are the 95 percent confidence intervals. When these brackets overlap with those for other point estimates, the differences are not statistically significant; when they do not overlap, we are highly confident in the estimated differences.

The results confirm the conclusions that one would draw from the earlier descriptive analysis. The first estimate, at the top of the figure, indicates not surprisingly that death rates were not much different from zero before military intervention. This was the period before factional warfare began. The next three rows present estimates for provinces where revolutionary committees were established early in 1967. The estimates for the first two groups among these localities are barely higher than for the period before military control. These were localities with very short periods of time without a political settlement—the short duration averaged 3.2 months, and the medium duration averaged 7.6. The estimate for the third period is more than twice as large, reflecting the much longer average duration in this group—19.3 months. The wide band of the confidence interval overlaps with those for the shorter durations, which indicates that the estimated difference is not statistically significant. This is likely due to the much smaller numbers of localities in this category (there were fewer than 400 cities and counties overall in these provinces), which resulted in a larger standard error for the estimate.

The results in the next three rows are for provinces placed under military control. Localities with a short duration (averaging 7.7 months) were the least violent. The estimated death rate is more than twice that of the first two periods in the "early revolutionary committee" provinces, and the difference is statistically significant. Of greatest relevance are the estimates for the longer durations in these provinces. This is where we should see the highest death rates as a symptom of escalation traps. The estimated death rates for both the medium and long duration groups (an average of 12.0 and 16.1 months, respectively) are 4 times larger than in localities with short durations, and more than 8 times larger than the estimates for the short and medium duration localities in the other group of provinces. These differences are statistically significant from all others by a wide margin. The final estimate presented at the bottom of the figure, for the period after the formation of a local and provincial revolutionary committee, indicates relatively low intensity of violence, equal to the levels observed in the short and medium duration localities in provinces with early revolutionary committees.[17]

These results provide further evidence for escalation traps in localities with long histories of conflict under military control. An early political settlement at the province level suppressed factional violence overall, while in provinces placed under military control for long periods, violence escalated over time, resulting in higher death rates in localities with longer periods without a political settlement. The longer that conflict continued, the more severe the perceived costs of losing, and the harder that factions pushed to mobilize combatants to prevail.[18]

Is there evidence that the costs of losing were more severe for groups that were defeated in these regions? Tanigawa found such evidence from his examination of county-level revolutionary committees in one particularly violent province where political settlements were long delayed. In 80 percent of the counties in Shaanxi where rebels were able to avoid defeat until after new army units were transferred into the province in late July 1968, both rebel factions were represented on local revolutionary committees. In every one of the revolutionary committees formed before that date, only one faction had representatives, indicating the defeat of the other faction. More than twice as many deaths were generated in subsequent political campaigns to consolidate political order in the counties where one faction had decisively lost.[19] More direct evidence of the dire consequences of defeat was the fate of the "April 22" faction in Guangxi, which fought one of the hardest last-ditch defenses in the country into the summer of 1968. After their final defeat at the hands of army units allied with their factional rivals, a wave of reprisal killings generated massive death tolls, in which members of April 22 comprised the overwhelming majority.[20] This was the anticipated outcome that drove escalation traps.

Final Factional Battles

To this point I have analyzed patterns of conflict in the abstract without describing the dramatic events that the patterns represent. Drawing on accounts of events during this period in the more detailed local annals, I will convey a descriptive sense of what this final wave of intensely violent factional warfare looked like on the ground.

In Shaanxi Province, which had some of the largest and most persistent factional warfare, combat escalated in the months leading up to the establishment of the provincial revolutionary committee in early May 1968. In Ziyang County, a cease-fire agreement between the two local factions broke down in March, and in April each side seized arms from the People's Armed Department and the local police. One of the factions, drawing on allies in nearby counties, armed themselves and formed fighting brigades that roamed across the county's smaller towns, fighting a series of pitched battles with their opponents that generated around 10 deaths in each encounter. As the fighters moved around the county they captured and tortured individuals aligned with the opposed faction and unaffiliated civilians, killing more than 400.[21] In Yan'an, the former capital of Mao's wartime base area, 110 died in fighting between rebel factions from May to July, including 30 who died in a single battle in nearby Fu County on June 3.[22] In Mian County, ten armed battles between April 5 and July 18 left 65 dead.[23]

In Sichuan province, the Beijing negotiations to form a provincial revolutionary committee began in March 1968. As these negotiations proceeded, armed battles intensified in and around the large prefecture-level city of Chongqing. In mid-March, fighting at a large steel complex shut it down completely. A single battle in suburban Changshou County left 42 dead. In early April combatants at a machinery plant fought a pitched battle with machine guns and artillery pieces. Near the end of the month, firemen on their way to extinguish a blaze set during an armed battle were fired upon by workers from a steel mill; 9 of them were killed and 17 wounded.[24] In Zhongjiang County, a distant suburb of the provincial capital of Chengdu, rebel fighters from 20 counties and 3 cities across Sichuan streamed in to take part in battles that began in mid-April. In fighting over the next 3 weeks the two sides, armed with antiaircraft guns and similar heavy weapons, suffered a total of 314 combat deaths. After the fighting was over, one faction marched 3,000 captives back to Zhongjiang and summarily executed 78 of them; more than a thousand refugees fled to Chongqing and other cities to avoid the fighting.[25] In remote Guangyuan County, located on Sichuan's border with Shaanxi, one faction captured the county seat on July 1 and in the ensuing battle to retake the town 190 people died.[26] In Yuechi County, 100 miles north of Chongqing, 2,000 fighters faced off in a battle on April 23 that left 53 dead and more than 100 wounded.[27]

The Sichuan Province Revolutionary Committee was established on the last day of May, but the province had experienced armed battles between well-armed factions for much of the past year. Some of the largest and most violent conflicts were still to come, as factions fought a last-ditch effort to avoid defeat in local rivalries. Luzhou, a county-level city on the Yangzi River 120 miles upstream from Chongqing, experienced one of the largest battles ever recorded. Luzhou had been the site of two large clashes during the summer of 1967, but the casualties appear to have been limited. The final battle between two large and heavily armed forces took place in July. More than 30,000 fighters from the surrounding region took part in the battles, employing firearms and gunboats in Luzhou and nearby counties, and coordinating their operations by radio. They killed close to 1,000 in battle, and captured around ten thousand prisoners, of whom more than 900 were summarily executed. Large parts of the city and its port lay in ruins. At a chemical plant 21 boats were destroyed. By the time the fighting ended, over 2,000 had been killed in Luzhou and an estimated 24,000 were wounded. Luzhou's revolutionary committee was not established until November 1968.[28] Violence persisted elsewhere in this prefecture, which proved particularly difficult to pacify. In Hejiang County, across the Yangzi

River from Luzhou, a skirmish between two factions in late September left 11 dead, and in the ensuing battle another 140 were killed. Hejiang did not establish its revolutionary committee until January 1969.[29]

Some of the worst recorded violence during this period occurred in Guangxi Province, where violent factional battles that preceded the establishment of the provincial revolutionary committee near the end of August frequently spurred the victorious combatants to engage in bouts of indiscriminate mass killings. A cease-fire between the two factions—Allied Command and April 22—had been reached through negotiations in Beijing near the end of 1967. The agreement broke down in March 1968 as counties and cities began to establish local revolutionary committees. Just over half of Guangxi's cities and counties had formed revolutionary committees in March, and close to 90 percent had done so by the end of April, but this appeared only to intensify the last-ditch armed resistance of the April 22 faction, which had stubbornly resisted military control. So long as a revolutionary committee was lacking at the province level, determined and even desperate resistance persisted at the local level.

In Guilin, a revolutionary committee was established for both the city and prefecture in mid-April, putting the Allied Command faction in control. But only 5 of the 12 counties in the prefecture had established similar revolutionary committees by the end of May, and fighters from the April 22 faction were not yet willing to give up. During a 7-week period from late June to early August, a continuous series of battles were fought in the city between the two factions. Both sides called in reinforcements of fighters from surrounding counties. Close to 8,000 members of militias from all 12 counties in the prefecture streamed into the city to reinforce their allies. A total of 604 deaths were recorded in the battles: 198 were combatants, but 406 were civilians who were trapped in districts with the heaviest fighting. Well over 1,000 were wounded, but large numbers of deaths and other casualties among the fighters from surrounding counties went unrecorded. Railway lines were cut, warehouses burned to the ground, factories closed, and public infrastructure was destroyed. The severity of the fighting is indicated by a partial count of the armaments recovered from combatants after the fact: 13,272 rifles, 80 artillery pieces, 8.7 million bullets, 19,090 artillery shells, and 230,000 hand grenades.[30]

As the battles were being waged in Guilin, factional fighters in towns and villages across the prefecture sought to "consolidate the rear" by engaging in sprees of mass killing. Xing'an County had sent 1,470 members of their militia, under the direction of their People's Armed Department, to take part in the Guilin battles. When they returned to Xing'an in late August after having lost 24 dead, they turned their attention to the remaining local forces of the April 22 faction. In the course of intensified armed battles with their opponents, the militias also went on a killing rampage against their family members and other unarmed civilians. During this short period 869 people were put to death in towns and villages in Xing'an. More than 8,500 noncombatants died in similar killing sprees during these weeks across Guilin prefecture.[31]

Sporadic fighting continued across China even after September 1968, largely in remote regions and on a much smaller scale. There were 3,926 factional battles recorded in the annals for 1967 and 1968, but only 372 afterwards, all but 7 of which occurred during 1969. The majority of these conflicts (210) occurred in four remote regions—Guizhou, Sichuan, Tibet, and Xinjiang. Only 46 of them reported at least 10 deaths, and only 72 at least 10 injuries. Only two incidents generated casualties on the scale observed during the final battles around the formation of revolutionary committees in 1968. In Yinjiang County, Guizhou, which contained a large population of Tujia and Miao minorities, factional fighting in June 1969 left 139 dead and 21 severely wounded. The fighting caused more than 2,000 local residents to flee the county to take refuge in neighboring Sichuan province.[32] Similar battles in Xichang County, a Tibetan region in far western Sichuan, left more than 600 dead and wounded from March to July 1969.[33]

The year 1970 marked the end of this era of violent warfare. Of the 4 clashes recorded in the annals for that year, 2 were in Xinjiang, and one each in Sichuan and Zhejiang. The last recorded factional battle, leaving 5 dead in August 1970, occurred in a county that spanned a chain of islands populated by fishermen off the coast of Zhejiang. That county also was the last known jurisdiction to establish a revolutionary committee—in November 1971.[34] These conflicts represented the last glowing embers of the conflagrations that raged across China for almost two years.

8

REPRESSION UNLEASHED

WE HAVE JUST EXAMINED the violence generated by clashes between rebel factions. Now I will turn to the impact of the repression exercised by military and civilian authorities as they imposed revolutionary committees. The final push to establish revolutionary committees relaxed remaining constraints on the use of military force. I will consider separately two distinct types of repression. The first is coercion deployed against armed rebel factions in order to create conditions for establishing a revolutionary committee, or to defend a revolutionary committee immediately after its establishment. The second is repression that was applied after the rebel factions were disarmed and disbanded—organized campaigns designed to consolidate political order in workplaces and communities. The first type of repression placed at risk active combatants in rebel insurgencies, and to some extent those connected to them by political or kinship ties. The second type, however, placed the entire adult population at risk, and resulted in far more casualties and political victims than anything previously observed during this entire period. As we shall see, the cure for factional warfare was far worse than the disease.

The Repression of Rebel Forces

Repression increased sharply during 1968. Figure 8.1 tracks repression against rebels and suspected sympathizers by local authorities—either mil-

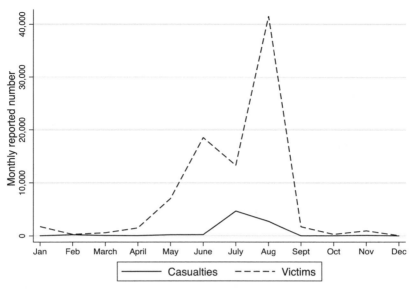

Figure 8.1. Indicators of Repression by Authorities, by Month, 1968

itary or civilian—during 1968. These actions were less commonly reported than insurgent activity (452 versus 2,139 total events that year), but
their impact was considerable. There are very few reports of repression until
May, when the numbers begin to rise sharply. The dashed line represents
"victims"—individuals reportedly arrested, captured, or subjected to some
form of mistreatment due to their activities or political sympathies. By this
measure, the impact of repression reaches a peak in the summer of 1968,
with close to 20,000 victims reported in June, rising to more than 40,000 in
August, before declining afterwards. The solid line represents violent
repression—total reports of injuries and deaths at the hands of authorities.
The numbers are negligible until the summer months, peaking in July at
close to 5,000 casualties.

Repression was closely associated with the formation of local revolutionary committees. For localities whose revolutionary committees were
formed during 1968, Figure 8.2 traces the number of casualties (deaths plus
injuries) associated with repression applied by authorities. Negative numbers indicate calendar months before, positive numbers after, with 0
representing the month that the revolutionary committee was formed.

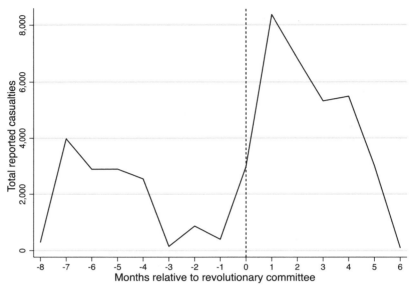

Figure 8.2. Casualties Generated by Repression, Relative to the Formation of Local Revolutionary Committees, 1968

Violent repression against rebels began some 6 to 7 months prior and continued at relatively high levels until around 3 months prior, when it subsided, perhaps indicating that rebel insurgencies had been quelled sufficiently to form a new government. Immediately upon the formation of a revolutionary committee, however, the number of casualties increased sharply, within two months rising to levels twice as high as the previous high point. Violent repression at this level was sustained until the fourth month subsequent to the revolutionary committee, at which point it dropped sharply.

Less violent forms of repression traced roughly the same pattern. Figure 8.3 traces the monthly number of victims—primarily arrests and political charges—excluding those reported as injured or killed. In the months prior to the formation of a revolutionary committee, there appears to have been an inverse relationship between casualties and other victims. In Figure 8.2 we saw that relatively high numbers of casualties 4 to 7 months prior to the revolutionary committee dropped to lower levels in the months immediately before. In Figure 8.3, by contrast, nonviolent forms of repression rise sharply as the revolutionary committee approaches and continues

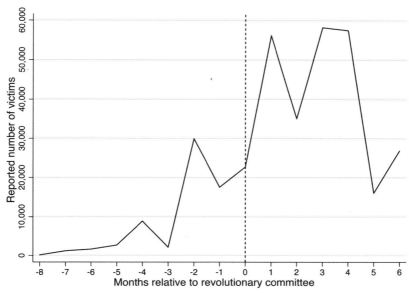

Figure 8.3. Victims Generated by Repression, Relative to the Formation of Local Revolutionary Committees, 1968

to rise afterwards. There are vastly more reported victims than casualties. A total of 336,662 victims and 46,140 casualties are represented in Figures 8.2 and 8.3.

Repression associated with the formation of revolutionary committees took two different forms. First, it represented the victimization of rebel factions who lost local struggles, the anticipated outcome that drove the escalation traps of 1968. Second, it represented a final armed offensive against local rebels who staged last-ditch resistance against the imposition of order by army units. The data do not permit the disaggregation of the two, but there is ample evidence for both in narrative accounts.

From Factional Warfare to Mass Repression

Narrative descriptions in published annals provide a vivid sense of the kinds of activities that generated these numbers. In Guangdong Province, close to 90 percent of cities and counties had established revolutionary committees by the end of April 1968, yet stubborn factional resistance persisted across the province. In July, the provincial revolutionary committee issued stern directives calling for its final suppression. Chenghai County had established its revolutionary committee in April, but armed opposition persisted in a number of villages. After a clash in one village left 22 dead in late July, local militia and regular army troops surrounded 8 holdout villages the following week, beating to death 69 and arresting more than 80. The prisoners were taken back to the county seat, where another 17 of them were beaten to death at the front gates of the public security bureau.[1] In Changjiang County, similarly harsh measures were taken to consolidate its revolutionary committee, which was established in April. Continued resistance was declared to be counterrevolution by the new county authorities, and militia forces were unleashed on the holdouts. During a one-month period that began near the end of July, more than 3,000 were arrested, more than 1,000 resisters were wounded, and 122 were killed.[2] In Wenchang County, which also established its revolutionary committee in April, a wave of arrests in July targeted rebel leaders and spread to individuals in politically suspect households. More than 200 were killed or committed suicide in a final wave of repression against active political opposition.[3]

In Huangmei County, Hubei, a revolutionary committee was formed in January 1968, and the new authorities conducted a large suppression campaign against the rebel faction that had fought against its establishment until the very end. From May until December, the campaign targeted close to 6,700 individuals for alleged counterrevolutionary activities. A total of 1,804 were arrested, subjected to harsh interrogation and various forms of physical torture. In the course of the campaign, 749 of these individuals were injured, 90 suffered permanent disabilities, and 129 were beaten to death in captivity.[4] These are precisely the kind of feared outcomes that drove the escalation traps observed in some regions—defeated factions feared violent retribution.

Frustrated by their inability to quell the disorders on China's border with Vietnam during the height of the U.S. escalation of the war, Mao issued an order in early July 1968 that made absolutely clear that continued resistance in Guangxi by armed factions would no longer be tolerated. Troops under the Guangxi Military District, supporting the Allied Command faction, moved into position in mid-July to direct the final campaign. A revolutionary committee had been established over the provincial capital of Nanning back in mid-April, anticipating a subsequent revolutionary committee for the province as a whole. Stubborn and well-armed fighters from the April 22 faction, however, still occupied several key buildings and neighborhoods in the capital and refused to surrender. The final battle to crush them destroyed large parts of downtown Nanning, and generated casualties on a scale comparable to those observed the previous month in the Sichuan river port of Luzhou.

The final battle began on July 15, when troops from the Guangxi Military District and rebels from the Allied Command surrounded and sealed off the downtown city blocks still occupied by April 22 forces. At noon the next day they began shelling the district, and the bombardment continued until nightfall. As the bombardment resumed the following day, squads of soldiers and Allied Command fighters tightened their cordon around the April 22 districts, and the two sides began to throw firebombs at one another, setting fire to commercial and residential buildings in the area. The main headquarters of April 22, in the city's largest department store, caught fire after being hit by mortar fire. Artillery bombardment concentrated on April 22 outposts along the nearby Yongjiang River port, setting alight thousands of barrels of gasoline and aviation fuel, gutting scores of river freighters along with their contents. On July 27, military units, unable to dislodge the defenders, brought more sophisticated weapons to bear, and began to use anti-aircraft weapons, recoilless cannons, surface-to-surface missiles, and tanks to pound the city blocks and buildings where April 22 fighters were concentrated. The indiscriminate bombardment set fire to residences and office buildings and reduced 33 city blocks to rubble. The April 22 fighters continued to resist with rifles and fire bombs until August 5, when the last holdouts along Liberation Road surrendered.

During the battle of Nanning, according to "incomplete statistics," 1,340 April 22 fighters were killed and 6,445 were taken prisoner, along with 2,500 residents suspected of supporting the rebels. As soldiers and Allied Command fighters marched hundreds of captives out of the rubble-strewn neighborhoods along Liberation Road that morning, 26 of them were summarily executed. During the entire campaign to pacify Nanning, a total of 1,587 combatants died (84 percent of whom were April 22 fighters) and 9,845 combatants and other suspects were taken prisoner. More than 7,000 of the April 22 prisoners were sent back to their home counties, where more than 2,300 were soon executed.[5]

As the fighting in Nanning reached its apex, repeated broadcasts of the July directive calling for the crushing of counterrevolutionary resistance set off a wave of mass killings across Guangxi. The victims included local rebels who were aligned with the April 22 faction, but the killings frequently spread to their family members and other people in stigmatized political categories. The worst reported death toll was in Binyang County, where mass killings took place in every one of its rural communes. During an 11-day period from July 26 to August 6, 3,681 individuals were put to death, at times in the most gruesome fashion. The killings were not limited to April 22 sympathizers or to adults in households stigmatized as former landlords and other kinds of class enemies. The massacres also included children and the elderly, and 176 households were entirely exterminated. This eruption of violence accounted for 93 percent of the total deaths recorded in Binyang County—a pattern repeated across Guangxi.[6] This extraordinary spasm of violence finally cleared the way for the imposition of Guangxi's revolutionary committee on August 26. Guangxi's was the 27th provincial revolutionary committee to be established. Only two remained—Xinjiang and Tibet, both of which followed 10 days later, on September 5.

Systematic Repression on a National Scale

The final suppression of factional conflict, after almost two years of endemic collective violence, might lead one to expect a rapid decline in the number of deaths, injuries, and in levels of political persecution. Revolutionary committees were established in many regions only after a final spasm of intense violence. Yet local annals describe a new wave of repression, conducted by revolutionary committees in the form of a campaign known in most localities as the "Cleansing of the Class Ranks" *(qingli jieji duiwu)*.

Table 8.1 illustrates the magnitude of the repression unleashed under revolutionary committees. It sorts into two groups the total number of reported deaths, injuries, and victims generated by the political conflicts of the period—or to be more precise, the subset of the reports that can be tied to specific events. In the first group are all reported deaths, injuries, and victims generated by political events from June 1966 until the month prior to the formation of a revolutionary committee in a city or a county (the median date was April 1968). In the second group are the same totals for the period beginning with the month that a local revolutionary com-

Table 8.1.   Reported Casualties and Victims, Relative to the Formation of Local Revolutionary Committees

Timing	Deaths (percent)	Injuries (percent)	Victims (percent)
Prior to Month the Revolutionary Committee Was Established	45,432 (24.7)	79,968 (32.3)	1,169,188 (11.1)
Month the Revolutionary Committee Was Established and Afterwards	138,348 (75.3)	167,506 (67.7)	9,373,596 (88.9)
Total	183,780 (100)	247,474 (100)	10,542,784 (100)

mittee was established, and through the end of 1971. The imbalance in casualty figures is striking: there were 3 times as many reported deaths in the latter period, 2 times as many injuries, and 8 times as many victims *after* the establishment of local revolutionary committees. What could possibly account for this?

Table 8.2 suggests an answer—the higher casualty rates were generated by organized political campaigns that were conducted almost simultaneously across the country. The table classifies all politically generated casualties reported during the entire period according to the type of activity described. The definition of deaths and injuries is clear (although local annals rarely distinguish permanently crippling injuries, other severe injuries, and minor wounds). The category of "victim" is more loosely defined. It includes anyone formally accused of a political crime, whether imprisoned or not; anyone who was fired from their jobs, expelled from their homes in the city and relocated to the countryside for political reasons (including family members expelled along with them); and anyone subjected to a violent struggle session or a harsh interrogation.

Two things stand out in Table 8.2. The first is that the actions of authorities generated far more reported deaths and victims than the actions of insurgents—by several orders of magnitude. The second is that the political campaign known as the "Cleansing of the Class Ranks" was by far the single most important generator of casualties and victims. Of the 183 thousand deaths recorded in local annals that are tied to a specific event or period of time, half are attributed to this campaign alone. And of the 13.4

Table 8.2. Summary Data on Deaths, Injuries, and Victims, by Reported Causes

Cause	Deaths	Injuries	Victims
Insurgents			
Insurgent Conflicts	30,412	101,051	16,690
Other Insurgent Actions	5,053	6,255	510,962
Total Insurgents	35,465	107,306	527,652
Authorities			
Suppression of Insurgents	34,129	39,542	1,954,584
Cleansing of Class Ranks	96,608	93,714	5,643,235
Other Campaigns*	9,323	595	2,093,393
Total Authorities	140,060	133,851	9,691,212
Other (unclear)	8,303	6,332	323,921
Total	183,828	247,489	10,542,785
Grand Total**	275,052	370,304^	13,410,207

 * Specifically, the "One strike, three anti" campaign *(yida sanfan)* and the campaign to investigate "May 16 elements" *(wuyaoliu fenzi);* these campaigns occurred primarily during 1970 and 1971.

 ** Includes summary data provided in annals that are not tied to specific dates or types of events.

 ^ Estimated based on ratio of deaths to injuries in the previous row.

million reported victims, no fewer than 42 percent were generated by this campaign, which typically commenced immediately after the formation of a revolutionary committee. Two other campaigns, known as the "One Strike, Three Anti" and the investigation of "May 16 Elements," typically began during 1970 and 1971, respectively, and fall after the period covered in this book. The two latter campaigns were much less violent but generated more than 2 million reported victims. These three campaigns, carried out in an organized fashion by established revolutionary committees, generated a reported total of 7.6 million victims, well over half of the total number of reported victims from all causes.

   Why were actions of authorities so much more damaging than the violent insurgencies that persisted across China for almost two years? And in particular, why did these late campaigns generate so many more reported casualties than the violent factional warfare of the earlier period? One possible interpretation is that there are simply more complete records for organized political campaigns than for the chaotic events in the prior period. It is likely that reports of casualties generated by factional clashes are less complete. But even if we could adjust for differences in reporting, large differences would likely remain.

The answer is more likely to lie in the process of restoring political authority at the level of local communities and workplaces. The establishment of a revolutionary committee over a city or county was only the first step in rebuilding political order. It generally marked the effective suppression of factional alliances that spanned across counties and cities, deeply crippling if not eliminating their ability to coordinate political action. This, however, only served to push factional antagonisms back into individual offices, factories, schools, and villages. The animosities and rivalries survived, but they were now bottled up in smaller settings. The heads of provincial revolutionary committees continued to complain about a plague of grass-roots factionalism in factories, offices, and local communities for a year or more after revolutionary committees were established.[7] Political authority still had to be reestablished at lower levels of social organization after a prolonged period when all manner of military and civilian authority had been openly defied. This was an intense period of state building at the grass roots. The reimposition of these highly intrusive and partially militarized state structures involved the intensive application of repression across all grass-roots social organizations.

While these campaigns targeted individuals with a history of challenging authority or who continued to defy the new order and pursue factional animosities, the Cleansing of the Class Ranks was explicitly designed to attack a much broader slice of the population. The campaign originated at the national level with an editorial in *People's Daily* on New Year's Day, 1968, which called for the cleansing from society of a variety of class enemies and traitors. A May 1968 report of how the campaign was conducted in a factory in Beijing served as a model for emulation throughout the country. The factory's military control committee, staffed by officers from an elite military unit, carried out a campaign that focused on older personnel who had worked in the factory under the Japanese occupation and the Nationalists. Mass meetings exposed alleged traitors and unmasked hidden counterrevolutionaries. The suspects were subjected to struggle sessions, forced to write confessions, and warned that leniency would be extended only to those who confessed fully.[8]

The Cleansing Campaign reached more localities than the 1967 wave of rebel power seizures, and it was conducted even in regions that never reported insurgent activity or factional battles. The annals from 89 percent of all localities reported activity related to the Cleansing Campaign, compared to 81 percent that reported a power seizure, 76 percent that reported insurgent activity, and 66 percent that reported violent factional battles. April to October 1968 was the high tide of the campaign's spread—the median date was August. Fewer than 6 percent of reports occur prior to the month that a local revolutionary committee was formed, and more than half of all reports are within the first 5 months after its establishment.

The campaign was organized in local government offices, factories, schools, and collective farms by "case groups" *(zhuan'an zu)* that were expected to bring charges against suspects. Political dossiers were scoured for evidence of suspicious behavior or past associations. As it unfolded across the country the case groups began with suspicions, moved to accusations, and then interrogated suspects with the aim of securing a confession. The questioning was typically harsh and threatening. Despite instructions from Beijing that only "principled" methods be employed, coercive interrogations and physical abuse were common. According to subsequent reports, sadistic tortures were applied by some of the more zealous case group interrogators. Many suspects died under interrogation or committed suicide. One of the reasons why the number of victims of this campaign was so high is that an admission to counterrevolutionary activity implied that one had co-conspirators. Those who named names under coercion, hoping to end their ordeal, served only to drag other suspects into the campaign's machinery. Suicide was considered an admission of guilt and was decried as a barrier to extracting the names of additional co-conspirators. Those judged guilty of particularly serious offenses were executed.[9]

But deaths due to executions, excessively brutal interrogations, and suicide were a tiny percentage of the numbers investigated and charged during the course of this campaign. In Shanghai, where it ran from January 1968 through April 1969, 169,000 individuals were placed under investigation, and the official death toll among these suspects (5,000, based on "partial" statistics) suggests that the death rate among those accused was roughly 3 percent.[10] These numbers fit broadly with the death rate implied by the casualty numbers for the Cleansing campaign in Table 8.2. Of the 5.6 million individuals who were reported in local annals to have been victimized nationwide during the campaign, 96 thousand reportedly died— 1.7 percent. Despite the low apparent death rates among victims, the wide scope of the campaign and the unpredictability about who might be accused was likely more than enough to deter any disgruntled rebels who still had thoughts of challenging authority. It seems likely that this was in fact the campaign's intent.

If the death rates during the campaign were so low, how did the overall death toll become so large, outstripping by a factor of 3 the total reported death toll due to all insurgent activities in the prior period? And how did the total number of victims become so large—more than 10 times the total number of reported victims of the rebel movement and related factionalism (a reported 5.6 million versus 527,000)?

The overall numbers might suggest that the Cleansing Campaign was conducted with a ferocity that far outstripped that of the violent period that preceded it. But there is a less dramatic and more plausible explanation. Unlike the factional warfare of 1967 and 1968, almost every adult in China was potentially at risk in the Cleansing Campaign. Only a fraction of the population joined a rebel faction, and even fewer were armed combatants. The majority of adults were uninvolved in the dramatic conflicts of the recent past. Combat between rival mass factions took place primarily outside of workplaces, across city districts, in nearby rural counties, or the streets of county towns. Moreover, while large factional battles were common in 1967 and 1968, they were brief events, and still relatively rare. There were 4,411 violent factional clashes mentioned at some point in time across 2,246 cities and counties. But only 66 percent of these cities and counties reported at least one violent clash. Even within the cities and counties that reported factional warfare, only small percentages of the adult population, primarily young males, would have participated actively in the combat brigades organized by rebel factions.

Direct evidence about the percentage of citizens who were involved in factional combat is very rare, but a local history for one county in Guizhou Province provides a detailed breakdown. The account states that at the height of factional warfare in late 1967, the two local factions were evenly matched, with 3,318 "hardcore rebels" (zaofan gugan) in one faction and 3,682 in the other. These two groups together represented roughly 11 percent of the total adult population of the county.[11] There were surely others who were associated with factions who did not participate in combat brigades, but they would not have been exposed to combat risks.

By contrast, the Cleansing Campaign was carried out in hundreds of thousands of grass-roots organizations—schools, urban workplaces, and collective farms—each of which was expected to find and punish political deviants. Unlike brief events connected with rebel insurgencies, the campaign was systematically applied over a sustained period. As people returned to their places of work, they were all exposed to the campaign, whether or not they had been involved in factional activities. The campaign's startling scope and the surprisingly large counts of casualties and victims are the consequence of this shift in organizational settings. One could escape from factional warfare simply by not participating, but very few adults who worked outside the home could escape exposure to the Cleansing Campaign.

This also helps us to understand how a certain kind of state capacity was restored so quickly after a near-complete collapse of civilian governments. The deeply militarized structure of the Chinese party-state, which predated this period, explains how order could be restored so quickly through a well-organized application of repression, once Beijing's support for the application of armed force was unambiguous. In reality, the core of the new government in the vast majority of localities was the party organization within the armed forces, which was still largely intact. "Party core groups" were established during this period, dominated by military officers and including selected civilian party officials—many of them previously "cadre rebels"—who survived the tumult and were offered positions on revolutionary committees. Cooperative leaders of favored mass factions that managed to survive the Cleansing Campaign were also included in these new leadership structures, though in practice they had little real authority.

Rebellion versus Repression over Time

The surprisingly high levels of repression so evident in this later period raise a broader question about the overall pattern of rebellion and repression from the beginning of these upheavals in mid-1966 to their end. How does the wave of repression that began in mid-1968 compare with the damage done by Red Guards and rebel insurgents during the previous two years? Figure 8.4 tracks the deaths generated by the activities of insurgents and by the actions of authorities over the 43 months from June 1966 to December 1969.[12] These trend lines make clear that the deaths generated by the actions of insurgents outstripped those due to repression by authorities until late 1967, when the armed forces were given greater freedom to use force to constrain the upsurge of factional warfare in August of that year. The early peak in the death count in the summer of 1966 corresponds

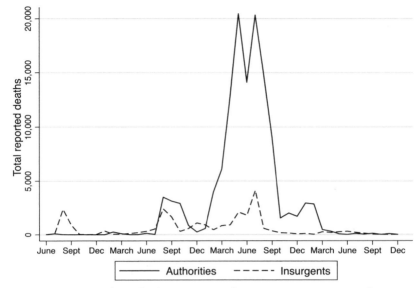

Figure 8.4. Reported Deaths due to Actions of Insurgents versus Actions of Authorities, by Month, June 1966–December 1969

with the violence of the early Red Guard movement. Interestingly, death counts during the wave of power seizures in early 1967 were considerably lower. Not until the summer of 1967 did insurgent violence generate death tolls comparable to this early period. Insurgent conflicts generated a much higher death count in mid-1968, during the last-ditch factional battles that coincided with the formation of revolutionary committees. The massive upsurge due to repression by authorities that ran from February to October 1968 was completely off-scale—far in excess of any previous actions by authorities, who were by comparison highly restrained prior to late 1967, and far in excess of the death tolls due to insurgent violence at any point in time.

How do these magnified death tolls relate to the formation of local revolutionary committees? Figure 8.5 arrays the same data in a way that is more meaningful in terms of local political conflicts, with "0" representing the calendar month that a local revolutionary committee was formed, negative numbers months before, and positive numbers months afterward. It shows that the death tolls from insurgent activity began to decline four months prior to the establishment of a revolutionary committee. The death

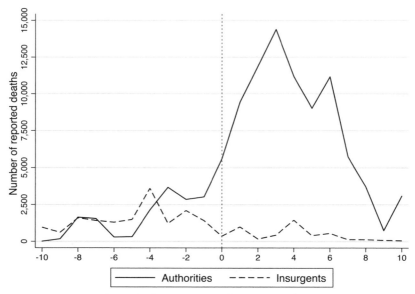

Figure 8.5. Reported Deaths due to Actions of Insurgents versus Actions of Authorities, Relative to the Formation of Local Revolutionary Committees

tolls due to repression by authorities did not surpass the insurgent death counts until three months prior and continued to increase in the months leading up to the restoration of local governments. They accelerated to unprecedented levels afterwards, despite the continuing decline of insurgent activity.[13]

Death tolls indicate the violence associated with rebellion and repression, but they are not an accurate reflection of overall levels of political persecution. Many more people were made to suffer in ways that did not involve deadly violence. The difference in the numbers victimized by insurgents versus authorities is much larger even than the gap for death tolls. More than 4 times as many people were reportedly killed by the authorities than by insurgents, but the authorities reportedly created more than 18 times as many victims as insurgents (calculated from numbers in Table 8.2). The reasons are the same—the victims of authorities were generated by political campaigns that were carried out in an organized fashion throughout the country in basic-level social organizations, exposing literally the entire population to a militarized new state structure.

The early Red Guard and rebel movements engaged in fierce persecutions in their initial months. Their activities were highly publicized, widely observed, and left deep impressions in popular memory. But the number of students and rebel activists was relatively small, and their persecutions were sporadic and unorganized. There is nonetheless some justification for the reputation of the Red Guard and rebel movements as particularly violent. There was one death for every 15 individuals reportedly persecuted by insurgents, while there was one death for every 70 people victimized by the authorities (calculated from figures in Table 8.2). Based on the information provided in local annals, it would appear that one's prospects for survival were much higher if one was targeted for persecution by authorities rather than insurgents.

A Broader View

By any comparative standard, the first three years of China's Cultural Revolution deserve to be ranked among the largest political upheavals in modern history. The accounts in local annals describe remarkable levels of political mobilization and collective violence. While these claims are plausible, they lack precision. How does China's upheaval of 1966–1969 compare with other major instances of domestic political conflict or state-directed repression? This question has both quantitative and qualitative dimensions.

The quantitative dimension is obscured by the partial nature of the accounts recorded in local annals. Only a fraction of the events that occurred in Chinese localities during these years were recorded in the annals. Of the events that were reported, only a fraction provided specific numbers of deaths, injured, or other victims. The potential scale of such underreporting is evident when one compares the numbers tabulated from city and county annals with totals occasionally provided for provinces as a whole—both published accounts and unpublished government reports. The two provinces that reported the highest numbers of deaths, reflecting considerable statistical detail in the annals, are Guangdong and Guangxi. The local annals in our database from Guangdong reported a total of 31,012 deaths related to the political events of the period. Summary figures for Guangdong published in China, however, report a total of 42,227 "abnormal" deaths during the same period.[14] Even larger gaps in reporting are evident when one compares published accounts with the classified internal investigation reports from Guangxi. The published annals from Guangxi reported a total of 55,651 deaths—by far the highest number for any province. The compilers of these accounts were able to provide such statistical detail due to the availability of unpublished investigation reports for every city and county in the province that recorded a much higher total—82,868.[15] Even in this instance, where the compilers of local annals had access to exhaustive and authoritative investigation reports, they chose to publish only two-thirds of the internal numbers.

The underreporting in the city and county annals for other provinces could be much more extreme. The annals for the urban districts and rural counties of Beijing reported a total of 5,807 deaths, while a published account for the city provided a figure of 10,275.[16] The Jiangsu local annals reported a total of 3,877 deaths, while a published provincial history reported more than 30,000.[17] In Shanxi, the same gap was 3,753 versus a number just under 20,000.[18] These examples suggest that at their most complete, local annals reported two thirds of the actual number of deaths (Guangxi), but others report well below 20 percent (Jiangsu and Shanxi). This assumes generously that published provincial figures are not themselves undercounts.

Editorial policies of provinces had a major influence on the detail provided in local annals. Journals devoted to the compilation of local annals conducted a spirited debate during the 1980s about how much detail to provide about the conflicts of this period.[19] Many provinces clearly chose to provide markedly less detail than others. The average number of reported deaths by provinces was in excess of 8,500, but the median was only 3,877, a highly skewed level of statistical detail. The average figure for provinces below the median is only 1,941.

Despite obvious and widespread underreporting, there were still 275,052 total deaths reported in the 2,246 city and county annals in our database. This clearly is only a fraction of the total number of deaths generated by the events described in this book, and by other events not recorded in local annals—but how small a fraction? In a separate publication, I have examined in considerable detail the differences between summary provincial figures and tabulations from city and county annals, and between published and unpublished accounts. I also employed sample selection models to predict the likely underlying numbers at the city and county level. This effort generated a deliberately conservative range of estimates that ran from a lower limit of 1.1 million to an upper limit of 1.6 million deaths. This would imply that the city and county annals reported anywhere from 17 to 25 percent of the underlying death count.[20]

After publishing these estimates, I encountered an article published in a Hong Kong magazine that was purportedly based on two classified investigations commissioned by the Central Committee of the Chinese Communist Party. I have not been able to obtain copies of these reports. The first investigation, compiled in 1978, reportedly counted a total of 1.25 million deaths. The second, completed in 1984, reportedly based on a longer and more thorough investigation, was said to have concluded that the actual death toll was 1.73 million. The close correspondence between these figures and the range of estimates that I generated independently by other means (1.1 to 1.6 million) gives me greater confidence in my earlier estimates and suggest that the underlying number actually is close to the higher end of my estimated range.

My confidence in the credibility of the article about the Central Committee estimates is enhanced by additional detail it provided. In my database, there were a total of 29,646 deaths directly linked to armed factional battles—close to 16 percent of reported deaths that could be linked to specific types of events. The comparable percentages for the Central Committee investigations described in the article were very close to this estimate: around 14 percent in both the 1978 and 1984 documents.[21] I therefore find this report to be credible, and am more confident than I was originally in an estimate at the upper limit of my previous estimated range—1.6 million deaths from all causes.[22]

The number of victims reportedly enumerated in the Central Committee report of 1978 also closely corresponds to my earlier estimates (there were no comparable tabulations for the 1984 report). That early investigation, which was of more limited scope than the second, reportedly counted 21.4 million people who were "accused and attacked," another 3.8 million who were "accused and investigated" and another 1.15 million "arrested and imprisoned"—a total of 26.4 million, close to the midpoint of my earlier published estimate of 22 to 30 million victims. The definition of "victim" covers only those directly attacked for political reasons during this period. It excludes the impact of these attacks on close family members of those accused, investigated, and imprisoned. During this period, one would generally assume that a nuclear family had 4 to 5 members, which would suggest, based on my estimated range of direct victims, that these persecutions directly affected anywhere from 106 to 150 million closely related individuals. The 1978 Central Committee investigation reported 123 million people who were "affected" in some way by these political attacks.[23]

These are very large numbers—do they confirm the idea that China's internal upheaval of the late 1960s was among the largest in modern history? As an aggregate number of deaths, 1.6 million would rank very high in any list of internal upheavals that did not involve sustained conventional warfare. Table 8.3 ranks China against some of the most notorious modern cases of internal civil strife and state-directed repression during the twentieth century. Only Cambodia under the Khmer Rouge surpasses the figure for the Cultural Revolution. China's death toll easily surpasses the high estimate for the "Great Terror" of the late 1930s in Stalin's USSR, and it doubles the estimate for the Rwandan genocide of 1994 and also the high estimate for the Indonesian massacres of 1965–66. Much lower down in these rankings are other episodes of extreme political violence. In terms of its magnitude, China's upheaval indeed does rank among the costliest episodes of political violence in modern history.

The magnitude of the death toll, however, tells us little about the intensity of violence and repression. The fact that events in China and Cam-

Table 8.3.   Ranking of Comparison Cases by Scale

Episode	Estimated Deaths
Cambodia—Khmer Rouge, 1975–1979	1.7 million
China, Cultural Revolution, 1966–1971	1.6 million
USSR, "Great Terror," 1937–1939	0.8–1.2 million
Rwanda, Massacre of Tutsi, 1994	800,000
Indonesia, Massacre of Suspected Communists, 1965–1966	400,000–800,000
Bosnia, Civil War and Ethnic Cleansing, 1991–1995	104,732
El Salvador—Civil War, 1980–1991	75,000
Guatemala—Counterinsurgency, 1980–1984	27,000
Taiwan, Nationalist Army Massacres, 1947	10,000–20,000

Sources: Bosnia (Zwierzchowski and Tabeau 2010); Cambodia (Cambodian Genocide Program 2013); El Salvador (Center for Justice and Accountability 2013); Guatemala (Ball, Kobrak and Spirer 1999, 119); Indonesia (Cribb 2002, 557–559; Robinson 2018, 120–121); Taiwan (Kerr 1965, 310); Rwanda (UNICEF 2013); USSR (Getty and Naumov 1999, 588–591; Werth 1999, 206–207).

Table 8.4.   Ranking of Comparison Cases by Intensity

Episode	(1) Estimated Deaths	(2) Base Population	(3) Deaths per Thousand
Cambodia—Khmer Rouge, 1975–1979	1.7 million	7.6 million	224
Rwanda, Massacres of Tutsi, 1994	800,000	6.0 million	133
Bosnia, 1992–1995	104,720	4.1 million	25.5
El Salvador—Civil War, 1980–1991	75,000	4.9 million	15.3
USSR, "Great Terror," 1937–1939	0.8–1.2 million	162 million	4.9–7.4
Indonesia, Massacres, 1965–1966	400,000–800,000	104 million	3.8–7.6
Guatemala, Counterinsurgency, 1980–1984	27,000	7.3 million	3.7
Taiwan, Nationalist Army Massacres, 1947	10,000–20,000	6.5 million	1.5–3.1
China, Cultural Revolution, 1966–1971	1.6 million	731 million	2.2

Sources: Table 8.3 and published population data.

bodia generated similar death tolls is remarkable—Cambodia's population was a tiny percentage of China's. An individual living in Cambodia under the Khmer Rouge was vastly more likely to be killed than an individual in China during the high tide of the Cultural Revolution. In other words, China's large death toll is partially an expression of its massive population. This makes it difficult to assess the intensity of China's upheaval in relation to severe episodes in much smaller political jurisdictions.

Table 8.4 sheds light on this question by ranking cases according to the proportion of their populations killed. By this metric, deaths per thousand, the Cultural Revolution ranks at the bottom of the same group of cases. Cambodia and Rwanda are extreme cases, where 224 and 133 per thousand of their total populations, respectively, were killed (that is, 22.4 and 13.3 percent). Of the others, only Bosnia (25.5 per thousand) and El Salvador (15.3 per thousand) had death rates higher than 1 percent. All of the other cases are a fraction of one percent (below 10 per thousand), and China's overall death rate was 2.2 per thousand. It is noteworthy that the death rate in China during the Cultural Revolution was roughly on a par with the death rate on Taiwan in 1946, when the Nationalist Army engaged in widespread massacres in response to a rebellion on the island against the imposition of Nationalist Chinese rule.

The figures in the table indicate that an individual in Cambodia under the Khmer Rouge was 110 times more likely to have been killed than an individual in China; in Bosnia, 12.5 times more likely. An individual in the Soviet Union during Stalin's "Great Terror" of the late 1930s would have been somewhere between 2.5 and 3.7 times more likely to be killed. Another way of illustrating these differences is to apply the death rates of these other cases to China's much larger population. If the intensity of violence and persecution in China had been the same as in Cambodia, China's death toll would have been 161 million; in Bosnia, 18.3 million; in the USSR or Indonesia, between 2.8 and 5.6 million. By these standards China's late 1960s upheaval did not approach the intensity of these other cases.

In a nation the size of China, however, there is ample room for wide regional variation. Were there regions where the intensity of violence approached any of these other cases? The obvious place to examine is Guangxi, which has a justified reputation for having unusually high death rates. The provincial population was 20.8 million in the census of 1964: the death toll in classified investigation reports of 82,868 implies a death rate just below 4 per thousand, which was twice the national average. This would place Guangxi on a par with Guatemala's fierce counterinsurgency campaign of the early 1980s, and near the lower end of the estimates for the Soviet Great Terror of the late 1930s and Indonesian massacres of the mid-1960s.

One would have to examine individual counties and cities to find death rates that were higher than the Guangxi average. There are 52 localities in the database where the reported death rates are above the Guangxi average of 4 per thousand—30 of them, not surprisingly, are in Guangxi, but another 22 are not. The largest number of these was in Inner Mongolia (8), which had an unusually intense suppression campaign that targeted ethnic Mongols.[24] There are only 5 counties in the database where the reported death rate exceeds 1 percent (or 10 per thousand). Three of them are in Inner Mongolia, and their death rates, based on published annals, ranged from 14 to 17 per thousand.[25] This was around 8 times higher than the national average—close to the death rates generated by El Salvador's long and bloody civil war, but still well short of the Bosnian genocide of the early 1990s. On a national scale violence of this intensity was very rare. Nonetheless, in relatively rare cases—in particular in Guangxi and Inner Mongolia—there were localities where the intensity of the violence would have ranked high among the most notorious cases in recent world history.

In qualitative terms these years in China differ in fundamental ways from these comparison cases, which represent a variety of different kinds of political activity. Cambodia was a systematic liquidation of alleged class enemies by trained cadres in a recently victorious communist insurgency. The Soviet Union was a case of state-directed terror by a well-established party-state. Rwanda and Indonesia were mass killings of targeted sub-populations by local activists who were actively assisted by civilian and military authorities. Bosnia was a case of ethnic cleansing by armed militants as part of a nationalist insurgency. El Salvador and Guatemala were cases of rebel insurgency and counterinsurgency. Taiwan represented military reprisals in response to a mass uprising.

What is distinctive about this period in China is that it is a mixture of qualitatively different elements that parallel the above cases only partially, and only part of the time. The first 18 months of the period we have examined was marked by a widespread insurgency of Red Guards, rebels, and rebel factions. There was no hint of this type of popular political mobilization in the cases of Cambodia or the Soviet Union—certainly no rebellion against established authority figures. There was widespread popular mobilization in Rwanda, Indonesia, and Bosnia, but the mobilizations were of militias that engaged in widespread mass killings of targeted ethnic groups or suspected political enemies. China's factional insurgencies of 1967 and 1968 bore certain resemblances to the conflicts in El Salvador, and the repression of rebel factions occasionally resembled the counterinsurgency campaign in Guatemala. But only a small fraction of the deaths generated in China were the due to these kinds of conflicts, and they were limited to the period prior to late 1968. China's Cleansing of the Class Ranks Campaign, on the other hand, bore a resemblance to the organized persecutions of the Soviet "Great Terror" of 1937–38, although it generated much lower death rates. The same is true of Cambodia under the Khmer Rouge. Some historians have suggested that Cambodia's unprecedented episode of mass killing was inspired by the ideology behind China's recent Cleansing Campaign, although the outcome in Cambodia was far more violent and deadly.[26] By contrast, only tiny percentages of those targeted in China's Cleansing Campaign were killed. Vastly higher percentages of those targeted as political enemies died in the USSR and Cambodia. The qualitative variation over time in the kinds of political activity we have examined in China during these years, and the shifting balance of rebellion and repression, make it difficult to find direct parallels, and add to the enigmatic quality of this remarkably complex upheaval.

What is most striking overall about this period of Chinese history, and what truly distinguishes it from comparable historical episodes, is how many people suffered severe forms of political persecution but nonetheless survived and lived well into the post-Mao period, sometimes rising once again into positions of authority. The same procedures utilized in estimating the death toll yield an estimate of roughly 26 million people who suffered direct persecution during this period, and perhaps another 100 million family members who were affected indirectly. The estimated death toll of 1.6 million implies that for each person killed during this upheaval, 16 victims survived. The overall number of victims was enormous, but the very high rate of survival is perhaps the most distinctive feature of this period of upheaval, and it is perhaps the reason why so many of those who lived through these years sought to document these events in ways that have made this book possible.

9
FINAL OBSERVATIONS

THIS BOOK HAS UNFOLDED AS A SERIES OF PUZZLES, compelling me to shuttle back and forth between description and explanation. Statistical patterns derived from city and county annals raised questions that required me to examine local narratives, and narrative accounts suggested possible answers that caused me to return to statistical patterns for confirmation. The final analysis is the product of this shuttling back and forth—from description to explanation, from statistical patterns to narrative. The central focus is the unfolding of events over time: their sequence and timing; shifts in national and local political contexts that presented evolving choices to local actors; the influence of prior events on subsequent actions; the influence of events at one level of the political hierarchy on the levels below; and the reshaping of political conflict through interactions between individuals and groups. Years ago, when I began this line of research, I shared my discipline's tendency to view rebellion as a function of the variable characteristics of groups and settings that promote or hinder political mobilization. The puzzles that have presented themselves along the way were not ones that I anticipated at the outset. Working on this subject has altered my understanding of this extraordinary period of recent Chinese history, and also my understanding of the sociology of politics.

The first of these puzzles is why and how power seizures spread so widely and so rapidly across the framework of the civilian party-state, despite the very limited prior spread of popular insurgencies. Prior research, to the extent that it explicitly addressed power seizures, unconsciously assumed that they were a product of popular rebellions that overwhelmed the state's capacity to respond. Observations of events in Shanghai and other provincial capitals encouraged this assumption, but as one moves the focus away from China's largest cities, the role of student and worker rebellions fades in significance and the role of cadre rebels moves to center stage. The extent to which China's state structures were overthrown rapidly across more than 2,100 small cities and rural counties has not previously been understood, nor has the role of party-state cadres in this process. The rapid collapse of state structures in early 1967 was not the contest between agents of the state and popular insurgents that is typically conceived in theories about rebellion and revolution. It was instead an inside-out process, in which the state's agents played a pivotal role in destroying the structures to which their group interests were intimately tied.

How could such a powerfully disciplined and centralized revolutionary state collapse so quickly? As it turns out, this was precisely because it was so disciplined and centralized. Even before the Red Guard movement was unleashed, the national political hierarchy was shaken by extensive nationwide loyalty investigations that purged large numbers of ranking officials and even larger numbers of lesser officials for alleged political offenses. These purges heightened the awareness of cadres across China that they needed to stay on the right side of these unfolding conflicts, in order to ensure that they did not themselves suffer a similar fate. Political authorities nationwide welcomed and encouraged Red Guard mobilization, following Mao's very public lead, but only so long as it was limited to the destruction of temples and attacks on leaders of schools and workplaces and other ordinary citizens. When a rebel wing began to target local governments, many cadres cooperated actively with their leaders' efforts to divert and blunt rebel attacks. But after these efforts were condemned in the October Party Conference in Beijing, cadres throughout China, whether or not they had been Scarlet Guards, were compelled to reassess their political stances. The Scarlet Guard organizations rapidly disbanded, and many of their members and other cadres formed rebel groups to challenge their superiors. When cadres in party and government organs were themselves in rebellion, the authority of local leaders was more deeply undermined than it was by student and worker demonstrations and their periodic office invasions.

The top-down cascade of power seizures in early 1967, combined with detailed accounts of the rise of the cadre rebels, revealed that these political processes, which were internal to the state's structures, were a type of collective behavior addressed in threshold and critical mass theories. These theories emphasize the ways that group action is an outcome of dynamic interactions: how individual decisions to act are contingent on the observed actions of others. In the wake of the collapse of communist regimes across Eastern Europe and Eurasia from 1989 to 1991, these models were applied to the sudden and unexpected upsurge of popular rebellions. As it turns out, these same collective processes apply equally to the agents of these unitary and centralized state structures, which suffer from none of the structural flaws identified in previous "state-centered" theories of revolution. It is highly likely that the same processes were at work in East Germany, Czechoslovakia, the Soviet Union, and elsewhere during the "mass extinction" of communist regimes.

In this case, however, I have modified a key assumption of these models. They typically assume, like interest group models, that the preferences of individuals are fixed—exogenous to the activities of interest. What changes in these models is the propensity of individuals to act on these preferences, something that is contingent on the actions of others. The cascade of internal power seizures by cadre rebels was a process that was subtly different. What we observe is not a shifting propensity to act on prior political preferences, but a shift in political preferences. The collective choices of cadres violated the interests that they presumably shared as a group—the preservation of a system in which they held high status. Their collective behavior served to undermine these structures and ushered in a period of extraordinary upheaval. In other words, threshold and critical mass models of collective behavior apply not solely to the propensity to act on stable interests. They apply also to the endogenous formation of political preferences.[1]

The second puzzle is why new factions formed in the wake of these power seizures, and why factional divisions intensified despite widespread military intervention ostensibly intended to support rebels who had seized power. The origins of these factional divisions, as we have seen, were the same structural features that promoted rapid mobilization of political action in schools, workplaces, and party and government agencies. Red Guard and rebel organizations grew out of the organized networks that ordinarily served as the regime's instruments of mobilization and control. The result was a pronounced pattern of bloc recruitment familiar to analysts in other political settings. This meant that rebel alliances prior to January 1967, even where they existed, were fragmented collections of smaller solidary groups, each of which had their own leaders. This grass-roots pattern promoted mobilization, but it also contained the seeds of later divisions that fatally divided rebel movements.

In the vast majority of localities, the move to seize power was actually the first occasion where local rebels attempted to forge a coalition. In the many small cities and rural counties where there was limited or only nascent rebel activity among students and workers, rebel cadres frequently coordinated rebel power seizures or seized power on their own. They moved quickly, under pressure created by power seizures in the province, cities, and prefectures above them. In the rush to act, many other rebel groups were inevitably left out of power seizures. When they protested their exclusion, and moved into opposition, the seeds for new factional alignments were sown. In short, the limited development of popular insurgencies, and the fragmented nature of rebel movements even where they flourished, were the foundation for the ubiquitous splits created by the rush to seize power across China in early 1967.

It was at this point that military intervention was crucial. The interventions of military actors in a setting of widespread rebel discord served to crystallize these nascent divisions and harden them into increasingly coherent and self-conscious political factions. The role of the armed forces in creating the foundations for more than a year of factional warfare was revealed when it became clear that military intervention was rapid and even more extensive than the wave of power seizures. Nascent divisions among rebel groups were crystallized and hardened by the interventions of army officers and local People's Armed Departments. The armed forces were forced to choose sides, often haltingly and unwillingly, in the disputes among rebel groups over power seizures, and their actions inevitably favored one side over another. The rebels who were favored by the army's decisions became their staunch supporters, while rebels whose claims were ignored or denied by the military became their opponents. Initial moves by the armed forces to suppress opposition hardened these splits, and the April 1967 orders that undercut army authority and ordered the release of all prisoners and the legalization of banned rebel organizations fueled anti-army rebellions. This, in turn, compelled rebel groups initially favored by the armed forces into a closely supportive alignment with them. In a period when their military backers were restrained from directly using force against their rebel opponents, their rebel supporters defended them, and in so doing defended their own claims against those of their rivals.

Support or opposition to local military control, then, did not express inherent stances of different social groups to the restoration of the status quo ante, nor was it a continuation in masked form of prior clashes between groups opposed to, and supportive of, now-deposed local officials. These factional stances, instead, were the product of contingent political interactions between the armed forces and rebel groups in the context of disputed claims about power seizures. If the armed forces supported your claims, you became their allies; if they supported your opponents and punished you for disputing their actions, you became their opponents. This undercut the core of the reasoning behind interest group explanations and forced me to think about contentious politics in ways different from the paradigm of fixed interests in dynamic circumstances. Factional orientations toward military control were an expression of histories of interaction among local rebels and military units, not of some preexisting orientation toward China's social and political order.

The third puzzle is why violent warfare between factions became so widespread, and why it escalated over time, reaching a crescendo in 1968. To explain the formation of factions does not in itself account for the violence between them. This puzzle forced me to reverse the emphases of many theories about rebellion, which focus on mobilizational capacity and repression, essentially how rebellions are sustained, and instead examine how rebellions end—exit from collective action. Closer examination of where and when violent warfare intensified led to the discovery of escalation traps in a limited number of regions that generated the largest casualties.

The regions that languished for the longest periods of time under military control without a final political settlement—defined as the establishment of a revolutionary committee at both the provincial and local level—accounted for the vast majority of the violence during 1967 and 1968. Moreover, in these regions, the intensity of factional warfare escalated over time, reaching a peak shortly before a final political settlement. When a province was placed quickly under a new form of government ratified by Beijing, and ultimately by Mao Zedong, local compromise between nascent factions was easier to obtain, and local revolutionary committees formed relatively quickly. Rebels who lost out in these settlements relinquished potential gains that would have come from victory, but they would not have faced severe retribution. These localities experienced almost none of the factional warfare observed in other regions of China. However, even within provinces that established revolutionary committees early in 1967, the establishment of local revolutionary committees came almost to a halt after strict limits were placed on military units in April 1967—and especially after challenges to military units were encouraged from Beijing in July of that year. After that point, even in provinces with early revolutionary committees, localities that remained under military control suffered relatively high levels of collective violence that escalated the longer that military control endured without a final political settlement.

The upsurge of violence as political settlements approached in these regions suggested that factions had fallen into a kind of escalation trap. After a certain threshold of violent warfare had been crossed, each side fought with increasing intensity to avoid the retribution that would likely follow from their defeat. Rebel factions opposed to military control fought with increasing intensity to force the removal and replacement of military commanders who supported their rivals, while the opposed factions fought equally hard to ensure that supportive military commanders would remain to impose order in the form of a revolutionary committee. Each side understood that there was no exit from local communities and workplaces. Departure for other regions of China was impossible, and they faced violent retribution in the short run and likely discrimination in the long run if antagonistic commanders and factions assumed control of a local revolutionary committee. This led to the otherwise somewhat anomalous pattern in which the intensity of violence escalated to unprecedented levels as overall levels of factional conflict declined. Patterns of suppression at the end of local insurgencies in these regions indicate that these expectations about violent retribution were realistic.

The fourth and final puzzle is why the largest numbers of casualties and victims during this entire period—by far—came only after the suppression of rebel insurgencies and the dismantling of their capacity to coordinate activities across workplaces. The casualties generated by the rebel insurgencies and violent factionalism of 1967 and 1968 were dwarfed by those due to the repression of rebel groups and the subsequent rebuilding of the political order. The vast majority of deaths and victims generated by the events of 1966–1969 were at the hands of military or civilian authorities. This may surprise those whose impressions of the Cultural Revolution are shaped by reading horrific accounts of cruelty and violence committed by the Red Guards and the rebels in schools and workplaces, or dramatic descriptions of chaotic civil unrest and armed battles during the upheavals of 1967 and 1968. As it turns out, the forces of order were far better organized and far more active across China's many political jurisdictions, and most of China's adult population, not just factional combatants, were exposed to risk. Where one might have expected ferocious and deadly persecution campaigns, the reality was more mundane—the simple arithmetic of a national political hierarchy, with enormous reach, that could generate a massive toll of victims with relatively small numbers targeted in each local community. Their application of force in the suppression of rebel organizations, and their conduct of the vast persecution campaigns designed to consolidate political order after the suppression of rebel insurgencies, generated far more deaths, and vastly more victims, than the disruptive insurgencies to which they were a response.

The analysis that I have offered in this book, which emphasizes events and processes, might appear to some readers to deny the salience of social structure. This is true only if one conceives of social structures as static regularities of the kind reflected in patterns of inequality, occupational categories, and formal organizations. In the analysis of political conflict in periods of severe disruption of existing institutions, however, one needs to be mindful of the idea that social structure is the product of regular patterns of social action, a "web of crystallized interactions."[2] What I have offered in this book is not a denial of structural explanation, but an emphasis on different conceptions of social structure and the relationships between these structures and political action. This analysis has been deeply informed by an emphasis on the organizational structures of the party-state, which under normal circumstances enhanced the unity and discipline of the state's agents, but that also compelled them in an altered context to turn against their own superiors. It also has emphasized the organization of workplaces, schools, and communities, which were also structured in ways designed to prevent independent political activity and to mobilize citizens toward regime-designated ends. In the altered context of late 1966, these same structures promoted the pronounced pattern of bloc mobilization that accounted for both the widespread mobilization of ordinary citizens, especially in large cities, and at the same time promoted the severe fragmentation and disunity that would serve to generate the factional rivalries that dominated Chinese politics in 1967 and 1968.

There are also strong reasons to suspect that micro-level patterns of informal social relationships, which are barely hinted at in the kind of sources employed in this study, played an important role in many of the initial rivalries that were reflected in patterns of bloc mobilization. There are hints in the most detailed local accounts of possible departmental rivalries between cadres in the police and security apparatus and those in economic planning departments. It is easy to imagine that the most active members of Scarlet Guard organizations had closer personal ties to their superiors than other cadres, who were not actively involved in them. It is also easy to imagine that relatively mundane personal rivalries and animosities proved to be the initial fracturing points for conflict at the outset of these events, and that they set into motion a train of events that would play out for many months thereafter. These are all elements of social structure that are highly relevant to the formation of factional conflict. They are not, however, readily observable at the level of analysis pursued in this book. To fully reveal them would require a detailed micro-level analysis of small-scale local settings. Findings from such a study, however, would not yield ready generalizations across local settings on a national scale, especially of the kind that interest group models derive from static categories based on occupational position or rank.

A final point about the kind of structural analysis pursued in this book is that the social structures that inform political action are no more static than the political orientations that evolve during sustained episodes of conflict. Moreover, the ones that matter most are not the ones that were exogenously given by prior social categories, but instead were generated by events endogenous to these conflicts. In the wake of power seizures, new political categories were created based on structurally equivalent positions vis-à-vis certain rebels' claims to have seized power. These new categories served as the foundation for new insurgent identities, and the intervention of military units served to crystallize these group differences and spur the formation of more solidary and self-conscious political factions. Their ties to one another strengthened along with the antagonisms and conflicts that developed with rival groups. The kinds of categories that help us to analyze a stable structure of social and political inequality have only a contingent relationship to patterns of political activity. In complex historical episodes, it would be a mistake to designate the groups defined by these static categories as interest groups, and interpret the resulting conflicts through such a lens without careful attention to the sequences of events and the processes through which collective actors form.

At the outset of this book I referred to this analysis as a variety of "state-centered" explanation, though one that is distinct from the static macro-comparative theories of revolution to which that term has previously been applied. Instead, the focus has been on the political behavior of agents of the party-state, and the crucial impact that they had on the unfolding of violent political events. The first such instance was the collective behavior of party-state cadres that generated the fast-developing internal rebellions against local leaders and the rapid collapse of local state structures in early 1967. The second was the interventions by military actors in the resulting discord among local rebels in the wake of that collapse. Their contingent interactions with rival rebels crystallized emergent local cleavages and hardened the solidarities that generated the collective violence to follow. The militarization of these conflicts, and the alignment of rebel factions for and against military control, escalated the violence and its associated casualties. Finally, the reimposition of order, especially in regions where military control had endured the longest without a political settlement, generated far more casualties and victims than the factional warfare that preceded it. Throughout this period, actors typically viewed as the forces of order fueled and accelerated the upheavals and the damage that they wrought in ways that could not have been anticipated by the presumed political interests of groups at the outset. This is the most sobering, and perhaps the most frightening, of the conclusions to be drawn from this study.

APPENDIX
LOCAL ANNALS DATA SET

THE ANALYSIS OF patterns of rebellion and repression presented in this book draws on a database of information extracted from local annals *(difang zhi)* published in China in recent decades. The central government mandated the publication of local annals for provinces, cities, and counties in the mid-1980s. They contain a wide range of information about local history, geography, climate, the economy, and local administration. These annals were published gradually, primarily during the 1990s. Only 14 percent of cities and counties had published one by 1990, but by 2001, more than 90 percent had done so. The last one consulted for this study was published in 2015. We found these volumes in a number of locations. In order of their importance, they were the Universities Service Centre Library of the Chinese University of Hong Kong; the Harvard-Yenching Library, the University of California-Berkeley East Asia Library; Stanford's East Asia Library, the Shanghai Municipal Library, and the Beijing National Library.

We scanned these narratives for accounts of specific kinds of political events. The events of interest were any report of political activity by civilian groups identified as Red Guards or rebels; and any reported political campaign or other actions by civilian or military authorities in response to independent political activity. Any actions that resulted in personal harm for at least one person, regardless of which actors were responsible, were also recorded.[1] The definition of "event" was of necessity somewhat flexible.

In some instances, the event was reported as a specific action that occurred on a single day; in other instances, certain types of events were reported as occurring repeatedly over a longer period of time. If the events in question could be dated to a specific calendar month, they were recorded in the database. Longer periods of time were treated as summary statements and not entered as single events in the database.

Like any source of information, users of a data set of events culled from printed sources need to be sensitive to potential sources of reporting bias. The first issue of potential concern is that these are retrospective accounts compiled by local governments 20 or more years afterwards. The sources do not approve of most of the activities that they describe, which raises questions about the political viewpoints of those who compiled the accounts. Some might argue that these accounts reflected the viewpoints of the victors, but it would be more accurate to say that they reflected the viewpoints of the survivors. These sources clearly disapprove of the disorders and violence of the period, but they never take sides in the factional conflicts that they describe.

What is perhaps most noteworthy about even the most detailed accounts is their striking lack of argumentation, analysis, and what passes for historical interpretation. This is most evident in the "chronologies of major events," but it is also characteristic of the more detailed historical narratives that are frequently included in the annals. There is almost no explicit effort to condemn or editorialize, nor is there any effort to explain. The annals describe factional battles, but they invariably take a strictly neutral tone: they do not portray one side as more commendable than another. Even the longest and most detailed of the supplementary narrative accounts are little more than chronological lists of events, sometimes accompanied by statistical detail. These sources are less elaborate and detailed than the press accounts that are commonly employed in analyzing protest movements in other settings.[2] Little more than factual chronologies of a stream of events, these accounts are especially useful for aggregation into a database that traces the unfolding of events over time.

These spare chronological accounts may nonetheless contain subtle biases introduced by the *types* of events that are more commonly reported, and the types about which they tend to be silent. The most obvious such bias is a clear reticence about reporting the activities of military units, especially those that place their activities in a negative light. The violent activities of civilian rebels receive extensive coverage, while direct description of the actions of military units are rare. There are 4,411 reports of violent clashes between rebel factions in the data set, 1,636 rebel actions against military units or military compounds, and another 753 actions by rebels against government officials or offices—almost half of all the events recorded in the database. Yet there are only 350 reports of any type of repressive action by military or civilian authorities against rebel groups—fewer than 3 percent of all reported events. Other sources consulted for this book make abundantly clear that military units played a central political role throughout this period, but this is not reflected in the event counts from these sources. For this reason, I have relied extensively on other sources in my analysis of the role of the military.

While there is little *direct* reporting of the activities of military units, there is an extraordinary amount of *indirect* evidence in these sources about their activities. This becomes abundantly clear when we consider the distribution of civilian casualties and other indicators of repression in the periods of time when military units were most active—in particular in the months leading up to and immediately after the formation of military-dominated revolutionary committees. Despite the reticence of local annals about direct description of military activities, it is precisely during the periods when army units fully exercised their powers of repression that casualties and other victims, as reported in local annals, reached unprecedented heights.

There is, therefore, a clear editorial slant toward reporting violent events by civilian rebels, and the implicit editorial tone is one of concern, if not outright condemnation. The party's official stance toward these events, formulated shortly after the death of Mao Zedong, is that they were a disaster for China—a clear reversal of what any account published during Mao's lifetime would have contended (and such accounts would surely have completely censored negative information). Yet despite this evident bias, the annals provide overwhelming evidence that the damage caused by rebel activity during the most chaotic period was only a fraction of that caused by repression at the hands of military units and revolutionary committees.

How might these biases in reporting certain kinds of events more than others subtly shape analyses based on these sources? There is an extensive literature on the evaluation of conflict data, much of it focused on the potential biases of newspaper reports, or of the differences between news sources and police or government records.[3] The most useful way to discuss this question is in relation to the major conclusions that I have drawn in this study. In particular, it is important to keep in mind that my analysis focuses very heavily not simply *what* happened, or *how often* something happened, but also *when* and *where* certain kinds of events are reported. The local annals do not describe Red Guard and rebel movements with approval, but they do make clear that they were widespread and created considerable havoc—but not everywhere, and not all at once. One of the key conclusions that I have drawn from accounts of the growth of student and worker rebellions is that they were not very far advanced prior to the wave of power seizures that began in late January 1967, and that therefore it is hard to credit popular insurgencies with the overthrow of local governments. It is hard to conceive of reasons for a bias toward *under*reporting rebel activity *prior to* the wave of power seizures. It is hard to think of how such a bias might cause them to report an upsurge of these events during 1967, only *after* the widespread interventions of military units, with which the chroniclers appear to be sympathetic. The annals may tend to report more of some kinds of activities than others, but it is hard to think of reasons why they would be more likely to report events during some periods of time rather than others.

Similarly, despite the widespread reporting of disorders due to rebel activity, and despite the implicitly favorable attitude of the chroniclers toward the restoration of order, the annals report far more casualties and victims at the hands of authorities than they do at the hands of rebels, and they report far more deaths and victims after the restoration of local governments in 1968 than they report at any time in the preceding period of rebellion and "chaos." In short, used with care, and with attention not simply to what is reported but when and where, one can extract a series of conclusions that are not plausibly related to the presumed biases of the annals, and that contradict what we might suspect are the compilers' implicit biases.

The entire database covers events from June 1966 to December 1971, although in this book I draw on evidence only through the end of 1969, by which point the suppression of the popular insurgencies of 1967–1968 was completed. It contains information about a range of political events in a total of 2,246 political jurisdictions.[4] This is 98 percent of the 2,293 counties and cities in existence in 1967.[5] Some of the jurisdictions in existence at that time have been abolished or combined with others; counties have become cities; and cities have absorbed counties into their boundaries. These changes have been reconciled by consulting standard compendia of administrative boundaries, along with local histories, to ensure that we have not omitted jurisdictions and that the information we have collected corresponds only to one location. Where we were unable to link information to the 1967 boundaries, we either left that jurisdiction as missing, or consolidated that information with a larger jurisdiction that merged earlier ones into a single unit.[6] There were very few cases that we were unable to resolve. The database contains information about close to 33,400 events dated to the month that they occurred, and somewhat more than half (17,800) according to the specific day that they occurred.

The work of locating these volumes and photocopying relevant sections for later analysis began in 1996, and was almost completed twelve years later. Two sections were the primary sources of relevant information. The first, included in almost every volume, is a "Chronology of Major Events" *(dashiji)*—a listing of notable events of all kinds. All but 19 of the local annals contained this standard chronology. The second are separate sections devoted to describing political events and Communist Party history—sometimes under the subheading "major political campaigns" or "Cultural Revolution." Only 65 percent of the annals contained relevant information about events in these other sections. In a small number of cases (104) we also recorded relevant information from other sources about specific jurisdictions.[7]

I have made this database publicly available, along with full documentation, code sheets, and instructions for coders. Those who are interested in the data and in the details of how the data set was compiled will find these materials online through my faculty page on the website of Stanford University's Department of Sociology.[8] I encourage interested scholars to analyze these data for themselves and publish their results. I will limit the discussion here to matters that will help readers understand the sources of information used in the tables and figures presented in this book. Those who want greater detail about specific subjects are free to explore the database and documentation on their own.

For statistical purposes, this data set should not be conceived as a sample of counties and cities—almost all of them are represented in the data set. It should be considered a non-probability sample of relevant local political events. The compilers of local annals decided which events to report, based on events about which they had information—which in turn was only a subset of all relevant events. Clearly, only a fraction of the political events that occurred nationwide during this period are recorded in local annals. This is true for all conflict data sets, whatever their source of information.[9] A probability sample would begin with a list of all localities and all relevant events, and would sample randomly from these lists. By definition, conflict data sets are never representative probability samples. Unlike most data sets of this type, this one includes information from the same kind of source for virtually every jurisdiction.[10] The primary concern, therefore, is variation in the likelihood that local annals will report events, which will reflect both editorial decisions and the resources devoted to compiling local histories.[11]

Excluded almost by definition are many hundreds of thousands of small-scale events—surely millions—that occurred within individual schools, factories, and collective farms. Only the largest and most consequential of these are mentioned in histories compiled at the county or city level. This is not a serious drawback. I am interested in insurgent activities that targeted provincial, city or county governments and their leaders, or actions by the forces of order to suppress rebellion. Activities that do not have an impact beyond the boundaries of schools or workplaces do not bear directly on the questions of interest in this book. In other words, the sources are biased toward reporting events that are relevant to the questions that I ask.

However, these materials also report only a fraction of the larger and more consequential events that *are* relevant to this inquiry—for example, invasions of government offices, clashes between rebel groups and the armed forces, armed battles between insurgent factions, seizures of party officials, and military suppression of armed insurgents. Even for the events that *are* recorded in these annals, information about their impact in terms of the number of people involved, or the number of deaths, injuries, or other consequences of the action is also incomplete. Due to limitations of information available to those who compiled local histories, the level of effort and resources put into the compilation, and the inherent biases reflected in what is considered appropriate or important enough to report, all data of this sort are filtered. The data set is a nonprobability sample from an underlying population of events, and any attempt to draw inferences from it must deal carefully with the potential biases of the sample.[12]

With newspaper data, there is no way to systematically gauge likely sample selection bias. With a virtually complete collection of local histories, however, the issue is not coverage but levels of detail. Each locality provides a narrative account, so the question of regional bias, so prevalent in news accounts, is not a concern. The problem, instead, is variation in levels of coverage of local events in these local histories. The level of relevant detail in local annals varied considerably at the level of counties, cities, and provinces as a whole. For each jurisdiction, the coders recorded the total number of Chinese characters devoted to describing all local events of whatever kind during this period of time. This is a way of gauging the quality and level of detail in local accounts, and how the length of an account influenced the level of statistical and narrative detail that it contained. In multivariate models, the length of the account can be employed in two-stage models designed to correct for sample selection.[13]

One Chinese character is not equivalent to one word in English: many Chinese words are compounds of two or more characters. To make variations in length more intelligible, I define one page as equal to 500 Chinese characters. The average number of relevant pages in local annals was 9.9 pages; the median was 7.4.[14] The number of pages is strongly related to level of urbanization, which in turn is related to the resources available to localities in compiling local histories. Annals from provincial capitals contain an average of 38.5 relevant pages; other prefecture-level cities, 19.9 pages; county-level cities, 15.1 pages; and counties, 9.0 pages. There are also wide differences in provincial averages. The most detailed annals by far were from Shaanxi Province (an average of 22.7 pages) and the two provincial-level cities of Beijing (20.7 pages), and Shanghai (16.7). At the opposite end of the range, 5 provinces averaged fewer than 6 pages—Jiangxi, Hubei, Anhui, Zhejiang, and Tibet. Tibet's were the least detailed—an average of only 3.3 pages. The provincial average was 10 pages, and the median was 9.6, which means that the provincial averages were not particularly skewed.[15]

The two most important determinants of the length of an account is the province in which it was published and the jurisdiction's level of urbanization. In a simple equation that predicts account length, province accounts for 15.7 percent of the variation (r-squared = .157). The second most important determinant is the size of the urban population, which alone accounts for another 13 percent of variation, and which together with province accounts for more than 27 percent of variation (adjusted r-squared = .271). A jurisdiction's total population is very weakly related to account length—it explains less than 5 percent of overall variation in account length by itself, and when added to an equation with province and urban population it does not have a significant net impact. This suggests that the length of accounts is a product of provincial editorial policy, as suggested by open debates conducted in journals devoted to the compilation of local annals during the 1980s, which pitted those who insisted that these politically sensitive events be chronicled only in "broad strokes," while others insisted on more extensive detail.[16] Also important is level of urbanization, which suggests that localities at higher levels of industrialization had more administrative resources to devote to the compilation of the historical sections of their annals.

The next question is how the length of accounts is related to the reporting of different kinds of events and related numbers of deaths, injuries, and victims. It should be evident that not all events of potential interest were reported in local annals, and not all of them provided similar levels of narrative or statistical detail. I assume that the length of an account is strongly related to the likelihood that an event would be reported, and especially to the likelihood that these events would be reported in detail. In reading large numbers of these accounts over the years it is clear that many annals describe major upheavals in highly cryptic terms, or refer to deaths or injuries without providing numbers. These broad references do not contribute evidence to the database, for the simple reason that a described event has to be dated at least to a specific month before it can be coded as an event for our purposes. Similarly, events that do qualify for inclusion, but that do not provide data about casualties or victims, are coded as reporting "0" casualties or victims, rather than treated as missing cases.

On the other hand, brief accounts might also indicate that there actually were few political events of interest during this period, and therefore that shorter accounts mean that there were fewer events to report. While this is surely true to some extent, the length of accounts is unlikely to correspond closely to the actual level of political conflict in the locality. One reason is that "chronologies of major events" are not limited to politics—they describe anything noteworthy that occurs. This can include the completion of major construction projects, natural disasters, epidemics, the implementation of government policies, local party conferences, and reports of bumper harvests or levels of industrial production. Variation in these sections reflects the level of resources devoted to the compilation and editing of annals, combined with editorial decisions about how to report sensitive topics. These sections sometimes betray obvious signs of this kind of self-censorship. One frequently finds that the sections devoted to major events for 1967 through 1971 are much shorter than for the immediately preceding or subsequent years. It may be the case that there were few conflict events during these periods, but it is highly unlikely that there were fewer events of *any* kind. In addition, the fact that local compilers chose not to provide a separate section that describes major political campaigns, or specialized historical accounts devoted to the Cultural Revolution, is itself a reflection of editorial decisions guided by political considerations, and to some extent perhaps a result of resource constraints.

Certain kinds of events were very widely reported—in particular many of the close to 19,000 events that were the "first report" of certain landmark events—for example, the first appearance of student Red Guards, the first appearance of "rebel" organizations that targeted local government officials, the date of the first local military intervention, the date of a power seizure that deposed the local government, and the date that a revolutionary committee was established. These events were reported by the vast majority of jurisdictions: 81 percent report a rebel power seizure over the local government; 90 percent reported the existence of local Red Guard activity; 93 percent reported the local intervention of military units; and more than 99 percent reported the establishment of a revolutionary committee. These figures make very clear that key events related to the major conflicts of this period occurred in the vast majority of local jurisdictions. The only significant variation for this subset of events is in their timing. Because such large percentages of localities reported these landmark events, and because there is no reason to suspect systematic bias in the reporting of the date that they occurred, we can be highly confident that the distribution of these events over time accurately portrays actual time trends.

Although the vast majority of localities reported these landmark events, they varied greatly in how much additional detail that they reported. Each jurisdiction could report no more than 1 "landmark" event, but there was no limit on the reporting of armed conflicts between mass factions, attacks by rebels on government agencies, clashes between rebels and military units, the armed suppression of rebels, or the conduct of political campaigns designed to suppress dissent. There was wide variation in detail on these kinds of events, and in addition, there was considerable variation in the extent to which local annals recorded statistics on the number of individuals killed, injured, or otherwise victimized by the events that *were* reported.

The total number of these "repeatable" events in the database is 14,259. No single province reported more than 10 percent of this number. Only 3 contributed more than 5 percent—Hebei (6.9 percent), Shaanxi (9.5 percent), and Sichuan (10 percent). At the opposite end of the distribution, 5 provincial jurisdictions contributed less than 1 percent of the total reported events, but all were jurisdictions with small populations (the cities of Beijing and Shanghai, and the provinces of Ningxia, Qinghai, and Tibet). The most common single type of event was an "armed battle" *(wudou)* between mass factions (4,390). The distribution across provinces in reporting this type of event was more skewed than for the overall number of events—the same 5 provinces that reported the lowest number of events overall also contributed fewer than 1 percent of the total number of armed battles. At the high end, the same three provinces were at the top of the distribution, and their respective contributions were 6.6 percent (Hebei), 10.5 percent (Sichuan), and 12.2 percent (Shaanxi). In sum, certain provinces appear to be more highly represented in the counts of events, but the variations appear to roughly correspond to the relative population numbers in these jurisdictions (for example, Sichuan's population was 10 times that of Beijing in 1967, and Shaanxi's was 10 times that of Qinghai).

Of greater concern are much wider disparities in the level of statistical detail linked to the reported events. Guangxi Province provided an unusually high level of statistical detail, even though its annals did not provide unusually high levels of narrative detail. As a result, this province, whose published annals contributed only 4 percent of the total number of events in the database, contributed 23 percent of the reported deaths.[17] The next highest number of deaths linked to specific events was in Guangdong Province, which contributed 9.9 percent of the total. The reporting of injuries linked to specific events was less skewed—Yunnan, Sichuan, and Inner Mongolia each contributed between 17.2 and 17.8 percent of the total number of reported injuries (Guangxi only 5.2 percent). The reporting of victims of some form of political persecution was even less skewed, with no province contributing more than 11.5 percent and another 5 contributing between 7.7 and 8.8 percent (Guangxi contributed only 4.8 percent).

The one concern raised by this discussion is the exaggerated role of Guangxi in reports of deaths. Because that one province contributed 23 percent of the total reported deaths from all conflict events, the distribution of deaths across event types or across time may distort our aggregate analysis for the country as a whole. The primary concern about Guangxi is only about the reporting of deaths—the province contributed only 4 percent of conflict events, and only 4.8 percent of victims of persecution. The distribution of event counts across the 11 different categories in our data set for Guangxi is almost identical to the distribution of reported event types in the rest of the country. However, the number of deaths that resulted from different types of events in Guangxi diverges from the averages for the rest of the country. A much smaller percentage of Guangxi's reported deaths come from armed battles between mass factions (6.6 versus 19.1 percent elsewhere); a much higher percentage of deaths come from the armed suppression of rebels (13.5 versus 0.7 percent elsewhere); and somewhat higher percentages of the deaths were due to other unspecified actions by authorities (20.5 versus 13.2 elsewhere). These differences reflect the extremely harsh armed suppression of rebel opposition in the summer of 1968, which is described in Chapter 8.

The distribution of deaths in Guangxi over the months of observation also diverges considerably from the rest of the country. The deaths reported for Guangxi are highly concentrated in a 5-month period from April to August 1968. These 5 months contained 85 percent of the total deaths reported in Guangxi for the entire 67 months from June 1966 to December 1971. Just below 30 percent of Guangxi's total occurred in one extraordinarily violent month—August 1968. The comparable percentage for the same 5-month period in the rest of the country is 56 percent, and for August 1968 only 12 percent.

Because of this concentration of deaths in a short period, and by a province that reported unusually high death counts, it is likely that Guangxi's experience distorts the national profile of violence over time. Figure A-1 helps us to visualize the way that the Guangxi data might alter our view of national trends.

The solid line represents China as a whole, including Guangxi, and the dashed line represents China as a whole, excluding Guangxi. The trend lines are almost identical until March 1968, at which point Guangxi's numbers begin to push the national totals upward. Guangxi's impact is first evident

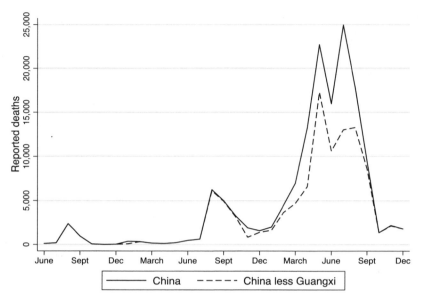

Figure A.1. Reported Monthly Death Counts, with and without Guangxi, June 1966–December 1968

in May, and is most pronounced during July and August. The concern about the distorting effect of Guangxi should be limited primarily to July and August.

This, however, raises a more difficult question. Because Guangxi's statistical reporting is unusually complete, and because the province has a deserved reputation for being particularly violent during these months, how can we decide how much of Guangxi's numbers distort national patterns, and how much the high death rates in Guangxi deserve to be included in the national totals? There is no easy answer to this question, but it is clear that any concerns that we have about Guangxi's oversized contribution to overall death rates should be focused on a few months in mid-1968. The close correspondence between the trend lines for Guangxi and the rest of the country, however, encourages confidence that any distortions will be relatively modest and easy to identify.

NOTES

I. AN ENIGMATIC UPHEAVAL

1. An analysis of Mao's political rationale, and a condensed overview of the period, are provided by Walder (2017).

2. For example, Andreas (2002); Blecher and White (1979); Chan, Rosen, and Unger (1980); Rosen (1981; 1982); Tang Shaojie (1999; 2003); Walder (1996; 2004; 2006b; 2009a); Yin Hongbiao (2009).

3. A near-exhaustive list of regional accounts would include Guangzhou (Hai Feng 1971; Yan 2015; 2018); Inner Mongolia (Yang Haiying 2014; Wu Di 2010); Jiangsu (Dong and Walder 2010; 2011a; 2011b; 2012a; 2018); Ningxia (Wu and Zhao 2007); Shaanxi (Tanigawa 2007; 2018); Shanghai (Li Xun 2015; Perry and Li 1997); Wuhan (Wang 1995); and Zhejiang (Forster 1990).

4. For example, MacFarquhar and Schoenhals (2006) tie their national narrative to an intensive analysis of politics in Beijing. One exception is Bu Weihua (2008), who provides a long series of capsule summaries of province-level developments.

5. Whyte (1975), Kraus (1977).

6. L. White (1989).

7. Lee (1975; 1978; 1979) was the first to pull these threads together into a coherent overall interpretation, the "radical-conservative hypothesis," which was a major interpretive breakthrough at the time.

8. For example, Hough (1977); Skilling (1970; 1983); Skilling and Griffiths (1970).

9. Skilling (1976).

10. As noted by Oksenberg (1968) and Vogel (1968; 1969, 321–347).

11. The canonical early statements were Oberschall (1973), Gamson (1975), McCarthy and Zald (1977), Tilly (1978), and McAdam (1982).

12. Rosen (1981); Walder (1978, 43–46; 1987); Gordon White (1974; 1980); Lynn White (1976).

13. Wu (2014a, 97–132).

14. The class label system is described in Walder (2015, 108–117). Its large impact on educational and career advancement has been demonstrated with retrospective life history data drawn from representative population samples (Walder and Hu 2009; Treiman and Walder 2019).

15. Andreas (2002); Chan, Rosen and Unger (1980); Rosen (1982); Unger (1982); Wu (2014a, 53–67).

16. Gordon White (1976); Wu (2014a, 67–82).

17. Walder (2009a, 123–154).

18. Walder (2009a, 136–154). The most penetrating and detailed analysis of this fascinating episode is Wu (2014a, 82–92).

19. Andreas (2009, 119–124); Walder (2004; 2006a).

20. Walder (2006b; 2009a, 27–87).

21. Walder (2006a; 2009a, 203–222).

22. Blecher and White (1979); Walder (1987; 1996).

23. Li Xun (2015, 381–416); Perry and Li (1997, 71–95); Walder (1978).

24. Dong and Walder (2010; 2018); Tanigawa (2007; 2018); Yan (2015; 2018). Xu Youyu (1999) was the first to criticize the common conflation of these early factional conflicts with the ones that emerged after the overthrow of local authorities.

25. The factional divisions within the party leadership of the factory originated during the recent Socialist Education Movement (also referred to as the "Four Cleans") in 1965 (Dong and Walder 2011a). Similar divisions due to the same campaign have been documented in a state-owned factory in Shanxi (Yang 2015), and in Shanghai (Wu 2014a, 134–136). Wu concluded that the factional divisions among officials at the Shanghai Diesel Engine Factory created splits among rank-and-file workers. In his words, this created a "swiftly shifting political field that exceeded the determination of its social composition" (Wu 2014a, 136).

26. Dong and Walder (2011b); Walder (2016).

27. In Xuzhou, for example, different rebel factions initially received support from military units in different military districts, and later, after military commanders split into factions, received it from different officers within the same military command (Dong and Walder 2018). Elsewhere in Jiangsu Province, officers from the Air Force supported rebel factions that sought to overthrow the regional military commander (Dong and Walder 2011b; 2012a). Similar patterns

have been documented in Shaanxi (Tanigawa 2007) and Ningxia (Wu and Zhao 2007).

28. Mehnert (1969); Unger (1991).

29. Wu (2014a, 158).

30. Wu (2014a, 141 and 170). Wu observed that "the emergent positions, identities, and politics of the recalcitrant rebels were the products of contingent, open-ended political processes" (Wu 2014a, 188) and that "Red Guard factionalism in Hunan was rooted in contingent political processes that may not be reducible to fixed social categories and interests . . . driven largely by organizational rivalry, personal power ambitions and local political accidents, originally minor incidents and conflicts became catalysts for widening antagonisms" (Wu 2014b, 26–27).

31. See, for example, the analysis of factions in the Beijing Red Guard movement (Walder 2006a) and three prominent Nanjing cases in Dong and Walder (2011a).

32. See, for example, Biggs's (2002) critique of variable-based approaches in the analysis of labor strikes, which is a concrete illustration of the more abstract distinction between variable-based and narrative approaches to explanation (Abbott 2001; Abell 2004).

33. Tilly (1964).

34. Tilly subsequently developed theories about collective protest that were a variety of interest group analysis and focused single-mindedly on processes of mobilization. He returned to an interactionist perspective much later, but in the trenchant critique of the tradition of analysis of contentious politics that he developed with others over the years, he neglected the insights developed in his first book (McAdam, Tarrow, and Tilly 2001).

35. Usually expressed as debates about the relative importance of rationality, structural constraints, or cultural understandings and personal identity (McAdam 1996).

36. Two excellent examples of this line of analysis are McAdam (1983) and Ganz (2000).

37. For example, Gusfield (1963); Kornhauser (1959); Lipset (1959); and Smelser (1959).

38. For example, Davies (1962); Gurr (1970); Johnson (1966); and Smelser (1962). An alternative early tradition is represented by the work of Moore (1966), who traced cross-national variations in political movements to class and community structures, and Gusfield (1963), who explained moral revitalization movements as a form of status politics.

39. Lodhi and Tilly (1973); Paige (1971); Shorter and Tilly (1968); Snyder and Tilly (1972).

40. See, for example, Oberschall's (1973, 104–113) critique of Kornhauser's theory about the vulnerability of "mass society" to extremist political movements.

41. Oberschall (1973, 118–119). McCarthy and Zald (1977, 1215), quoting from Turner and Killian (1972, 251), made an even more widely known statement of the same principle: "We are willing to assume . . . that there is always enough discontent in any society to supply the grass-roots support for a movement if the movement is effectively organized and has at its disposal the power and resources of some established elite group."

42. For a more detailed presentation of this argument, see Walder (2009b). Notable exceptions to this overall trend are scholars who continued to focus on the social origins of varied political orientations of rural rebellions (Paige 1975; Perry 1980), trade union movements (Kimeldorf 1988; Perry 1993), and the conditions under which class, ethnic or alternative identities find political expression (Hechter 1975; 2000; 2004; 2013; Kalyvas 2008; Olzak 1992).

43. Fearon (2004); Fearon and Laitin (2003); Toft (2003).

44. Cunningham (2011); Cunningham, Blake, and Seymour (2012); Kalyvas (2006; 2008); Pearlman and Cunningham (2012); Staniland (2012).

45. Kalyvas (2008, 1043).

46. Long ago, Oberschall (1973, 26) observed: "In situations of conflict where the aggregate outcome is determined by the intersection of several mutually dependent choices that cannot be treated as independent events, an interaction model of the process . . . is the appropriate model."

47. Parenthetically, this is why there is almost always a very large "error term" in regression equations, because variable based models often do not capture these "stochastic" processes.

48. The term and definition are Roger Gould's (1995). This is entirely different from the psychological conceptions of personal identity that some analysts claim to be crucial for political commitment and activism.

49. Zheng (2006); Walder (2009a, 211–215). A contrasting interpretation of this case is by Andreas (2009, 111–130), who emphasizes the fact that the two rebel factions that eventually emerged at Tsinghua expressed different stances toward the university's status quo. While demonstrating convincingly that there were no systematic differences in the membership or leadership of the two factions, he nonetheless treats the content of the factions' rhetoric as expressions of underlying orientations that were presumably stable.

50. As argued by Wu (2014b).

51. Munson (2008).

52. Markoff (1996); Markoff and Shapiro (1985).

53. Lee (1979, 302–322) offered a content analysis of factional newspapers in Guangzhou to substantiate his claim that the factions had different orientations toward the status quo. The most pronounced difference, not surprisingly, was toward the armed forces (p. 318). More recent work (Yan 2015) has shown that these political stances were adopted only after rebel disputes over the provincial power seizure and different responses to the imposition of military control. Yan showed that the faction originally deemed "radical" for opposing what they claimed was a "fake" power seizure was later portrayed "conservative" for supporting the armed forces for their unwillingness to ratify that power seizure.

54. Two classic works that deploy this concept with great effect are McAdam (1982), and Tarrow (1989). More recent developments of the concept are Koopmans (1993); Meyer and Staggenborg (1996); and Meyer and Minkoff (2004).

55. See Dong and Walder (2011b; 2012a); MacFarquhar and Schoenhals (2006, 99–101); and Walder (2015, 202–207; 253–262).

56. An early review of this work by Olzak (1989) distinguished usefully between static, cross-sectional research designs and dynamic analyses of sequences of events. The precursor of contemporary research in this vein was Sorokin (1937, 383–506), whose work strongly influenced Charles Tilly. Examples of the analysis of long-term patterns of change include a range of studies of 19th and 20th century Europe (Shorter and Tilly 1968; Tilly 1995b; Tilly, Tilly, and Tilly 1975); and ethnic conflict and racial violence in the United States (Olzak 1992; Tolnay and Beck 1995). Examples of the analysis of relatively brief and intense episodes of conflict include analyses of the French Revolution and its immediate aftermath (Markoff 1996; 1997; Markoff and Shapiro 1985), a tumultuous decade of protest and disorder in postwar Italy (Tarrow 1989); and the regional mobilizations that led to the sudden collapse of the Soviet Union (Beissinger 2002).

57. Organization Department, CCP Central Committee (2000, 12:1227; 16:1331).

58. Tilly (1986, 5).

59. Tilly (1995a).

60. Tilly (1986, 8).

61. Rowe (2007); Tong (1991).

62. For example, Kuran (1989; 1991) and Lohmann (1994).

63. For example, Skocpol (1979), Goodwin and Skocpol (1989), Goldstone (1991).

64. Walder and Su (2003); Walder (2014).

2. MOBILIZING A NATION

1. The scope and impact of this unprecedented free circulation of information is detailed by Schoenhals (2015).

2. Shirk (1982); Unger (1982).

3. Whyte (1974); Whyte and Parish (1984); Walder (1986).

4. Oi (1989); Parish and Whyte (1978).

5. First emphasized by Oberschall (1973), this later became known as "bloc recruitment." One variant of this idea was the "ecological" model that Zhao (1998) employed to explain the rapid mobilization of university students in Beijing in 1989.

6. MacFarquhar and Schoenhals (2006, 32–51).

7. MacFarquhar and Schoenhals (2006, 63–65).

8. This is explicitly mentioned as a motivation for regional leaders in the published memoirs of an official who was First Party Secretary of Jiangsu Province at the time (Jiang Weiqing 1996, 513).

9. CCP Central Committee (1966a; 1966b).

10. Bu Weihua (2008, 103–104).

11. Bu Weihua (2008, 105).

12. In Beijing, various sources indicate that in June 1966 more than 7,200 individuals were sent to "educational and cultural units" in the capital; over 6,000 to universities and institutes under central government industrial ministries; more than 1,000 were sent to institutes under the Ministry of Culture; and more than 5,500 sent to the city's middle schools (Walder 2002, 445 n. 11). In Shanghai on June 3, 168 work teams were sent to universities and high schools (Li Xun 2015, 76–77). Similar efforts were organized in the provinces: Jiangsu's provincial party committee dispatched more than 840 work teams to universities and government offices in mid-June (Jiangsu Provincial Annals Editorial Committee 2003, 314–315). Guangdong Province sent 900 investigators to colleges on June 7 (Guangdong Party History Research Office 2004, 205).

13. Su Hua (1987, 136); Su Hua and Hou Yong (1992, 111).

14. Fujian Province Annals Editorial Committee (2000, 370–371).

15. Contemporary China Editorial Committee (1992, 114–115); Gansu Province Annals (1989, 431).

16. Guangxi Cultural Revolution Chronology (1990, 2).

17. Tibetan Autonomous Region Party Committee Party History Research Office (2005, 240–241); Organization Department, CCP Central Committee (2000, 9:746, 752–753).

18. Bu Weihua (2008, 96–97).

19. Guangxi Party Committee (1987, 18:8–9).

20. Linzhi County Annals (2014, 224).

21. These events are detailed in Walder (2009a, 28–87, 123–133).

22. MacFarquhar and Schoenhals (2006, 84–85); Organization Department, CCP Central Committee (2000, 10:23).

23. CCP Central Committee (1966c); MacFarquhar and Schoenhals (2006, 86–92).

24. MacFarquhar and Schoenhals (2006, 106–110).

25. CCP Central Committee (1966d, 1966e).

26. CCP Central Committee (1966f).

27. The only provincial capital whose local annals did not report any Red Guard activity through the end of 1966 was Lhasa, the capital of Tibet.

28. Walder (2015, 135–151).

29. Walder (2009a, 88–173) details this progression in Beijing, and similar patterns have been documented for Shanghai (Li Xun 2015, 163–195).

30. MacFarquhar and Schoenhals (2006, 136–140); Organization Department, CCP Central Committee (2000, 10:23).

31. Beijing Party Committee (1966); CCP Central Committee (1966h).

32. State Statistical Bureau (1983, 511); China Education Yearbook (1984, 1001, 1005).

33. Li Xun (2015, 249–256).

34. This account is based on Nanjing Archives Bureau (1985, 4–6); and a longer narrative account in Dong and Walder (2011a, 18–22).

35. CCP Central Committee (1966g).

36. Li Xun (2015, 209–213). Over the next decade, Wang Hongwen would rise into political prominence in Shanghai and Beijing, only to be purged shortly after Mao's death in 1976 as a member of the "Gang of Four."

37. Li Xun (2015, 263, 266–288).

38. Li Xun (2015, 289–298).

39. Li Xun (2015, 303–335). Zhang Chunqiao, like the Shanghai rebel leader Wang Hongwen, would rise into the national leadership shortly afterward, only to be purged in 1976 as a member of the "Gang of Four."

40. For minutes of Politburo discussions of the issue on December 4, see CCP Politburo (1966); CCP Central Committee (1966i).

41. Nanjing Archives Bureau (1985, 9).

42. Guangxi Party Committee (1987, 17:801).

43. The formation of Scarlet Guards within individual party and government administrative offices is described in the province-level organs in Nanning

(Guangxi Party Committee 1987, vol. 18); in the prefectural administrations of Yulin and Qinzhou (Guangxi Party Committee 1987, 1:76–77; 13:248–249); in the municipal administrations of Guilin and Nanning, (Guangxi Party Committee 1987, 6:241–242; 13:68–69); and in Guiping, Lingshan, Lingui, Mengshan, Pubei, and Wuming Counties (Guangxi Party Committee 1987, 1:454–457; 3:117–118; 6:325–326; 13:209, 370–371, 506–507).

44. Guangxi Party Committee (1987, 13:248–249).

45. Guangxi Party Committee (1987, 13:209).

46. Guangxi Party Committee (1987, 6:325–326).

47. It seems likely that many rank and file workers without strong party affiliations would have been pressured to participate in these activities, forcing them to choose between Scarlet Guard and rebel groups.

48. This account is based on Nanjing Archives Bureau (1985, 6–12).

49. This summarizes a much longer and more detailed account by Li Xun (2015, 381–416).

50. Li Xun (2015, 503–563).

51. See Walder (2016).

52. Zhejiang Provincial Organs (1966).

53. Zhejiang Party History Research Office (2000, 240).

54. Mao Zedong, 9 January 1967, in Cultural Revolution Database (2002). The original source is unclear.

55. Perry and Li (1997, 14–18).

56. This condenses a longer and more detailed account in Li Xun (2015, 447–502).

57. Nanjing Archives Bureau (1985, 9–13).

58. Guangxi Party Committee (1987, 16:1, 16; 17:801–802).

59. Guangxi Party Committee (1987, 13:69–73).

60. Guangxi Party Committee (1987, 13:250–251).

61. Guangxi Party Committee (1987, 6:328).

62. Guangxi Party Committee (1987, 2:234).

63. Guangxi Party Committee (1987, 3:514).

64. Guangxi Party Committee (1987, 13:370–371).

65. Cases where it was not possible to determine clearly whether insurgents or authorities were responsible for the victimization are excluded from these figures.

66. For example, Walder (2009a).

3. THE PACE OF REBEL INSURGENCIES

1. These figures are calculated from the information in the database, which in turn is based on local annals and population yearbooks.

2. Local attacks on party and government organs persisted well into 1969, but 90 percent of them had occurred by the summer of 1968. This number does not include invasions of party and government headquarters that occurred during a rebel power seizure. Rebel power seizures, all but one of which occurred after the end of 1966, are analyzed separately in Chapter 4.

3. Beijing, a province-level jurisdiction like Shanghai, was also the seat of the national government, and many of the central government ministries and central party agencies were deeply disrupted during the last half of 1966. However, the national insurgency was also directed by the Maoist core of the central party-state, which was never subjected to rebel attacks in ways that party authorities were elsewhere. Moreover, the Beijing city government and party organization were devastated by the purges of May and June 1966, which removed at a stroke the incumbent officials who became the targets of rebel movements in other cities in subsequent months. Tianjin did not become a province-level city until late in 1967; it was still a county-level city in Hebei Province.

4. Shanghai Bureau of Statistics (1990, 60, 74).

5. Shanghai Bureau of Statistics (1990, 343, 348).

6. Li Xun (2015, 92, 121, 127, 130–137).

7. Li Xun (2015, 178–183, 187–188).

8. Li Xun (2015, 190–193).

9. Li Xun (2015, 423–443).

10. Li Xun (2015, 504–505).

11. Li Xun (2015, 508–515).

12. Li Xun (2015, 516–561).

13. Nanjing Annals Editorial Committee (1986, 92, 283, 677, and 686).

14. This account is based on a detailed chronology compiled by the Nanjing Archives Bureau (1985, 6–11).

15. This account is based on Guangzhou City Annals (1998, 113–119, 460–465), supplemented with material from Hai Feng (1971, 42–71).

16. Guangzhou Statistical Yearbook (1999, 47, 59).

17. Guangzhou City Annals (1999, 76, 193, 211).

18. Nanning Statistical Yearbook (2000, 117, 126).

19. Nanning City Annals (1998, 43 and 77). Guangxi University, the city's largest, had a total enrollment of only 1,525 (Guangxi University Annals 1998, 33).

20. This account is based on Guangxi Party Committee (1987, 13:63–74).

21. Guangxi Party Committee (1987, 17:801).

22. The cases that I describe here are based on the three most detailed chronologies for prefecture-level cities, which range from 72 to 107 standard pages in length. A "page" is defined as containing 500 Chinese characters (see the Appendix).

23. Qiqihaer Population Annals (1992, 15); Qiqihaer Labor Annals (1994, 77).

24. Qiqihaer Education Annals (1993, 84, 119, 149, 165, 180).

25. This account is based on Qiqihaer Archives Bureau (1985, 1–3), and Qiqihaer City Annals (1998, 164–167).

26. Qingdao Labor Annals (1999, 41).

27. Qingdao Education Annals (1994, 363 and 366).

28. This account is based on Qingdao Historical Annals Office (2000, 324–331).

29. CCP Central Committee (1966f).

30. Wuzhou City Annals (2000, 179, 2945, 2947, 3232, 3242–3243).

31. This account is based on Guangxi Party Committee (1987, 9:660–667).

32. The three examples that I describe here are drawn from the 8 most detailed accounts for county-level cities, which range from 60 to 70 pages in length.

33. Shijiazhuang City Annals (1995, 166); Shijiazhuang City Annals (1999, 194).

34. Shijiazhuang Education Annals (1992, 106, 180).

35. This account is based on Shijiazhuang Party History Research Office (1997, 3, 20–21).

36. Anshun City Annals (1995, 212, 1243, 1262).

37. This account is based on Anshun City Annals (1995, 51–53, 420–421).

38. Beihai City Annals (2002, 167, 1266, 1381).

39. This account is based on Guangxi Party Committee (1987, 12:587–592).

40. To ensure that the comparisons do not express simply the level of detail in local histories, I draw all of these examples from the most detailed accounts for counties—those longer than 40 pages, in the top 5 percent by length.

41. Ankang County Annals (1989, 605–606, 663).

42. This account is based on Ankang County Annals (1989, 897–901).

43. Yulin City Annals (1993, 157, 848, 964).

44. This account is based on Guangxi Party Committee (1987, 12:6–16, 101–109).

45. Zengcheng County Annals (1995, 119, 649–650).

46. This account is based on Zengcheng County Annals (1995, 33, 561–564).

47. Shanglin County Annals (1989, 46, 354–355, 426).

48. This account is based on Guangxi Party Committee (1987, 8:208–213).

49. Zichang County Annals (1993, 195, 614).

50. This account is based on Zichang County Annals (1993, 30, 828–833).

51. The 1964 national census counted 1,993 people as part of the "nonagricultural" population. State Statistical Bureau Population Statistics Office (1986, 77); Zhang County Annals (2005, 905). The county's annals do not report any salaried employment figures until the 1980s, suggesting that the county was purely agricultural at the time.

52. This account is based on Zhang County Annals (2005, 84–86, 710).

4. THE IMPLOSION OF THE PARTY-STATE

1. See Li Xun (2015, 617–653); Perry and Li (1997, 86–88, 114–116); Walder (1978, 46–50); and Wu (2014a, 108–115).

2. Li Xun (2015, 665–742); MacFarquhar and Schoenhals (2006, 163–169); Wu (2014a, 120–131).

3. MacFarquhar and Schoenhals (2006, 165–166).

4. Among them were 7 counties and 1 other city, scattered widely across China. In fact, the first power seizure reported in local annals was not Shanghai, but Kaifeng County in Henan Province, whose local annals report a power seizure almost two weeks earlier, on December 24, 1966. The action was taken by high school Red Guards in collaboration with Scarlet Guards in the county government offices. The involvement of the latter group appears to distinguish it from the rebel power seizures that came later (Kaifeng County Annals, 1992, 29). The prefecture-level city of Jinzhou, in Liaoning province, reported a power seizure on January 6, the same day as Shanghai (Jinzhou City Annals 1997, 251). There may have been other power seizures during the first week of January, but not all of the annals that reported power seizures in January provided specific dates.

5. I write "no fewer than" because the accounts from 392 of the 1,089 localities that reported power seizures during January did not provide a specific date.

6. People's Daily (1967a, 1967b).

7. The full Chinese name of the cadre rebel alliance was *shengji jiguan geming zaofan lianhe zong zhihui bu*. Zhejiang Party History Research Office (2000, 242).

8. Ministry of Civil Affairs (1998, 2210).

9. Organization Department (2000, 16:1331, 1335–1340).

10. I report median ratios in this column because averages are highly skewed by extremely high ratios in counties where there are tiny numbers of salaried workers or no workers at all.

11. These numbers are tabulated from the chronicles of major events contained in Guangxi Party Committee (1987, vols. 8–15).

12. MacFarquhar and Schoenhals (2006, 137).

13. For example, in Lingui County: Guangxi Party Committee (1987, 6:328).

14. Rebel groups formed even in the administrative offices of the Guangxi Party Committee itself. By the end of December there were 8 small rebel "fighting groups" among the cadres and staff who worked in the party's own offices (Guangxi Party Committee (1987, 17:802).

15. Guangxi Party Committee (1987, 13:69–73).

16. Guangxi Party Committee (1987, 13:249).

17. Guangxi Party Committee (1987, 6:328).

18. Guangxi Party Committee (1987, 2:234).

19. Guangxi Party Committee (1987, 3:514).

20. Guangxi Party Committee (1987, 13:370–371).

21. Guangxi Party Committee (1987, 13:307–308).

22. Guangxi Party Committee (1987, 4:197–198).

23. Guangxi Party Committee (1987, 1:76–77).

24. Guangxi Party Committee (1987, 13:508–509).

25. Guangxi Party Committee (1987, 3:114–120).

26. Guangxi Party Committee (1987, 6:328–329; 13:8–9, 251; 13:210; 13:308, 374).

27. I conducted these interviews in 2007. I have not masked the name of the county because my research there has been described in a local publication issued by the county government (Zhao Yonggang 2013, 59–60).

28. Zouping County Annals (1992, 197, 326–327, 774).

29. Student rebels who tried to seize power in Beijing's city government departments in January 1967 found that their staff were already organized into opposed factions of rebel groups (Walder 2009a, 203–207).

30. More detail on the activities in individual offices and bureaus are provided in Guangxi Party Committee (1987, vol. 17).

31. Guangxi Party Committee (1987, 13:73–75).

32. Guangxi Party Committee (1987, 1:514–518).

33. The counties administered by Nanning Prefecture were in the city's suburbs, some distance away. Any student or worker rebels active in those counties would have focused their activities in the county seat. Rebels in the city of Nanning would have ignored the prefecture offices, which did not have jurisdiction over the city.

34. Guangxi Party Committee (1987, 11:152–153). The group's name was *shi zhi jiguan zhigong ganbu geming zaofan tuan.*

35. Guangxi Party Committee (1987, 3:639–642). The Guilin Prefecture offices were located in Guilin City, but it governed only the rural counties in the prefecture, which were distant from the city itself. For this reason the city's rebels ignored them, as was the case also for Nanning Prefecture.

36. Guangxi Party Committee (1987, 4:214–216).

37. Guangxi Party Committee (1987, 1:77–78).

38. Guangxi Party Committee (1987, 3:177–180).

39. Guangxi Party Committee (1987, 3:221–223).

40. Guangxi Party Committee (1987, 1:175–176).

41. Guangxi Party Committee (1987, 13:211).

42. Guangxi Party Committee (1987, 5:172–174).

43. Guangxi Party Committee (1987, 13:508–509).

44. Guangxi Party Committee (1987, 2:235–236).

45. Guangxi Party Committee (1987, 5:108–109; 13:377).

46. Guangxi Party Committee (1987, 1:456–457).

47. Guangxi Party Committee (1987, 2:193–194).

48. Guangxi Party Committee (1987, 13:309).

49. Guangxi Party Committee (1987, 4:169–171).

50. Guangxi Party Committee (1987, 4:333–335).

51. Guangxi Party Committee (1987, 3:514–516).

52. Guangxi Party Committee (1987, 4:492–496).

53. Guangxi Party Committee (1987, 3:339–340).

54. For example, Hechter (1995); Kuran (1989; 1991); Tilly (1995b).

55. Granovetter (1978); Marwell and Oliver (1993).

56. Examples of the former are Kuran (1989); Lohmann (1994); and Oberschall (1994); of the latter, Opp (1994); Opp and Gern (1993); Pfaff (1996); and Pfaff and Kim (2003). Kurzman (1996) offered similar ideas in relation to the Iranian revolution of 1979.

57. Goldstone (1991); Goodwin (2001); Goodwin and Skocpol (1989); Skocpol (1979).

58. Tarrow (1989, 223).

59. Biggs (2005); Conell and Cohn (1995); Koopmans (1993); Myers (1997); Pitcher, Hamblin and Miller (1978); Tarrow (1994, 223–230).

60. Soule (1997).

61. For example, Cunningham and Phillips (2007); Gould (1991), Hedstrom (1994); Hedstrom, Sandel and Stern (2000); Kim and Pfaff (2012); Myers (2000); Tolnay, Deane, and Beck (1996) and Wang and Soule (2012).

62. Andrews and Biggs (2006); Myers (2000).

63. For example, Biggs (2003; 2005); Conell and Cohn (1995); Tarrow (1994).

64. For example, Andrews and Biggs (2006); McAdam (1983); Minkoff (1997); Soule (1997); Wang and Soule (2012); Traugott (2010).

65. Walder and Lu (2017).

66. At the prefecture level, within the same province; at the county level, within the same prefecture.

5. THE FORMATION OF FACTIONS

1. Oberschall (1973, 117–125). Later memorable applications of this idea are McAdam (1986) and Hirsch (1990). The latter explained the upsurge of labor strife in late 1800s Chicago as bloc mobilization of ethnic loyalties among immigrant groups.

2. Oberschall (1973, 143) observed, "A heterogeneous leadership and membership, loosely held together in their pursuit of some common goals, comes into being. . . . Yet, the movement will have little central organization, and the primary loyalties of the members may be to the component groups, leaders, and associations, and not to the overarching movement itself. Each group seeks to have its leaders recognized. . . . There are no preestablished norms for choosing or establishing top leaders, and their authority does not rest on institutional positions. There are no agreed upon, legitimized procedures for reaching collective decisions."

3. Walder (2009a, 174).

4. Zhejiang Party History Research Office (2000, 242).

5. Guangdong Provincial History Editorial Committee (2005, 592).

6. Guangxi Party Committee (1987, 17:802).

7. Zhenyuan County Party History (2008, 253–254).

8. Guangxi Party Committee (1987, 13:69–73, 249).

9. This description of Shanghai events is based on Li Xun (2015, 743–852); Perry and Li (1997, 20–21, 119–144); and Walder (1978, 46–60).

10. This condenses a more detailed account in Dong and Walder (2010, 679–690).

11. This account of events in Guangzhou is based on Yan (2015, 173–182) and Yan (2018).

12. The same initial pattern occurred in the Hubei Province capital of Wuhan. Hurried negotiations to form a power seizure alliance stalled and several rebel alliances moved forward with a power seizure without the participation of one of the largest and most important rebel coalition in the city. The two sides immediately faced off in a furious propaganda campaign that led quickly to street confrontations (Wang 1995, 114–119).

13. This account is based on Guangxi Party Committee (1987, 13:75–79).

14. Guangxi Party Committee (1987, 1:77–82).

15. Guangxi Party Committee (1987, 3:177–183).

16. Guangxi Party Committee (1987, 3:639–642).

17. Guangxi Party Committee (1987, 3:516–517).

18. Guangxi Party Committee (1987, 4:169–171).

19. Guangxi Party Committee (1987, 4:301–305, 492–497).

20. Guangxi Party Committee (1987, 13:508–509).

21. Guangxi Party Committee (1987, 4:332–335).

22. CCP Central Committee (1967a); Central Military Commission (1967a).

23. Nelsen (1972).

24. Central Military Commission (1967a).

25. Nelsen (1972); Nelsen (1981, 7–9, 115–123); and Chinese People's Liberation Army History Editorial Group (2011, 37–38).

26. This is based on the first mention in local annals of intervention by military units to "support the left."

27. This account is based on Dong and Walder (2011b, 430–431).

28. This account is based on Yan (2015, 181–183, 186–187).

29. Wang (1995, 119–124).

30. This account is based on Dong and Walder (2018).

31. This statement is based on examining the relevant pages of county-level Communist Party organizational histories.

32. Guangxi Party Committee (1987, 10:12–18).

33. Guangxi Party Committee (1987, 1:175–176; 12:158–161).

34. Guangxi Party Committee (1987, 3:339–340).

35. Hannan (1992).

36. Tilly (2003, 29–32).

37. This is analogous to the more general processes through which factions and parties form in a variety of settings (Martin 2009, 305–308).

38. As famously emphasized by Simmel (1955 [1922], 87–93), and as elaborated by Coser (1956).

39. Burt (1978; 1980).

6. THE EMERGENCE OF FACTIONAL WARFARE

1. The measure for faction merges two kinds of information: an explicit description in a local account of the formation of two opposed factions or, failing such an explicit statement, the first mention of a violent clash between rebel factions.

2. The development of factions even where there had been no power seizure should not be surprising. Many of these localities had active rebel groups that had seized power in their offices or places of work, but had not yet attempted to seize power over the entire government. In these localities rebel movements were also fragmented, and they presented many of the same dilemmas to army units.

3. MacFarquhar and Schoenhals (2006, 175).

4. Bu Weihua (2008, 306–307; 383–392); MacFarquhar and Schoenhals (2006, 171–173).

5. Dong and Walder (2010); Walder (2015, 239–242).

6. Dong and Walder (2010); Yan (2015).

7. Dong and Walder (2011b), Yan (2015)

8. Xining City Annals (1998, 169); MacFarquhar and Schoenhals (2006, 178–181).

9. Wu (2014a, 152–153).

10. MacFarquhar and Schoenhals (2006, 191–197).

11. CCP Central Committee (1967b); Central Military Commission (1967b; 1967c; 1967d).

12. MacFarquhar and Schoenhals (2006, 180–181).

13. The statement was made by Kang Sheng (Zhou Enlai and Kang Sheng 1967).

14. CCP Central Committee (1967c).

15. The classic and highly influential statement of this interpretation was Lee (1978).

16. These shifts are described in considerable detail in Dong and Walder (2010, 2011b) and Yan (2015; 2018).

17. Yan (2015).

18. Haifeng County Annals (2005, 696–697).

19. Haifeng County Annals (2005, 696–697). The background to these events is described in Galbiati (1985, 369–373).

20. Dong and Walder (2011b, 427–428).

21. Bu Weihua (2008, 409–410).

22. Guangxi Cultural Revolution Chronology (1990, 22–25). Zhou Enlai gave the order on March 13 and key provincial organs were placed under military control on March 23.

23. Guangxi borders North Vietnam. When Zhou Enlai authorized Wei Guoqing to enforce military control, he gave this as an important reason: "Guangxi is on the front lines of the effort to assist Vietnam in resisting American imperialism" (Guangxi Cultural Revolution Chronology 1990, 22). Perhaps also relevant is the fact that Wei Guoqing was one of the only ethnic Zhuang officials in the top regional leadership, and Guangxi Province was officially known as the Guangxi Zhuang Autonomous Region (Organization Department, CCP Central Committee 2000, 9:656–657).

24. Guangxi Cultural Revolution Chronology (1990, 26–29). Guangxi Organization Department (1995, 8–9; 430; 514–516).

25. These numbers are based on tabulations from detailed local histories contained in Guangxi Party Committee (1987, vols. 8–15).

26. Shijiazhuang Party History Research Office (1997, 23).

27. Schoenhals (2005, 280–281).

28. Dong and Walder (2011b); Dong and Walder (2018).

29. MacFarquhar and Schoenhals (2006, 199–207); Wang (1995, 112–149); Wang (2006, 243–249).

30. MacFarquhar and Schoenhals (2006, 207–212); Wang (1995, 149–157); and Wang (2006, 249–261).

31. MacFarquhar and Schoenhals (2006, 212–216); Wang (1995, 157–160); and Wang (2006, 261–265).

32. Schoenhals (2005, 286–289).

33. MacFarquhar and Schoenhals (2006, 214–216); Schoenhals (2005).

34. See, for example, Dong and Walder (2011b; 2012a).

35. Sichuan Province Annals (1999, 138).

36. The events in these paragraphs are described in Chongqing City Annals (1992, 109–111); Sichuan Province Annals (1999, 139); Tongliang County Annals (1991, 30); and Tongliang Historical Materials (2002, 4).

37. Xiangtan City Annals (1997, 237–239).

38. Changzhou City Annals (1995, 101–102, 1106).

39. Zaozhuang City Annals (1992, 73–74).

40. Jinzhou City Annals (1997, 251–252).

41. Gan County Annals (1991, 13).

42. Sheng County Annals (1989, 29).

43. Yongning County Annals (1995, 29).

44. Tongshan County Annals (1993, 74). The background to this fighting is described in Dong and Walder (2018).

45. Hanshou County Annals (1993, 280).

46. Liuzhou Chronology (1995, 240).

47. Wanxian City Annals (2001, 23).

48. MacFarquhar and Schoenhals (2006, 231).

49. For example, Xu Shiyou, commander of the Nanjing Military Region (Dong and Walder 2011b, 438).

50. MacFarquhar and Schoenhals (2006, 229–231); Schoenhals (2005, 294–297).

51. Dong and Walder (2011b, 437–438); Schoenhals (2005, 297).

52. CCP Central Committee (1967d).

53. Schoenhals (2005, 297).

54. Detailed descriptions of the process are in Dong and Walder (2012a; 2018).

7. THE DYNAMICS OF REGIONAL ESCALATION

1. Wu (2014a, 144–145). The order went out on September 5, 1967 (Union Research Institute 1968, 505–510).

2. The events include violent clashes between rebel factions, rebel attacks on military or government installations, and any other action by rebels that generated victims or casualties.

3. The numbers for 1968 were inflated by a month-long battle in the city of Luzhou, Sichuan, which generated a reported 2,000 deaths. This created the large spike in deaths in July 1968. Even if we discount that extreme case, it is still clear that levels of violence escalated as the number of violent events declined.

4. For example, Tarrow (1989, 305–310) explained the escalation of violence near the end of a cycle of protest in Italy in the early 1970s as a strategic response by small groups to revive a dying movement in the face of an overall decline in large-scale protest.

5. This has been documented in considerable detail in Nanjing (Dong and Walder 2011b), Xuzhou (Dong and Walder 2018), and Shaanxi Province (Tanigawa 2018).

6. In Guangxi, the "April 22" faction, which opposed forces under the military district commander, relied heavily on the support of PLA unit 6984 for its survival. When they learned that the unit was to be transferred elsewhere, they pleaded with the commander to disobey his orders. Their departure was delayed for only a month, until February 1968, sealing the fate of this "anti-army" rebel faction, and ushering in the massacres that made Guangxi's death tolls the highest in the country (Guangxi Cultural Revolution Chronology 1990, 69–70).

7. There was no power seizure over Beijing's city government, where a revolutionary committee was imposed in April.

8. MacFarquhar and Schoenhals (2006, 245–246).

9. Dong and Walder (2012b, 901).

10. MacFarquhar and Schoenhals (2006, 246).

11. Tanigawa (2007, 278) was able to document 21 county-level revolutionary committees in Shaanxi dominated by one faction, and 16 with even representation, out of the 75 counties in the province.

12. See, for example, a detailed account of this process in Jiangsu Province (Dong and Walder 2012a).

13. The mix of coercion and negotiation employed in Jiangsu province is described in Dong and Walder (2012a). See also the account of the process nationwide by MacFarquhar and Schoenhals (2006, 239–246).

14. Strictly speaking, the theory behind escalation traps would predict more intense violence near the end of long periods under military control—that is, the intensity of collective violence increases over time. This statistical model, however, examines average intensity of violence across entire durations of different length. By averaging across the entire duration, this would tend to weaken the measurable impact of escalation near the end, and therefore makes it somewhat less likely that we will detect differences across periods of different duration.

15. See the longer discussion in Walder (2014).

16. Full details about the statistical procedures, including the regression results from the model described above, is provided in Walder and Chu (2018).

17. Attentive readers will note that there is a degree of endogeneity that contributes to these statistical results—that is, regions with more severe violence will likely delay the formation of local revolutionary committees, leading to longer periods under military control. This is unlikely to make these results spurious, however. Figure 7.2 indicates that violence escalated over time in all regions, and

Figure 7.7 indicates that it escalated over time in regions that still lacked a political settlement. Moreover, the duration of the period without a political settlement is jointly defined as a revolutionary committee at both the provincial and local level. In 36 percent of the 1,853 localities in provinces placed under military control, the local revolutionary committee was established during the same month as the provincial revolutionary committee, or earlier. In these cases, the length of time without a political settlement would not be an endogenous outcome of the intensity of *local* conflicts.

18. As noted in Figure A.1, in the Appendix, death tolls in Guangxi Province during the period from April to August 1968 formed an especially large percentage of the nationwide total. This raises the possibility that the statistical results I have just reported are biased by extreme events in Guangxi. A close examination of the data set rules out this possibility. Of the 235 insurgent clashes in the database from April through August 1968 that were included in the analysis presented in Figure 7.8, only 6 percent were from Guangxi, with an average death toll of 7.8 per event (compared to an average of 4.5 deaths for this subset of events). Shaanxi province, by contrast, contributed 25 percent of the cases in this group, and they averaged 9.0 deaths per event. The very high overall death tolls in Guangxi noted in the Appendix were generated almost exclusively by repression of rebel insurgents or by mass reprisals carried out by the victorious faction, and almost all of them occurred only after an imposed political settlement. These cases by definition were not among the factional clashes represented in Figures 7.7 and 7.8.

19. Tanigawa (2007, 278–279).

20. Yan Lebin (2012, 15). The author was a member of an investigation team sent to Guangxi from Beijing in the early 1980s to investigate the mass killings, which local authorities were still covering up.

21. Ziyang County Annals (1989, 523).

22. Yan'an City Annals (1994, 30 and 827–828).

23. Mian County Annals (1989, 456–458).

24. Sichuan Province Annals (1999, 142).

25. Zhongjiang County Annals (1994, 445).

26. Guangyuan County Annals (1994, 54).

27. Yuechi County Annals (1993, 27).

28. Luzhou City Annals (1998, 38); Sichuan Province Annals (1999, 139–140)

29. Hejiang County Annals (1993, 41).

30. Guangxi Party Committee (1987, 3:648–655).

31. Guangxi Party Committee (1987, 3:650; 653–655; 10:98–99); Xing'an County Annals (2002, 21).

32. Yinjiang County Annals (1992, 43).

33. Xichang County Annals (1996, 27).

34. Putuo County Annals (1991, 1076). In September 1972 "former members of the two mass factions" got into a fight in a village in Xinjiang Province that left 16 injured, but this was long after organized factional activity had been suppressed (Miquan County Annals 1998, 35).

8. REPRESSION UNLEASHED

1. Chenghai County Annals (1992, 57–58).

2. Changjiang County Annals (1998, 46).

3. Wenchang County Annals (2000, 30 and 756).

4. Huangmei County Annals (1999, 23).

5. The account in these paragraphs is drawn from Guangxi Cultural Revolution Chronology (1990, 106–116), and Guangxi Party Committee (1987, 13:110–111). The former source gives a somewhat smaller number for combatant deaths—1,470. Photographs of the surrender and summary executions were published in the front matter of the former publication, and several are reproduced in Walder (2015).

6. Guangxi Cultural Revolution Chronology (1990, 111). Su (2006; 2011) analyzes these mass killings in considerable detail.

7. See, for example, the problems encountered in Jiangsu Province (Dong and Walder 2012a, 24–26).

8. MacFarquhar and Schoenhals (2006, 254–255).

9. MacFarquhar and Schoenhals (2006, 254–259).

10. Xu Jiangang (1990).

11. Zhenyuan County Party History (2008, 254).

12. The deaths due to insurgencies include armed factional battles, rebel attacks on military or government compounds, and any other deaths attributable to unspecified actions by insurgents. The deaths due to actions by authorities include repression by local governments (party and government organs before power seizures, revolutionary committees after their establishment) or by military units, deaths due to the Cleansing and other campaigns, and any other deaths attributable to unspecified actions by authorities. Instances where it was not possible to classify the deaths in this fashion (5 percent of the total) are excluded from these figures.

13. Instead of reporting all deaths associated with the Cleansing Campaign during the month that it began, I have distributed them equally over a 4-month period

after the reported initiation of the campaign. This results in a more accurate portrayal of the distribution—a shorter initial surge immediately after a revolutionary committee, but more sustained numbers of deaths afterwards.

14. Guangdong Local History Office (2005, 229–30).

15. Based on tabulating the summary figures provided in the 18 volumes of investigation reports compiled by the provincial authorities (Guangxi Party Committee 1987).

16. Contemporary China Editorial Committee (1989a, 165–166).

17. Contemporary China Editorial Committee (1989b, 121).

18. Contemporary China Editorial Committee (1991, 155).

19. See Walder and Su (2003, 79–80).

20. Walder (2014). The same procedures yielded an estimate of 22 to 30 million victims, which implies that the local annals reported much more complete numbers about this item—some 45 to 61 percent of the underlying totals.

21. The detailed statistical report on the two purported Central Committee investigations is in Li Zijing (1996, 17). The article's sensationally inaccurate title claims a death toll of 26 million, confusing the death toll with the number of reported victims—see the following discussion.

22. The Central Committee numbers evidently covered the entire decade from 1966 to 1976, but levels of violence and the intensity of persecution campaigns subsided greatly after 1971, the last year covered by my database. Because insurgent activity ebbed rapidly during 1968, I do not analyze events beyond 1969 in this book.

23. Li Zijing (1996, 17).

24. See Wu Di (2010) and Yang Haiying (2014).

25. One of the five was Dao County, Hunan, where startlingly widespread mass killings directed by authorities in late 1967 resulted in a reported death toll of 4,519, just below 1.2 percent of the population at the time. The case has been documented in great detail, based on classified investigation reports, by Zhang Cheng (2001, 66–67) and Tan Hecheng (2017).

26. See Chandler (1999, 66–67) and Kiernan (2002, 330).

9. FINAL OBSERVATIONS

1. Individual action in these models is typically interpreted in purely strategic terms, but this is not logically necessary. The same actions can just as readily be interpreted as efforts to act in conformity with moral or political commitments. In the case of cadre rebels (and even the Scarlet Guards), for example, their changing stances toward their superiors can be interpreted either as a rational

and strategic response designed to ensure personal survival, or as a realization that their previous loyalties were based on a misunderstanding of the correct actions expected by loyal Communists—or both.

2. The phrasing is Martin's (2009, 2), describing the approach to social structure central to the sociology of Georg Simmel (1955 [1922]).

APPENDIX

1. The persons harmed were counted in nonoverlapping categories as deaths, injuries, or "victims." The last category included anyone who was targeted by a political accusation, mistreated in rallies, held captive, imprisoned, removed from their jobs or from urban residence, or physically abused.

2. For example, Tarrow (1989, 357–366).

3. For example, Davenport and Ball (2002); Earl, Martin, McCarthy, and Soule (2004); Franzosi (1987); McCarthy, McPhail, and Smith (1996); Mueller (1997); Myers and Caniglia (2004); Oliver and Maney (2000); Oliver and Myers (1999); White (1993).

4. To be more precise, 84 prefecture-level cities *(diji shi)*, 90 county-level cities *(xianji shi)*, and 2,072 other county-level units (1,945 counties [*xian*], 67 autonomous counties [*zizhi xian*], 54 banners [*qi*], and 6 nonstandard county-level jurisdictions—towns [*zhen*] special districts [*tequ*] and forestry districts [*linqu*]).

5. All but 3 of the 47 missing localities are in Tibet (39) or a Tibetan prefecture in Qinghai (5). There is one missing jurisdiction each from Xinjiang, Inner Mongolia, and Guangdong (Hainan).

6. The source used to track these changes is Ministry of Civil Affairs, People's Republic of China (1998), which provides annual lists of local cities and counties, by province, and provides explanations of boundary changes.

7. In 86 of these cases we extracted only summary statistical data on numbers of deaths, injuries, and victims from 18 volumes of detailed internal investigation reports for Guangxi Province (Guangxi Party Committee 1987). In the remaining 18 cases, from 11 other provinces, we drew upon published communist party histories, separate compilations of local historical materials, or unpublished chronologies of "major events" during the Cultural Revolution, and coded all of the reported events as a supplement to or substitute for less detailed published annals. The Guangxi statistical data will be drawn upon only at the end of chapter 8, where I develop estimates of the overall death toll during this period. The extremely detailed narrative accounts in these reports, however, are drawn upon repeatedly to document conflict processes below the level of provincial capitals.

8. At the time of publication, the web address that provides access to the data set and documentation was https://stanford.app.box.com/s/1p228gewy2pjd3817ksq

9kd4d6cz3jy8. In subsequent years the data set will be placed in a public data repository.

9. The key concern from a sampling perspective is whether the absence of a report signifies the absence of a conflict event (Danzger 1975; Franzosi 1987; Mueller 1997; Myers and Caniglia 2004; Oliver and Maney 2000; Snyder and Kelly 1977). This is a classic problem of sample selection bias.

10. Most studies of this type rely on information culled from newspapers, which raises concern about biases in regional coverage, especially when national-level newspapers or a small number of large regional newspapers are employed (Earl, Martin, McCarthy and Soule 2004).

11. The parallel concern with newspaper-derived data is selectivity in editorial decisions about what kinds of events are considered newsworthy (McCarthy, McPhail and Smith 1996). Government-compiled data sets are affected by potential biases in legal regimes and policing practices.

12. In particular, one must consider the likelihood that the reporting of events or of detail about them will be censored by editorial decisions or by different levels of effort put into the compilation of local histories. A more extended discussion of these problems for the current data set is in Walder (2014).

13. Two of the most common are Heckman two-step estimators and zero-inflated negative binomial regression. The former was employed to estimate the underlying number of deaths and victims in Walder (2014); the latter was employed to test arguments about the escalation of violence in Chapter 7.

14. The average number is skewed by a small number of very long accounts. For example, 6 annals, all from major cities, had accounts longer than 78 pages, and by far the longest—for Guangzhou—was 176 pages.

15. By contrast, the 18-volume compilation of investigation reports for Guangxi, which became available only after the database was in its final stages of preparation, contain an average of just under 50 pages for its 86 cities and counties (Guangxi Party Committee 1987).

16. See the debate described in Walder and Su (2003, 79–80).

17. Here I refer to the statistics linked to specific events in Guangxi's published local annals, not the summary statistics contained in the much more detailed internal investigation reports. Guangxi's high level of published statistical detail was surely due to the compilation of detailed investigation reports for every city and county in the province during the mid-1980s. This classified 18-volume compendium (Guangxi Party Committee 1987) was available to compilers of local annals.

REFERENCES

Abbott, Andrew. 2001. *Time Matters: On Theory and Method.* Chicago: University of Chicago Press.

Abell, Peter. 2004. "Narrative Explanation: An Alternative to Variable-Based Explanation?" *Annual Review of Sociology* 30: 289–310.

Andreas, Joel. 2002. "Battling over Political and Cultural Power during the Chinese Cultural Revolution." *Theory and Society* 31, no. 4 (August): 463–519.

———. 2009. *The Rise of the Red Engineers: The Cultural Revolution and the Origins of China's New Class.* Stanford, Calif.: Stanford University Press.

Andrews, Kenneth A., and Michael Biggs. 2006. "The Dynamics of Protest Diffusion: Movement Organizations, Social Networks, and News Media in the 1960 Sit-ins." *American Sociological Review* 71, no. 5 (October): 752–777.

Ankang County Annals. 1989. *Ankang xian zhi* (Ankang County Annals). Xi'an: Shaanxi renmin chubanshe.

Anshun City Annals. 1995. *Anshun shi zhi, shang ce* (Anshun City Annals, Vol. 1). Guiyang: Guizhou renmin chubanshe.

Ball, Patrick, Paul Kobrak, and Herbert F. Spirer. 1999. *State Violence in Guatemala, 1960–1996.* Washington, D.C.: American Association for the Advancement of Science.

Beihai City Annals. 2002. *Beihai shi zhi* (Beihai City Annals). Nanning: Guangxi renmin chubanshe.

Beijing Party Committee. 1966. "Zhonggong Beijing shiwei guanyu gei geming qunzhong pingfan jinji tongzhi" (Beijing Party Committee's urgent notice on the rehabilitation of revolutionary masses). November 15.

Beissinger, Mark R. 2002. *Nationalist Mobilization and the Collapse of the Soviet State.* New York: Cambridge University Press.

Biggs, Michael. 2002. "Strikes as Sequences of Interaction: The American Strike Wave of 1886." *Social Science History* 26, no. 3 (Fall): 583–617.

———. 2003. "Positive Feedback in Collective Mobilization: The American Strike Wave of 1886." *Theory and Society* 32, no. 2 (April): 217–254.

————. 2005. "Strikes as Forest Fires: Chicago and Paris in the Late Nineteenth Century." *American Journal of Sociology* 110, no. 6 (May): 1684–1714.

Blecher, Marc J., and Gordon White. 1979. *Micropolitics in Contemporary China: A Technical Unit during and after the Cultural Revolution.* White Plains, N.Y.: M. E. Sharpe.

Bu Weihua. 2008. *Zalan jiu shijie: Wenhua da geming de dongluan yu haojie* (Smashing the Old World: The Catastrophic Turmoil of the Cultural Revolution). Hong Kong: Zhongwen daxue chubanshe.

Burt, Ronald S. 1978. "Cohesion versus Structural Equivalence as a Basis for Network Subgroups." *Sociological Methods and Research* 7, no. 2 (November): 189–212.

————. 1980. "Models of Network Structure." *Annual Review of Sociology* 6: 79–141.

Cambodian Genocide Program. 2013. https://gsp.yale.edu/case-studies/cambodian -genocide-program.

CCP Central Committee. 1966a. "Zhonggong zhongyang, guowuyuan, guanyu gongye jiaotong qiye he jiben jianshe danwei ruhe kaizhan wenhua da geming yundong de tongzhi" (Central Committee and State Council circular on how to unfold the Cultural Revolution campaign in industrial and transportation enterprises and basic construction units). Document [66] No. 336, July 2.

————. 1966b. "Zhonggong zhongyang, guowuyuan guanyu gongye jiaotong qiye he jiben jianshe danwei ruhe kaizhan wenhua da geming yundong de buchong tongzhi" (Supplementary circular of the Central Committee and State Council on how to unfold the Cultural Revolution campaign in industrial and transportation enterprises and basic construction units). Document [66] No. 373, July 22.

————. 1966c. "Zhonggong zhongyang zhuanfa Mao Zedong de 'paoda silingbu (wo de yizhang dazibao)'" (Central Committee transmits Mao Zedong's 'Bombard the headquarters [my big character poster]'). Document [66], no. 407, August 17.

————. 1966d. "Zhonggong zhongyang tongyi gonganbu guanyu yanjin chudong jingcha zhenya geming xuesheng yundong de guiding" (Central Committee approves Ministry of Public Security regulation strictly prohibiting the dispatch of police to suppress the revolutionary student movement). Document [66], No. 410, August 22.

————. 1966e. "Zong canmou bu, zong zhengzhi bu guanyu juedui bu xu dongyong budui wuzhuang zhenya geming xuesheng yundong de guiding" (PLA General Staff Headquarters and General Political Department regulations absolutely prohibiting the use of armed troops to suppress the revolutionary student movement). Document [66], No. 416, August 21.

————. 1966f. "Zhonggong zhongyang zhuanfa Mao zhuxi guanyu buzhun tiaodong gong nong bing ganyu xuesheng yundong de jueding" (Central Committee transmits Chairman Mao's decision prohibiting the incitement of workers, peasants, and soldiers to interfere with the student movement). Document [66], No. 468, September 11.

———. 1966g "Zhonggong zhongyang guanyu nongcun, gongkuang qiye, shiye danwei, dangzheng jiguan, qunzhong tuanti bu chengli hongweibing deng zuzhi de pishi" (Central Committee comments on the directive forbidding the establishment of red guard and other organizations in villages, factories and mines, social institutions, party and government organs, and mass organizations). Document [66], No. 509, September 25.

———. 1966h. "Zhonggong zhongyang guanyu chuli wuchan jieji wenhua da geming zhong dang'an cailiao wenti de buchong guiding" (Central Committee supplementary regulations on the question of handling archival materials during the Great Proletarian Cultural Revolution). Document [66], No. 553, November 16.

———. 1966i. "Zhonggong zhongyang guanyu zhua geming, cu shengchan de shitiao guiding (caoan)" (Central Committee's ten-point directive on stressing revolution while promoting production). Document [66], No. 603, December 9.

———. 1967a. "Zhonggong zhongyang, guowuyuan, zhongyang junwei, zhongyang wen'ge xiaozu guanyu renmin jiefang jun zhichi geming zuopai qunzhong de jueding" (Decision of the CCP Central Committee, State Council, Central Military Commission and Central Cultural Revolution Group regarding the People's Liberation Army providing support for the revolutionary leftist masses). Document [67], No. 27, January 23.

———. 1967b. "Zhonggong zhongyang zhuanfa zhongyang guanyu Anhui wenti de jueding ji fu jian" (CCP Central Committee transmits the Center's decision regarding the Anhui question and attachments). Document [67], No. 117, April 1.

———. 1967c. "Zhonggong zhongyang guanyu jinzhi tiaodong nongmin jincheng wudou de tongzhi" (CCP Central Committee directive regarding the incitement of peasants to enter cities for armed conflicts). Document [67], No. 218, July 13.

———. 1967d. "Zhonggong zhongyang, guowuyuan, zhongyang junwei, zhongyang wen'ge xiaozu guanyu buzhun qiangduo renmin jiefangjun wuqi, zhuangbei he gezhong junyong wuzi de mingling" (Orders of the CCP Central Committee, State Council, Central Military Commission, and the Central Cultural Revolution Group forbidding the seizure of weapons, materials, and other military supplies from the People's Liberation Army). Document [67], No. 288, September 5.

CCP Politburo. 1966. "Zhongyang zhengzhiju huiyi tingqu guanyu 'gongjiao zuotanhui' de huibao" (CCP Politburo receives report on the 'Industry and Transportation Conference'). Excerpts of minutes, December 4 and 6. In Cultural Revolution Database (2002).

Center for Justice and Accountability. 2013. https://cja.org/where-we-work/el -salvador/.

Central Military Commission. 1967a. "Zhongyang junwei batiao mingling." (Eight orders of the Central Military Commission), January 28.

———. 1967b. "Zhonggong zhongyang junwei gei Dongbei Ju de wudian zhishi." (Five directives of the Central Military Commission issued to the Northeast Bureau), April 1.

———. 1967c. "Zhongyang junwei shitiao mingling." (Ten orders of the Central Military Commission), April 6.

———. 1967d. "Zhongyang junwei guanyu buren quanxian he chuli cuobu, qudi de qunzhong zuzhi wenti de liangge wenjian." (Two documents of the Central Military Commission regarding the authority to make arrests and handling the problem of those wrongly arrested and the suppression of mass organizations), May 3.

Chan, Anita, Stanley Rosen, and Jonathan Unger. 1980. "Students and Class Warfare: The Social Roots of the Red Guard Conflict in Guangzhou (Canton)." *China Quarterly* 83 (September): 397–446.

Chandler, David P. 1999. *Brother Number One: A Political Biography of Pol Pot.* Boulder, Colo.: Westview Press.

Changjiang County Annals. 1998. *Changjiang xian zhi* (Changjiang County Annals). Zhengzhou: Xinhua chubanshe.

Changzhou City Annals. 1995. *Changzhou shi zhi* (Changzhou City Annals), 3 vols. Beijing: Zhongguo shehui kexue chubanshe.

Chenghai County Annals. 1992. *Chenghai xian zhi* (Chenghai County Annals). Shaoguan: Guangdong renmin chubanshe.

China Data Center, University of Michigan. 2005. "Historical China County Population Census Data with GIS Maps (1953–2000)" (http://chinadatacenter .org/Data/).

China Education Yearbook. 1984. *Zhongguo jiaoyu nianjian 1949–1981* (China Education Yearbook 1949–1981). Beijing: Zhongguo da baike quanshu chubanshe.

Chinese People's Liberation Army Editorial Group. 2011. *Zhongguo renmin jiefang jun junshi, di liu juan (1966 nian 5 yue–1978 nian 12 yue)* (History of the People's Liberation Army, Vol. 6 [May 1966–December 1978]). Beijing: Junshi kexue chubanshe.

Chongqing City Annals. 1992. *Chongqing shi zhi (di yi juan)* (Chongqing City Annals [Vol. 1]). Chongqing: Sichuan daxue chubanshe.

Conell, Carol, and Samuel Cohn. 1995. "Learning from Other People's Actions: Environmental Variation and Diffusion in French Coal Mining Strikes, 1890–1935." *American Journal of Sociology* 101, no. 2 (September): 366–403.

Contemporary China Editorial Committee. 1989a. *Dangdai Zhongguo de Beijing* (Contemporary China: Beijing). Beijing: Zhongguo shehui kexue chubanshe.

———. 1989b. *Dangdai Zhongguo de Jiangsu* (Contemporary China: Jiangsu). Beijing: Zhongguo shehui kexue chubanshe.

———. 1991. *Dangdai Zhongguo de Shanxi* (Contemporary China: Shanxi). Beijing: Zhongguo shehui kexue chubanshe.

———. 1992. *Dangdai Zhongguo de Gansu* (Contemporary China: Gansu). Beijing: Dangdai Zhongguo chubanshe.

Coser, Lewis. 1956. *The Functions of Social Conflict*. Glencoe, Ill.: The Free Press.

Cribb, Robert. 2002. "Unresolved Problems in the Indonesian Killings of 1965–1966." *Asian Survey* 42, no. 4 (July–August): 550–563.

Cultural Revolution Database. 2002. *The Chinese Cultural Revolution Database* (CD-ROM). Song Yongyi (ed.). Hong Kong: Universities Service Centre for China Studies, Chinese University of Hong Kong. Online version: http://ccrd .usc.cuhk.edu.hk.

Cunningham, David, and Benjamin T. Phillips. 2007. "Contexts for Mobilization: Spatial Settings and Clan Presence in North Carolina, 1964–1966." *American Journal of Sociology* 113, no. 2 (November): 781–814.

Cunningham, Kathleen Gallagher. 2011. "Divide and Conquer or Divide and Concede: How Do States Respond to Internally Divided Separatists?" *American Political Science Review* 105, no. 2 (May): 275–297.

Cunningham, Kathleen Gallagher, Kristin M. Baake, and Lee J. M. Seymour. 2012. "Shirts Today, Skins Tomorrow: Dual Contests and the Effects of Fragmentation in Self-Determination Disputes." *Journal of Conflict Resolution* 56, no. 1 (February): 67–93.

Danzger, M. Herbert. 1975. "Validating Conflict Data." *American Sociological Review* 40, no. 5 (October): 570–584.

Davenport, Christian, and Patrick Ball. 2002. "Views to a Kill: Exploring the Implications of Source Selection in the Case of the Guatemalan Terror, 1977–1995." *Journal of Conflict Resolution* 46, no. 3 (June): 427–450.

Davies, James C. 1962. "Toward a Theory of Revolution." *American Sociological Review* 27, no. 1 (February): 5–19.

Dong Guoqiang and Andrew G. Walder. 2010. "Nanjing's Failed 'January Revolution' of 1967: The Inner Politics of a Provincial Power Seizure." *China Quarterly* 203 (September): 675–692.

———. 2011a. "Factions in a Bureaucratic Setting: The Origins of Cultural Revolution Conflict in Nanjing." *China Journal* 65 (January): 1–25.

———. 2011b. "Local Politics in the Chinese Cultural Revolution: Nanjing under Military Control." *Journal of Asian Studies*, 70, no. 2 (May): 425–447.

———. 2012a. "From Truce to Dictatorship: Creating a Revolutionary Committee in Jiangsu." *China Journal* 68 (July): 1–32.

———. 2012b. "Nanjing's 'Second Cultural Revolution' of 1974." *China Quarterly* 212 (December): 893–918.

———. 2018. "Forces of Disorder: The Army in Xuzhou's Factional Warfare, 1967–1969." *Modern China* 44, no. 2 (March): 139–169.

Earl, Jennifer, Andrew Martin, John D. McCarthy, and Sarah A. Soule. 2004. "The Use of Newspaper Data in the Study of Collective Action." *Annual Review of Sociology* 30: 65–80.

Fearon, James D. 2004. "Why Do Some Civil Wars Last So Much Longer Than Others?" *Journal of Peace Research* 41, no. 3 (May): 275–301.

Fearon, James D., and David D. Laitin. 2003. "Ethnicity, Insurgency, and Civil War." *American Political Science Review* 97, no. 1 (February): 75–90.

Forster, Keith. 1990. *Rebellion and Factionalism in a Chinese Province: Zhejiang, 1966–1976.* Armonk, N.Y.: M.E. Sharpe.

Franzosi, Roberto. 1987. "The Press as a Source of Socio-Historical Data: Issues in the Methodology of Data Collection from Newspapers." *Historical Methods* 20, no. 1 (Winter): 5–16.

Fujian Province Annals Editorial Committee. 2000. *Fujian sheng zhi, dashiji* (Fujian Province Annals, Chronology). Beijing: Fangzhi chubanshe.

Galbiati, Fernando. 1985. *P'eng P'ai and the Hai-Lu-Feng Soviet.* Stanford, Calif.: Stanford University Press.

Gamson, William A. 1975. *The Strategy of Social Protest.* Homewood, Ill.: Dorsey.

Gan County Annals. 1991. *Gan xian zhi* (Gan County Annals). Tangshan: Xinhua chubanshe.

Gansu Province Annals 1989. *Gansu sheng zhi, di er juan, dashiji* (Gansu Province Annals, Vol. 2, Chronology). Lanzhou: Gansu renmin chubanshe.

Ganz, Marshall. 2000. "Resources and Resourcefulness: Strategic Capacity in the Unionization of California Agriculture, 1959–1966." *American Journal of Sociology* 105, no. 4 (January): 1003–1062.

Getty, J. Arch, and Oleg V. Naumov. 1999. *The Road to Terror: Stalin and the Self-Destruction of the Bolsheviks, 1932–1939.* New Haven: Yale University Press.

Goldstone, Jack A. 1991. *Revolution and Rebellion in the Early Modern World.* Berkeley: University of California Press.

Goodwin Jeff. 2001. *No Other Way Out: States and Revolutionary Movements, 1945–1991.* New York: Cambridge University Press.

Goodwin, Jeff, and Theda R. Skocpol. 1989. "Explaining Revolutions in the Contemporary Third World." *Politics and Society* 17, no. 4 (December): 489–509.

Gould, Roger V. 1991. "Multiple Networks and Mobilization in the Paris Commune, 1871." *American Sociological Review* 56, no. 6 (December): 716–729.

———. 1995. *Insurgent Identities: Class, Community, and Protest in Paris from 1848 to the Commune.* Chicago: University of Chicago Press.

Granovetter, Mark. 1978. "Threshold Models of Collective Behavior." *American Journal of Sociology* 83, no. 6 (May): 1420–1443.

Guangdong Local History Office. 2005. *Dangdai Guangdong jianshi* (Brief History of Contemporary Guangdong). Beijing: Dangdai Zhongguo chubanshe.

Guangdong Party History Research Office. 2004. *Zhongguo gongchandang Guangdong lishi dashiji* (Historical Chronology of the Chinese Communist Party in Guangdong). Guangzhou: Guangdong renmin chubanshe.

Guangdong Provincial History Editorial Committee. 2005. *Guangdong sheng zhi: dashiji* (Guangdong Province Annals: Chronology). Guangzhou: Guangdong renmin chubanshe.

Guangxi Cultural Revolution Chronology 1990. *Guangxi wen'ge dashi nianbiao* (Chronology of the Cultural Revolution in Guangxi). Nanning: Guangxi renmin chubanshe.

Guangxi Organization Department. 1995. *Zhongguo gongchandang Guangxi Zhuangzu Zizhiqu zuzhishi ziliao* (Materials on the Organizational History of the Chinese Communist Party in the Guangxi Zhuang Autonomous Region). Nanning: Guangxi renmin chubanshe.

Guangxi Party Committee. 1987. *Guangxi 'wen'ge' dang'an ziliao (Archival Materials on the Guangxi 'Cultural Revolution')*, 18 vols. Nanning: Zhonggong Guangxi Zhuangzu Zizhiqu weiyuanhui, zhengdang lingdao xiaozu bangongshi.

Guangxi University Annals. 1998. *Guangxi daxue xiao zhi* (Guangxi University Annals). Nanning: Guangxi kexue jishu chubanshe.

Guangyuan County Annals. 1994. *Guangyuan xian zhi* (Guangyuan County Annals). Chengdu: Sichuan cishu chubanshe.

Guangzhou City Annals. 1998. *Guangzhou shi zhi, juan er* (Guangzhou City Annals, Vol. 2). Guangzhou: Guangzhou chubanshe.

Guangzhou City Annals. 1999. *Guangzhou shi zhi, juan shisi* (Guangzhou City Annals, Vol. 14). Guangzhou: Guangzhou chubanshe.

Guangzhou Statistical Yearbook. 1999. *Guangzhou tongji nianjian 1999* (Guangzhou Statistical Yearbook 1999). Guangzhou: Guangzhou tongji chubanshe.

Gurr, Ted Robert. 1970. *Why Men Rebel*. Princeton: Princeton University Press.

Gusfield, Joseph R. 1963. *Symbolic Crusade: Status Politics and the American Temperance Movement*. Urbana: University of Illinois Press.

Hai Feng. 1971. *Guangzhou diqu wen'ge licheng shulüe* (An Account of the Cultural Revolution in the Canton Area). Hong Kong: Youlian yanjiusuo.

Haifeng County Annals. 2005. *Haifeng xian zhi (shang)* (Haifeng County Annals [vol. 1]). Guangzhou: Guangdong renmin chubanshe.

Hannan, Michael T. 1992. "Rationality and Robustness in Multilevel Systems." Pp. 120–136 in *Rational Choice Theory: Advocacy and Critique*, ed. James S. Coleman and Thomas J. Fararo. Newbury Park, Calif.: Sage.

Hanshou County Annals. 1993. *Hanshou xian zhi* (Hanshou County Annals). Beijing: Renmin chubanshe.

Hechter, Michael. 1975. *Internal Colonialism: The Celtic Fringe in British National Development*. Berkeley: University of California Press.

———. 1995. "Reflections on Historical Prophecy in the Social Sciences." *American Journal of Sociology* 100, no. 6 (May): 1520–1527.

———. 2000. *Containing Nationalism*. Oxford: Oxford University Press.

———. 2004. "From Class to Culture." *American Journal of Sociology* 110, no. 2 (September): 400–445.

———. 2013. *Alien Rule*. Cambridge: Cambridge University Press.

Hedström, Peter. 1994. "Contagious Collectivities: On the Spatial Diffusion of Swedish Trade Unions, 1890–1940." *American Journal of Sociology* 99, no. 5 (March): 1157–1179.

Hedström, Peter, Rickard Sandell, and Charlotta Stern. 2000. "Mesolevel Networks and the Diffusion of Social Movements: The Case of the Swedish Social Democratic Party." *American Journal of Sociology* 106, no. 1 (July): 145–172.

Hejiang County Annals. 1993. *Hejiang xian zhi* (Hejiang County Annals). Chengdu: Sichuan kexue jishu chubanshe.

Hirsch, Eric L. 1990. *Urban Revolt: Ethnic Politics in the Nineteenth-Century Chicago Labor Movement.* Berkeley: University of California Press.

Hough, Jerry F. 1977. *The Soviet Union and Social Science Theory.* Cambridge, Mass.: Harvard University Press.

Huangmei County Annals. 1999. *Huangmei xian zhi, xiajuan* (Huangmei County Annals, Vol. 2). Beijing: Zhonghua shuju.

Jiang Weiqing. 1996. *Qishi nian zhengcheng: Jiang Weiqing huiyilu* (Seventy Year Journey: The Memoirs of Jiang Weiqing). Nanjing: Jiangsu renmin chubanshe.

Jiangsu Provincial Annals Editorial Committee. 2003. *Jiangsu sheng zhi: Zhonggong zhi* (Jiangsu Provincial Annals: Chinese Communist Party Annals). Nanjing: Jiangsu renmin chubanshe.

Jinzhou City Annals. 1997. *Jinzhou shi zhi (zhengzhi wenhua juan)* (Jinzhou City Annals [Politics and Culture]). Beijing: Zhongguo tongji chubanshe.

Johnson, Chalmers A. 1966. *Revolutionary Change.* Boston: Little-Brown.

Kaifeng County Annals. 1992. *Kaifeng xian zhi* (Kaifeng County Annals). Zhengzhou: Zhongzhou guji chubanshe.

Kalyvas, Stathis N. 2006. *The Logic of Violence in Civil War.* New York: Cambridge University Press.

———. 2008. "Ethnic Defection in Civil War." *Comparative Political Studies* 41, no. 8 (August): 1043–1068.

Kerr, George H. 1965. *Formosa Betrayed.* Boston: Houghton Mifflin.

Kiernan, Ben. 2002. *The Pol Pot Regime,* 2nd ed. New Haven: Yale University Press.

Kim, Hyojoung, and Stephen Pfaff. 2012. "Structure and Dynamics of Religious Insurgency: Students and the Spread of the Reformation." *American Sociological Review* 77, no. 2 (April): 188–215.

Kimeldorf, Howard. 1988. *Reds or Rackets? The Making of Radical and Conservative Unions on the Waterfront.* Berkeley: University of California Press.

Koopmans, Ruud. 1993. "The Dynamics of Protest Waves: West Germany, 1965 to 1989." *American Sociological Review* 58, no. 5 (October): 637–658.

Kornhauser, William. 1959. *The Politics of Mass Society.* Glencoe, Ill.: Free Press.

Kraus, Richard Kurt. 1977. "Class Conflict and the Vocabulary of Social Analysis in China." *China Quarterly* 69 (March): 54–74.

Kuran, Timur. 1989. "Sparks and Prairie Fires: A Theory of Unanticipated Revolutions." *Public Choice* 61, no. 1 (April): 41–74.

———. 1991. "Now Out of Never: The Element of Surprise in the East European Revolutions of 1989." *World Politics* 44, no. 1 (October): 7–48.

Kurzman, Charles. 1996. "Structural Opportunity and Perceived Opportunity in Social Movement Theory: The Iranian Revolution of 1979." *American Sociological Review* 61, no. 1 (February): 153–170.

Lee, Hong Yong. 1975. "The Radical Students in Kwangtung During the Cultural Revolution." *China Quarterly* 64 (December): 645–683.

———. 1978. *The Politics of the Chinese Cultural Revolution: A Case Study.* Berkeley: University of California Press.

———. 1979. "Mao's Strategy for Revolutionary Change: A Case Study of the Cultural Revolution." *China Quarterly* 77 (March): 50–73.

Li Xun. 2015. *Geming zaofan niandai: Shanghai wen'ge yundong shi gao* (Decade of Revolutionary Rebellion: A History of Shanghai's Cultural Revolution), 2 vols. Hong Kong: Oxford University Press.

Li Zijing. 1996. "Zhonggong an cheng Mao bao zheng haiguo yangmin: liangqian liubai wan ren cansi" (CCP Accounting of the Mao-Inspired Disasters Inflicted on the Country and People: 26 Million Violent Deaths). *Zheng Ming* 228 (October), 14–17.

Linzhi County Annals. 2014. *Linzhi xian zhi* (Linzhi County Annals). Beijing: Zhongguo zangxue chubanshe.

Lipset, Seymour Martin. 1959. "Social Stratification and 'Right-Wing Extremism.'" *British Journal of Sociology* 10, no. 4 (December): 346–382.

Liuzhou Chronology. 1995. *Liuzhou dashiji* (Liuzhou Chronology). Liuzhou: Guangxi renmin chubanshe.

Lodhi, Abdul Quaiyum, and Charles Tilly. 1973. "Urbanization, Crime, and Collective Violence in 19th-Century France." *American Journal of Sociology* 79, no. 2 (September): 296–318.

Lohmann, Susanne. 1994. "The Dynamics of Informational Cascades: The Monday Demonstrations in Leipzig, East Germany, 1989–1991." *World Politics* 47, no. 1 (October): 42–101.

Luzhou City Annals. 1998. *Luzhou shi zhi* (Luzhou City Annals). Beijing: Fangzhi chubanshe.

MacFarquhar, Roderick, and Michael Schoenhals. 2006. *Mao's Last Revolution.* Cambridge, Mass.: Harvard University Press.

Markoff, John. 1996. *The Abolition of Feudalism: Peasants, Lords, and Legislators in the French Revolution.* University Park, PA: Penn State University Press.

———. 1997. "Peasants Help Destroy an Old Regime and Defy a New One: Some Lessons from (and for) the Study of Social Movements." *American Journal of Sociology* 102, no. 4 (January): 1113–1142.

Markoff, John, and Gilbert Shapiro. 1985. "Consensus and Conflict at the Onset of Revolution: A Quantitative Study of France in 1789." *American Journal of Sociology* 91, no. 1 (July): 28–53.

Martin, John Levi. 2009. *Social Structures.* Princeton, N.J.: Princeton University Press.

Marwell, Gerald, and Pamela Oliver. 1993. *The Critical Mass in Collective Action: A Micro-Social Theory.* New York: Cambridge University Press.

McAdam, Doug. 1982. *Political Process and the Development of Black Insurgency, 1930–1970.* Chicago: University of Chicago Press.

———. 1983. "Tactical Innovation and the Pace of Insurgency." *American Sociological Review* 48, no. 6 (December): 735–754.

———. 1986. "Recruitment to High-Risk Activism: The Case of Freedom Summer." *American Sociological Review* 92, no. 1 (July): 64–90.

———. 1996. "Conceptual Origins, Current Problems, Future Directions." Pp. 23–40 in *Comparative Perspectives on Social Movements: Political Opportunities, Mobilizing Structures, and Cultural Framings,* ed. Doug McAdam, John D. McCarthy, and Mayer N. Zald. New York: Cambridge University Press.

McAdam, Doug, Sidney Tarrow, and Charles Tilly. 2001. *Dynamics of Contention.* Cambridge: Cambridge University Press.

McCarthy, John D., Clark McPhail, and Jackie Smith. 1996. "Images of Protest: Dimensions of Selection Bias in Media Coverage of Washington Demonstrations, 1982 and 1991." *American Sociological Review* 61, no. 3 (June): 478–499.

McCarthy, John D., and Mayer N. Zald. 1977. "Resource Mobilization and Social Movements: A Partial Theory." *American Journal of Sociology* 82, no. 6 (May): 1212–1241.

Mehnert, Klaus. 1969. *Peking and the New Left: At Home and Abroad.* Berkeley: Center for Chinese Studies, University of California.

Meyer, David S., and Debra C. Minkoff. 2004. "Conceptualizing Political Opportunity." *Social Forces* 82, no. 4 (June): 1457–1492.

Meyer, David S., and Suzanne Staggenborg. 1996. "Movements, Counter-Movements, and the Structure of Political Opportunity." *American Journal of Sociology* 101, no. 6 (May): 1628–1660.

Mian County Annals. 1989. *Mian xian zhi* (Mian County Annals). Beijing: Dizhen chubanshe.

Ministry of Civil Affairs, People's Republic of China. 1998. *Zhonghua renmin gongheguo xingzheng qufen (1949–1997)* (Administrative Jurisdictions of the People's Republic of China [1949–1997]). Beijing: Zhongguo shehui chubanshe.

Minkoff, Debra C. 1997. "The Sequencing of Social Movements." *American Sociological Review* 62, no. 5 (October): 779–799.

Miquan County Annals. 1998. *Miquan xian zhi* (Miquan County Annals). Wulumuqi: Xinjiang renmin chubanshe.

Moore, Barrington Jr. 1966. *Social Origins of Dictatorship and Democracy: Lord and Peasant in the Making of the Modern World.* Boston: Beacon.

Mueller, Carol. 1997. "International Press Coverage of East German Protest Events, 1989." *American Sociological Review* 62, no. 5 (October): 820–832.

Munson, Ziad W. 2008. *The Making of Pro-Life Activists: How Social Movement Mobilization Works.* Chicago: University of Chicago Press.

Myers, Daniel J. 1997. "Racial Rioting in the 1960s: An Event History Analysis of Local Conditions." *American Sociological Review* 62, no. 1 (February): 94–112.

———. 2000. "The Diffusion of Collective Violence: Infectiousness, Susceptibility, and Mass Media Networks." *American Journal of Sociology* 106, no. 1 (July): 173–208.

Myers, Daniel J., and Beth Schaefer Caniglia. 2004. "All the Rioting That's Fit to Print: Selection Effects in National Newspaper Coverage of Civil Disorders, 1968–1969." *American Sociological Review* 69, no. 4 (August): 519–543.

Nanjing Annals Editorial Committee. 1986. *Nanjing jian zhi* (Nanjing Annals, Abridged). Nanjing: Jiangsu guji chubanshe.

Nanjing Archives Bureau. 1985. *Nanjing 'wenhua da geming' dashiji (chu gao)* (Nanjing 'Cultural Revolution' Chronology [unpublished draft]). Nanjing: Nanjing shi dang'an guan.

Nanning City Annals. 1998. *Nanning shi zhi, wenhua zhi* (Nanning City Annals: Culture). Nanning: Guangxi renmin chubanshe.

Nanning Statistical Yearbook. 2000. *Nanning tongji nianjian 2000* (Nanning Statistical Yearbook 2000). Nanning: Zhongguo tongji chubanshe.

Nelsen, Harvey W. 1972. "Military Forces in the Cultural Revolution." *China Quarterly* 51 (July–September): 444–474.

———. 1981. *The Chinese Military System: An Organizational Study of the Chinese People's Liberation Army.* Second ed., revised and updated. Boulder, Colo.: Westview Press.

Oberschall, Anthony. 1973. *Social Conflict and Social Movements.* Englewood Cliffs, N.J.: Prentice-Hall.

———. 1994. "Rational Choice in Collective Protests." *Rationality and Society* 6, no. 1 (January): 79–100.

Oi, Jean C. 1989. *State and Peasant in Contemporary China.* Berkeley: University of California Press.

Oksenberg, Michel. 1968. "Occupational Groups in Chinese Society and the Cultural Revolution". Pp. 1–44 in *The Cultural Revolution: 1967 in Review,* ed. Michel Oksenberg, Carl Riskin, Robert A. Scalapino, and Ezra F. Vogel. Ann Arbor: Center for Chinese Studies, University of Michigan.

Oliver, Pamela E., and Gregory M. Maney. 2000. "Political Processes and Local Newspaper Coverage of Protest Events: From Selection Bias to Triadic Interactions." *American Journal of Sociology* 106, no. 2 (September): 463–505.

Oliver, Pamela E., and Daniel J. Myers. 1999. "How Events Enter the Public Sphere: Conflict, Location, and Sponsorship in Local Newspaper Coverage of Public Events." *American Journal of Sociology* 105, no. 1 (July): 38–87.

Olzak, Susan. 1989. "Analysis of Events in the Study of Collective Action." *Annual Review of Sociology* 15: 119–141.

———. 1992. *The Dynamics of Ethnic Competition and Conflict.* Stanford, Calif.: Stanford University Press.

Opp, Karl-Dieter. 1994. "Repression and Revolutionary Action: East Germany in 1989." *Rationality and Society* 6, no. 1 (January): 101–138.

Opp, Karl-Dieter, and Christiane Gern. 1993. "Dissident Groups, Personal Networks, and Spontaneous Cooperation: The East German Revolution of 1989." *American Sociological Review* 58, no. 5 (October): 658–680.

Organization Department, CCP Central Committee. 2000. *Zhongguo gongchandang zuzhishi ziliao 1921–1997* (Materials on the Organizational History of the Chinese Communist Party, 1921–1997), 19 vols. Beijing: Zhonggong dangshi chubanshe.

Paige, Jeffery M. 1971. "Political Orientation and Riot Participation." *American Sociological Review* 36, no. 5 (October): 810–820.

———. 1975. *Agrarian Revolution: Social Movements and Export Agriculture in the Underdeveloped World*. New York: Free Press.

Parish, William L., and Martin K. Whyte. 1978. *Rural Life in Contemporary China*. Chicago: University of Chicago Press.

Pearlman, Wendy, and Kathleen Gallagher Cunningham. 2012. "Nonstate Actors, Fragmentation, and Conflict Processes." *Journal of Conflict Resolution* 56, no. 1 (February): 3–15.

People's Daily. 1967a. "Wuchan jieji geming pai da lianhe, duo ziben zhuyi dangquan pai de quan!" (Proletarian revolutionaries, join together and seize power from capitalist powerholders!). *Renmin ribao*, January 22, p. 1.

———. 1967b. "Zaofan jiushi yao duoquan" (To rebel is to seize power). *Renmin ribao*, January 22, p. 1.

Perry, Elizabeth J. 1980. *Rebels and Revolutionaries in North China, 1845–1945*. Stanford, Calif.: Stanford University Press.

———. 1993. *Shanghai on Strike: The Politics of Chinese Labor*. Stanford, Calif.: Stanford University Press.

Perry, Elizabeth J., and Li Xun. 1997. *Proletarian Power: Shanghai in the Cultural Revolution*. Boulder, Colo.: Westview Press.

Pfaff, Steven. 1996. "Collective Identity and Informal Groups in Revolutionary Mobilization: East Germany in 1989." *Social Forces* 75, no. 1 (September): 91–117.

Pfaff, Steven, and Hyojeong Kim. 2003. "Exit-Voice Dynamics in Collective Action: An Analysis of Emigration and Protest in the East German Revolution." *American Journal of Sociology* 109, no. 2 (September): 401–444.

Pitcher, Brian L., Robert L. Hamblin, and Jerry L. L. Miller. 1978. "The Diffusion of Collective Violence." *American Sociological Review* 43, no. 1 (February): 23–35.

Putuo County Annals. 1991. *Putuo xian zhi* (Putuo County Annals). Hangzhou: Zhejiang renmin chubanshe.

Qingdao Education Annals. 1994. *Qingdao shi zhi: jiaoyu zhi* (Qingdao City Annals: Education). Qingdao: Xinhua chubanshe.

Qingdao Historical Annals Office. 2000. *Qingdao shi zhi: dashiji* (Qingdao City Annals: Chronology). Beijing: Wuzhou chuanbo chubanshe.

Qingdao Labor Annals. 1999. *Qingdao shi zhi: laodong zhi* (Qingdao City Annals: Labor). Qingdao: Xinhua chubanshe.

Qiqihaer Archives Bureau. 1985. *Qiqihaer shi "wen'ge" dashiji 1966.5–1976.10* (Qiqihaer 'Cultural Revolution' Chronology, May 1966–October 1976). Qiqihaer: Qiqihaer shi dang'an guan.

Qiqihaer City Annals. 1998. *Qiqihaer shi zhi, zonghe juan* (Qiqihaer City Annals, Overview). Hefei: Huangshan shushe.

Qiqihaer Education Annals. 1993. *Qiqihaer shi zhi gao, jiaoyu zhi* (Qiqihaer City Annals Draft, Education). Qiqihaer: Qiqihaer shi zhi zong bianjibu.

Qiqihaer Labor Annals. 1994. *Qiqihaer shi zhi gao, laodong zhi* (Qiqihaer City Annals Draft, Labor). Qiqihaer: Qiqihaer shi zhi zong bianjibu.

Qiqihaer Population Annals. 1992. *Qiqihaer shi zhi gao, renkou zhi* (Qiqihaer City Annals Draft, Population). Qiqihaer: Qiqihaer shi zhi zong bianjibu.

Robinson, Geoffrey W. 2018. *The Killing Season: A History of the Indonesian Massacres, 1965–66*. Princeton, N.J.: Princeton University Press.

Rosen, Stanley. 1981. *The Role of Sent-Down Youth in the Chinese Cultural Revolution: The Case of Guangzhou*. Berkeley: Institute of East Asian Studies, University of California.

———. 1982. *Red Guard Factionalism and the Cultural Revolution in Guangzhou (Canton)*. Boulder, Colo.: Westview Press.

Rowe, William T. 2007. *Crimson Rain: Seven Centuries of Violence in a Chinese County*. Stanford: Stanford University Press.

Schoenhals, Michael. 2005. "'Why Don't We Arm the Left?' Mao's Culpability for the Cultural Revolution's 'Great Chaos' of 1967." *China Quarterly* 182 (June): 277–300.

———. 2015. "China's 'Great Proletarian Information Revolution' of 1966–1967." Pp. 230–258 in *Maoism at the Grass Roots: Everyday Life in China's Era of High Socialism*, ed. Jeremy Brown and Matthew Johnson. Cambridge, Mass.: Harvard University Press.

Shanghai Bureau of Statistics. 1990. *Shanghai tongji nianjian 1990* (Shanghai Statistical Yearbook 1990). Beijing: Zhongguo tongji chubanshe.

Shanglin County Annals. 1989. *Shanglin xian zhi* (Shanglin County Annals). Nanning: Guangxi renmin chubanshe.

Sheng County Annals. 1989. *Sheng xian zhi* (Sheng County Annals). Hangzhou: Zhejiang renmin chubanshe.

Shijiazhuang City Annals. 1995. *Shijiazhuang shi zhi, di yi juan* (Shijiazhuang City Annals, vol. 1). Beijing: Zhongguo shehui chubanshe.

Shijiazhuang City Annals. 1999. *Shijiazhuang shi zhi, di si juan* (Shijiazhuang City Annals, vol. 4). Beijing: Zhongguo shehui chubanshe.

Shijiazhuang Education Annals. 1992. *Shijiazhuang shi jiaoyu zhi* (Shijiazhuang Education Annals). Shijiazhuang: Hebei jiaoyu chubanshe.

Shijiazhuang Party History Research Office. 1997. *Shijiazhuang wenhua da geming dashiji (1966.5—1978.12)* (Shijiazhuang Cultural Revolution Chronology

[May 1966—December 1978]). Shijiazhuang: Shijiazhuang shiwei dangshi yanjiushi.

Shirk, Susan L. 1982. *Competitive Comrades: Career Incentives and Student Strategies in China.* Berkeley: University of California Press.

Shorter, Edward, and Charles Tilly. 1968. *Strikes in France, 1830–1968.* New York: Cambridge University Press.

Sichuan Province Annals. 1999. *Sichuan sheng zhi: dashi jishu (xia juan)* (Sichuan Province Annals: Narrative of Major Events [vol. 3]). Chengdu: Sichuan kexue jishu chubanshe.

Simmel, Georg. 1955 [1922]. "The Web of Group Affiliations." Pp. 127–195 in *Conflict and the Web of Group Affiliations,* trans. by Reinhard Bendix. Glencoe, Ill.: The Free Press.

Skilling, H. Gordon. 1970. "Group Conflict and Political Change." Pp. 215–234 in *Change in Communist Systems,* ed. Chalmers Johnson. Stanford: Stanford University Press.

———. 1976. *Czechoslovakia's Interrupted Revolution.* Princeton: Princeton University Press.

———. 1983. "Interest Groups and Communist Politics Revisited." *World Politics* 36, no, 1 (June): 1–27.

Skilling, H. Gordon, and Franklyn Griffiths, eds. 1970. *Interest Groups in Soviet Politics.* Princeton: Princeton University Press.

Skocpol, Theda. 1979. *States and Social Revolutions: A Comparative Analysis of France, Russia, and China.* Cambridge: Cambridge University Press.

Smelser, Neil J. 1959. *Social Change in the Industrial Revolution.* Chicago: University of Chicago Press.

———. 1962. *Theory of Collective Behavior.* New York: Free Press.

Snyder, David, and William R. Kelly. 1977. "Conflict Intensity, Media Sensitivity and the Validity of Newspaper Data." *American Sociological Review* 42, no. 1 (February): 105–123.

Snyder, David, and Charles Tilly. 1972. "Hardship and Collective Violence in France, 1830 to 1960." *American Sociological Review* 37, no. 5 (October): 520–532.

Sorokin, Pitirim. 1937. *Social and Cultural Dynamics, Volume Three: Fluctuation of Social Relationships, War, and Revolution.* New York: American Book Company.

Soule, Sarah A. 1997. "The Student Divestment Movement in the United States and Tactical Diffusion: The Shantytown Protest." *Social Forces* 75, no. 3 (March): 855–882.

Staniland, Paul. 2012. "Between a Rock and a Hard Place: Insurgent Fratricide, Ethnic Defection, and the Rise of Pro-State Paramilitaries." *Journal of Conflict Resolution* 56, no. 1 (February): 16–40.

State Statistical Bureau. 1983. *Zhongguo tongji nianjian 1983* [China Statistical Yearbook 1983]. Hong Kong: Xianggang jingji daobao she.

State Statistical Bureau Population Statistics Office. 1986. *Zhonghua renmin gongheguo di erci renkou pucha tongji shuzi huibian* (Compilation of Data from the Second Population Census of the People's Republic of China). Beijing: Guojia tongji ju renkou tongji si.

Su Hua, ed. 1987. *Dangdai Anhui dashiji* (Chronology of Contemporary Anhui). Hefei: Anhui renmin chubanshe.

Su Hua, and Hou Yong, eds. 1992. *Dangdai Zhongguo de Anhui* (Contemporary China: Anhui). Beijing: Dangdai Zhongguo chubanshe.

Su, Yang. 2006. "Mass Killings in the Cultural Revolution: A Study of Three Provinces." Pp. 96–123 in *The Chinese Cultural Revolution as History*, ed. Joseph W. Esherick, Paul G. Pickowicz, and Andrew G. Walder. Stanford: Stanford University Press.

———. 2011. *Collective Killings in China during the Cultural Revolution*. New York: Cambridge University Press.

Tan Hecheng. 2017. *The Killing Wind: A Chinese County's Descent into Madness during the Cultural Revolution*. New York: Oxford University Press.

Tang Shaojie. 1999. "Cong Qinghua daxue de liangpai tan 'wenhua da geming' qunzhong zuzhi jiegou, gongneng." (Structure and Function of 'Cultural Revolution' Mass Organizations: The Case of the Two Factions at Tsinghua University). *Zhonggong dangshi ziliao* 72 (September): 66–81.

———. 2003. *Yiye zhi qiu: Qinghua daxue 1968 nian 'bairi da wudou'"* (An Episode in the Cultural Revolution: The 1968 Hundred Day War at Tsinghua University). Hong Kong: Zhongwen daxue chubanshe.

Tanigawa, Shinichi. 2007. *The Dynamics of the Chinese Cultural Revolution in the Countryside: Shaanxi, 1966–1971*. Doctoral Dissertation, Department of Sociology, Stanford University.

———. 2018. "The Policy of the Military 'Supporting the Left' and the Spread of Factional Warfare in China's Countryside: Shaanxi, 1967–1968." *Modern China* 44, no. 1 (January): 35–67.

Tarrow, Sidney G. 1989. *Democracy and Disorder: Protest and Politics in Italy, 1965–1975*. New York: Oxford University Press.

———. 1994. *Power in Movement: Social Movements and Contentious Politics*. Cambridge: Cambridge University Press.

Tibetan Autonomous Region Party Committee Party History Research Office, ed. 2005. *Zhongguo gongchandang Xizang lishi dashiji, 1949–2004* (Chronology of the History of the Chinese Communist Party in Tibet, 1949–2004). Beijing: Zhonggong dangshi chubanshe.

Tilly, Charles. 1964. *The Vendée*. Cambridge, Mass.: Harvard University Press.

———. 1978. *From Mobilization to Revolution*. Reading, Mass.: Addison-Wesley.

———. 1986. *The Contentious French: Four Centuries of Popular Struggles*. Cambridge, Mass.: Harvard University Press.

———. 1995a. *Popular Contention in Great Britain, 1758–1834*. Cambridge, Mass.: Harvard University Press.

———. 1995b. "To Explain Political Processes." *American Journal of Sociology* 100, no. 6 (May): 1594–1610.

———. 2003. *The Politics of Collective Violence.* Cambridge: Cambridge University Press.

Tilly, Charles, Louise Tilly, and Richard Tilly. 1975. *The Rebellious Century, 1830–1930.* Cambridge, Mass.: Harvard University Press.

Toft, Monica Duffy. 2003. *The Geography of Ethnic Violence: Identity, Interests, and the Indivisibility of Territory.* Princeton: Princeton University Press.

Tolnay, Stewart E., and E. M. Beck. 1995. *A Festival of Violence: An Analysis of Southern Lynchings, 1882–1930.* Urbana: University of Illinois Press.

Tolnay, Stewart E., Glenn Deane, and E. M. Beck. 1996. "Vicarious Violence: Spatial Effects on Southern Lynching, 1890–1919." *American Journal of Sociology* 102, no. 3 (November): 788–815.

Tong, James. 1991. *Disorder Under Heaven: Collective Violence in the Ming Dynasty.* Stanford, Calif.: Stanford University Press.

Tongliang County Annals. 1991. *Tongliang xian zhi* (Tongliang County Annals). Chongqing: Chongqing daxue chubanshe.

Tongliang Historical Materials. 2002. *Tongliang wenshi ziliao, di shi'er ji (wen'ge shinian)* (Tongliang Historical Materials, no. 12 [Cultural Revolution decade]). Unpublished draft, November.

Tongshan County Annals. 1993. *Tongshan xian zhi* (Tongshan County Annals). Beijing: Zhongguo shehui kexue chubanshe.

Traugott, Mark. 2010. *The Insurgent Barricade.* Berkeley: University of California Press.

Treiman, Donald J., and Andrew G. Walder. 2019. "The Impact of Class Labels on Life Chances in China." *American Journal of Sociology* 124, no. 4 (January 2019): 1125–1163.

Turner, Ralph H., and Lewis M. Killian. 1972. *Collective Behavior,* 2nd edition. Englewood Cliffs, N.J.: Prentice-Hall.

Unger, Jonathan. 1982. *Education Under Mao: Class and Competition in Canton Schools, 1960–1980.* New York: Columbia University Press.

———. 1991. "Whither China? Yang Xiguang, Red Capitalists, and the Social Turmoil of the Cultural Revolution." *Modern China* 17, no. 1 (January): 3–37.

UNICEF. 2013. "Rwanda: Ten years after the genocide." www.unicef.org /infobycountry/ rwanda_genocide.html.

Union Research Institute. 1968. *CCP Documents of the Great Proletarian Cultural Revolution.* Hong Kong: Union Research Institute.

Vogel, Ezra F. 1968. "The Structure of Conflict: China in 1967." Pp. 97–125 in *The Cultural Revolution: 1967 in Review,* ed. Michel Oksenberg, Carl Riskin, Robert A. Scalapino, and Ezra F. Vogel. Ann Arbor: Center for Chinese Studies, University of Michigan.

———. 1969. *Canton Under Communism: Programs and Politics in a Provincial Capital, 1949–1968.* Cambridge, Mass.: Harvard University Press.

Walder, Andrew G. 1978. *Chang Ch'un-ch'iao and Shanghai's January Revolution.* Michigan Papers in Chinese Studies, No. 32. Ann Arbor: Center for Chinese Studies, University of Michigan.

———. 1986. *Communist Neo-Traditionalism: Work and Authority in Chinese Industry.* Berkeley: University of California Press.

———. 1987. "Communist Social Structure and Workers' Politics in China." Pp. 45–89 in *Citizens and Groups in Contemporary China,* ed. Victor Falkenheim. Michigan Monographs in Chinese Studies No. 56. Ann Arbor: University of Michigan, Center for Chinese Studies.

———. 1996. "The Chinese Cultural Revolution in the Factories: Party State Structures and Patterns of Conflict." Pp. 167–198 in *Putting Class in its Place: Worker Identities in East Asia,* ed. Elizabeth J. Perry. Berkeley: University of California, Institute of East Asian Studies.

———. 2002. "Beijing Red Guard Factionalism: Social Interpretations Reconsidered." *Journal of Asian Studies* 61, no. 2 (May): 437–471.

———. 2004. "Tan Lifu: A 'Reactionary' Red Guard in Historical Perspective." *China Quarterly* 180 (December): 965–988.

———. 2006a. "Ambiguity and Choice in Political Movements: The Origins of Beijing Red Guard Factionalism." *American Journal of Sociology* 112, no. 3 (November): 710–750.

———. 2006b. "Factional Conflict at Beijing University, 1966–1968." *China Quarterly* 188 (December): 1023–1047.

———. 2009a. *Fractured Rebellion: The Beijing Red Guard Movement.* Cambridge, Mass.: Harvard University Press.

———. 2009b. "Political Sociology and Social Movements." *Annual Review of Sociology* 34: 393–412.

———. 2014. "Rebellion and Repression in China, 1966–1971." *Social Science History* 38, nos. 3–4 (Fall–Winter): 513–539.

———. 2015. *China Under Mao: A Revolution Derailed.* Cambridge, Mass.: Harvard University Press.

———. 2016. "Rebellion of the Cadres: The 1967 Implosion of the Chinese Party-State." *China Journal* 75 (January): 102–120.

———. 2017. "The Chinese Cultural Revolution." Pp. 220–243 in *The Cambridge History of Communism, Vol. 2,* ed. Norman Naimark, Silvio Pons, and Sophie Quinn-Judge. Cambridge: Cambridge University Press.

Walder, Andrew G., and James Chu. 2018. "Pathways to Violent Insurgency: China's Factional Warfare of 1967–1968." Working Paper, Department of Sociology, Stanford University.

Walder, Andrew G., and Songhua Hu. 2009. "Revolution, Reform, and Status Inheritance: Urban China, 1949–1996." *American Journal of Sociology* 114, no. 5 (March): 1395–1427.

Walder, Andrew G., and Qinglian Lu. 2017. "The Dynamics of Collapse in an Authoritarian Regime: China in 1967." *American Journal of Sociology* 122, no. 2 (January): 1144–1182.

Walder, Andrew G., and Yang Su. 2003. "The Cultural Revolution in the Country-side: Scope, Timing, and Human Impact." *China Quarterly* 173 (March): 74–99.

Wang, Dan J., and Sarah Soule. 2012. "Social Movement Organizational Collaboration: Networks of Learning and the Diffusion of Protest Tactics, 1960–1995." *American Journal of Sociology* 117, no. 6 (May): 1674–1722.

Wang, Shaoguang. 1995. *Failure of Charisma: The Cultural Revolution in Wuhan.* Oxford: Oxford University Press.

———. 2006. "The Wuhan Incident Revisited." *Chinese Historical Review* 13, no. 2 (Fall): 241–270.

Wanxian City Annals. 2001. *Wanxian shi zhi* (Wanxian City Annals). Chongqing: Chongqing chubanshe.

Wenchang County Annals. 2000. *Wenchang xian zhi* (Wenchang County Annals). Nanjing: Fangzhi chubanshe.

Werth, Nicolas. 1999. "A State against its People: Violence, Repression and Terror in the Soviet Union," Pp. 33–268 in *The Black Book of Communism: Crimes, Terror, Repression,* ed. S. Courtois, N. Werth, J.-L. Panné, A. Paczkowski, K. Bartošek, and J.-L. Margolin. Cambridge, Mass.: Harvard University Press.

White, Gordon. 1974. "The Politics of *Hsia-hsiang* Youth." *China Quarterly* 59 (July–September): 491–517.

———. 1976. *The Politics of Class and Class Origin: The Case of the Cultural Revolution.* Contemporary China Papers 9. Canberra: Australian National University, Contemporary China Centre.

———. 1980. "The Politics of Demobilized Soldiers from Liberation to Cultural Revolution." *China Quarterly* 82 (June): 187–213.

White, Lynn T., III. 1976. "Workers' Politics in Shanghai." *Journal of Asian Studies* 36, no. 1 (November): 99–116.

———. 1989. *Policies of Chaos: The Organizational Causes of Violence in China's Cultural Revolution.* Princeton, N.J.: Princeton University Press.

White, Robert W. 1993. "On Measuring Political Violence: Northern Ireland, 1969 to 1980." *American Sociological Review* 58, no. 4 (August): 575–585.

Whyte, Martin K. 1974. *Small Groups and Political Rituals in China.* Berkeley: University of California Press.

———. 1975. "Inequality and Stratification in China." *China Quarterly* 64 (December): 684–711.

Whyte, Martin K., and William L. Parish. 1984. *Urban Life in Contemporary China.* Chicago: University of Chicago Press.

Wu Di. 2010. *Neimeng wen'ge shilu: "minzu fenlie" yu "wasu yundong"* (The Cultural Revolution in Inner Mongolia: "Ethnic Divisions" and "Elimination Campaigns"). Hong Kong: Tianxing jian chubanshe.

Wu Lili and Zhao Dingxin. 2007. "Kelisima quanwei de kunjing: Ningxia wen'ge wudou de qiyuan" (The Limits of Charismatic Authority: Origins of Factional Warfare in Ningxia's Cultural Revolution). *Ershiyi shiji shuangyue kan* 101 (June): 58–70.

Wu, Yiching. 2014a. *The Cultural Revolution at the Margins: Chinese Socialism in Crisis*. Cambridge, Mass.: Harvard University Press.

———. 2014b. "The Great Retreat and its Discontents: Re-Examining the Shengwulian Episode in the Cultural Revolution." *China Journal* 72 (July): 1–28.

Wuzhou City Annals. 2000. *Wuzhou shi zhi* (Wuzhou City Annals). Nanning: Guangxi renmin chubanshe.

Xiangtan City Annals. 1997. *Xiangtan shi zhi, di yi juan* (Xiangtan City Annals, Vol. 1). Beijing: Zhongguo wenshi chubanshe.

Xichang County Annals. 1996. *Xichang xian zhi* (Xichang County Annals). Chengdu: Sichuan renmin chubanshe.

Xing'an County Annals. 2002. *Xing'an xian zhi* (Xing'an County Annals). Nanning: Guangxi renmin chubanshe.

Xining City Annals. 1998. *Xining shi zhi: dashiji* (Xining City Annals: Chronology). Xi'an: Shaanxi renmin chubanshe.

Xu Jiangang. 1990. "'Siren bang' pohai Shanghai ganbu qunzhong de sanchang yundong" (Three Campaigns by the 'Gang of Four' that Persecuted Cadres and Masses in Shanghai). *Shanghai dangshi* 12 (December): 18–25.

Xu Youyu. 1999. *Xingxing sese de zaofan: Hongweibing jingshen suzhi de xingcheng ji yanbian* (Rebellion of all Hues: The Formation and Evolution of Red Guard Mentalities). Hong Kong: Zhongwen daxue chubanshe.

Yan, Fei. 2015. "Rival Rebels: The Political Origins of Guangzhou's Mass Factions in 1967." *Modern China* 41, no. 2 (March): 168–196.

———. 2018. "Political Dynamics of Mass Factionalism: Rethinking Factional Conflict in Guangzhou, 1967." *China: An International Journal* 16, no. 4 (October): 1–25.

Yan Lebin. 2012. "Wo canyu chuli Guangxi wen'ge yiliu wenti" (I Participated in the Handling of Problems Left Over from the Cultural Revolution in Guangxi), *Yanhuang chunqiu* 11 (November): 13–20.

Yan'an City Annals. 1994. *Yan'an shi zhi* (Yan'an City Annals). Xi'an: Shaanxi renmin chubanshe.

Yang Haiying. 2014. *Mei you mubei de caoyuan: Menggu ren yu wen'ge da tusha* (Grasslands without Tombstones: Massacres of Mongols During the Cultural Revolution). Xin Taibei: Baqi wenhua chubanshe.

Yang Lijun. 2015. "From the 'Four Cleans' Movement to the Cultural Revolution: The Origins of Factional Conflict." *China: An International Journal* 13, no. 3 (December): 1–24.

Yin Hongbiao. 2009. *Shizongzhe de zuji: Wenhua da geming qijian de qingnian sichao* (Footprints of the Missing: Ideological Trends Among Youth During the Cultural Revolution). Hong Kong: Zhongwen daxue chubanshe.

Yinjiang County Annals. 1992. *Yinjiang tujia zu miao zu zizhi xian zhi* (Yinjiang Tujia and Miao Autonomous County Annals). Guiyang: Guizhou renmin chubanshe.

Yongning County Annals. 1995. *Yongning xian zhi* (Yongning County Annals). Yinchuan: Ningxia renmin chubanshe.

Yuechi County Annals. 1993. *Yuechi xian zhi* (Yuechi County Annals). Chengdu: Dianzi keji daxue chubanshe.

Yulin City Annals. 1993. *Yulin shi zhi* (Yulin City Annals). Nanning: Guangxi renmin chubanshe.

Zaozhuang City Annals. 1992. *Zaozhuang shi zhi* (Zaozhuang City Annals). Beijing: Zhonghua shuju.

Zengcheng County Annals. 1995. *Zengcheng xian zhi* (Zengcheng County Annals). Foshan: Guangdong renmin chubanshe.

Zhang Cheng. 2001. "Dao xian da tusha: 1967 nian Hunan Dao xian sharen shijian jishi" (The Great Dao County Massacre: An Account of the 1967 Killings in Dao County, Hunan). *Kaifang zazhi* 7 (July): 63–80.

Zhang County Annals. 2005. *Zhang xian zhi* (Zhang County Annals). Lanzhou: Gansu wenhua chubanshe.

Zhao, Dingxin. 1998. "Ecologies of Social Movements: Student Mobilization during the 1989 Protest Movement in Beijing." *American Journal of Sociology* 103, no. 6 (May): 1493–1529.

Zhao Yonggang, ed. 2013. *Kua shiji de chuangkou: Meiguo xuezhe zai Zouping shehui kaocha tupianji* (Window Across Centuries: A Pictorial History of American Scholars' Social Investigations in Zouping). Ji'nan: Shandong youyi chubanshe.

Zhejiang Party History Research Office. 2000. *Dangdai Zhejiang jian shi* (Brief History of Contemporary Zhejiang). Beijing: Dangdai Zhongguo chubanshe.

Zhejiang Provincial Organs. 1966. *Sheng ji jiguan sishiwu ge danwei de geming ganbu jiefa pipan zichan jieji fandong luxian shishi dahui fayan gao xuanbian* (Selected Compilation of Speeches by Revolutionary Cadres from 45 Provincial Organs at the Mass Rally to Expose and Criticize the Bourgeois Reactionary Line). Mimeographed pamphlet, 56 pp, October.

Zheng, Xiaowei. 2006. "Passion, Reflection, and Survival: Political Choices of Red Guards at Qinghua University, June 1966–July 1968." Pp. 29–63 in *The Chinese Cultural Revolution as History,* ed. Joseph W. Esherick, Paul G. Pickowicz, and Andrew G. Walder. Stanford: Stanford University Press.

Zhenyuan County Party History. 2008. *Zhongguo gongchandang Zhenyuan xian lishi (1919–2006)* (History of the Chinese Communist Party in Zhenyuan County [1919–2006]). Beijing: Zhonggong dangshi chubanshe.

Zhongjiang County Annals. 1994. *Zhongjiang xian zhi* (Zhongjiang County Annals). Chengdu: Sichuan renmin chubanshe.

Zhou Enlai and Kang Sheng. 1967. "Zhou Enlai Kang Sheng jiejian Shandong daibiaotuan Wang Xiaoyu Yang Dezhi deng ren de jianghua" (Statements by Zhou Enlai and Kang Sheng in a Meeting with a Shandong Delegation of Wang Xiaoyu, Yang Dezhi and Others). In Cultural Revolution Database (2002).

Zichang County Annals. 1993. *Zichang xian zhi* (Zichang County Annals). Xi'an: Shaanxi renmin chubanshe.

Ziyang County Annals. 1989. *Ziyang xian zhi* (Ziyang County Annals). Xi'an: Sanqin chubanshe.

Zouping County Annals. 1992. *Zouping xian zhi* (Zouping County Annals). Beijing: Zhonghua shuju.

Zwierzchowski, Jan, and Ewa Tabeau. 2010. "The 1992–95 War in Bosnia and Herzegovina: Census-Based Multiple System Estimation of Casualties' Undercount." Berlin: Households in Conflict Network and Institute for Economic Research.

ACKNOWLEDGMENTS

In pursuing this project, I have accumulated a large number of debts. Over the years, a long list of graduate students, mostly at Stanford University, have contributed to the photocopying, coding, and compilation of the data set employed in this book. They include Yang Su, Fei Yan, Lizhi Liu, Shinichi Tanigawa, Zheng Lu, Songhua Hu, Weiwei Shen, Xiaobin He, Dian Yang, Chunlei Wang, Timothy Wai-keung Tam, and Litao Zhao. Several of them deserve special thanks. Yang Su directed the compilation of a smaller early version of the data set and devised many of the coding schemes that were revised and adapted for the final product. He also employed part of the early data set in his dissertation, which later yielded an award-winning book on collective killings in severely affected regions of China. Lizhi Liu, Weiwei Shen, Xiaobin He, and Fei Yan were core members of the research team that helped to test and revise the final codebook and to code the materials included in the completed data set. Fei Yan worked closely with me in the first phases of data cleaning and provided indispensable assistance in bringing the final product to completion. He has also utilized part of these materials in his own research and publications on Guangzhou.

Funding for this project was generously provided over the years by several entities at Stanford University: the Shorenstein Asia-Pacific Research Center, the Freeman-Spogli Institute for International Studies, and the School of Humanities and Sciences. The National Science Foundation (Grant SES-1021134) provided funding for the final revision and testing of the codebook, the process of coding and data entry, and the initial process of data cleaning.

I also owe thanks to faculty colleagues and graduate students who participated over the years in the Political Sociology, Collective Action and Social Movements Workshop in Stanford's Department of Sociology. I have subjected members of that workshop to several presentations related to this book, ranging from the first draft of the grant proposal to a series of draft chapters. I have benefited greatly from the reactions of workshop participants to my preliminary drafts, and I owe special thanks to Susan Olzak, Doug McAdam, and Gi-Wook Shin, who have repeatedly provided fruitful suggestions and encouragement. I also owe a debt of thanks to members of Stanford's

China Social Science Workshop—in particular Xueguang Zhou and Jean Oi—who pointed out serious flaws in an earlier version of one of the chapters. Qinglian Lu was a creative co-author on an article on the diffusion of power seizures in early 1967, and I have included some of the observations from that article in Chapter 4. I was also fortunate to collaborate with James Chu on an analysis of factional formation and escalation processes, and some of these analyses have been incorporated into Chapter 7. Doug McAdam, Yang Su, and Shinichi Tanigawa provided detailed critical reviews of this book's very different first draft, and I also benefited from detailed comments by two reviewers for Harvard University Press, one of whom was Dingxin Zhao.

Those who have read my co-authored publications with Dong Guoqiang of Shanghai's Fudan University will recognize that some of the arguments that we have developed during our long collaboration on the history of conflict in Jiangsu Province deeply inform the analyses that I offer here. While I have not incorporated material from our publications into this book, I feel compelled to acknowledge my debt to Professor Dong.

This book expands on ideas presented in "Rebellion and Repression in China, 1966–1971," *Social Science History* 38, 3/4 (Fall–Winter 2014) © Cambridge University Press; "Rebellion of the Cadres: The 1967 Implosion of the Chinese Party-State," *The China Journal* 75 (January 2016), © The University of Chicago Press; and "The Dynamics of Collapse in an Authoritarian Regime: China in 1967," *American Journal of Sociology* 122, 4 (January 2017), © The University of Chicago Press. I am grateful to those publishers for the opportunity to share my work.

INDEX

Figures indicated by page numbers in italics